A TEXTBOOK OF ENGINEERING MATHEMATICS

A TEXTBOOK OF

ENGINEERING MATHEMATICS

For

B. Tech. II Year (*III Semester*)
University of Calicut, Kerala

By

N.P. BALI
Formerly, Principal
S.B. College, Gurgaon
Haryana

JAMEELA BEEVI U.S.
Asst. Professor & Head
Department of Mathematics
MES College of Engineering, Kuttippuram
Kerala

UNIVERSITY SCIENCE PRESS

(An Imprint of Laxmi Publications (P) Ltd.)

BANGALORE • CHENNAI • COCHIN • GUWAHATI • HYDERABAD
JALANDHAR • KOLKATA • LUCKNOW • MUMBAI • RANCHI
NEW DELHI • BOSTON, USA

Published by :

UNIVERSITY SCIENCE PRESS

(An Imprint of Laxmi Publications (P) Ltd.)

113, Golden House, Daryaganj,
New Delhi-110002

Phone : 011-43 53 25 00
Fax : 011-43 53 25 28

www.laxmipublications.com
info@laxmipublications.com

First Edition : 2013

OFFICES

© **Bangalore**	080-26 75 69 30	© **Jalandhar**	0181-222 12 72
© **Chennai**	044-24 34 47 26	© **Kolkata**	033-22 27 43 84
© **Cochin**	0484-237 70 04, 405 13 03	© **Lucknow**	0522-220 99 16
© **Guwahati**	0361-251 36 69, 251 38 81	© **Mumbai**	022-24 91 54 15, 24 92 78 69
© **Hyderabad**	040-24 65 23 33	© **Ranchi**	0651-220 44 64

UEM-9679-125-ENGG MATH III UC (KE)-JAM **C—**

Typeset at : Excellent Graphics, Delhi. *Printed at* : Repro Knowledgecast Limited, Thane

CONTENTS

PREFACE TO THE FIRST EDITION

This book is prepared in accordance with the latest syllabus for 3rd Semester B. Tech. Course (Common for all branches) of University of Calicut, Kerala. This book is based on the experience and notes while taking classes for B. Tech. students for more than 14 years.

This book consists of three Units. First Unit covers topics of both I and II Modules, Second Unit covers topics of IV Module and Third Unit that of III Module. Solved University Questions of previous years have been included in each unit, to let the students understand the various skills necessary to solve the problems. More university questions with answers have also been included in each unit for practice.

Intimations of errors and suggestions for improvement will be highly appreciated and gratefully acknowledged.

—Authors

SYLLABUS

EN09 301: ENGINEERING MATHEMATICS III

(Common for all branches)

Teaching scheme **Credits: 4**

3 hours lecture and 1 hour tutorial per week

Objectives

- *This course provides a quick overview of the concepts and results in complex analysis that may be useful in engineering.*
- *Also it gives an introduction to linear algebra and Fourier transform which has good wealth of ideas and results with wide area of application.*

Module I: Functions of a Complex Variable **(13 hours)**

Functions of a Complex Variable – Limit – Continuity – Derivative of a Complex function – Analytic functions – Cauchy-Riemann Equations – Laplace Equation – Harmonic Functions – Conformal Mapping – Examples: Z^n, $\sin z$, $\cos z$, $\sinh z$, $\cosh z$, $(z + 1/z)$ – Mobius Transformation.

Module II: Functions of a Complex Variable **(14 hours)**

Definition of Line integral in the complex plane – Cauchy's integral theorem (Proof of existence of indefinite integral to be omitted) – Independence of path – Cauchy's integral formula – Derivatives of analytic functions (Proof not required) – Taylor series – Laurent series – Singularities and Zeros – Residues – Residue Integration method – Residues and Residue theorem – Evaluation of real integrals.

Module III: Linear Algebra – Proofs not required **(13 hours)**

Vector spaces – Definition, Examples – Subspaces – Linear Span – Linear Independence – Linear Dependence – Basis – Dimension – Ordered Basis – Coordinate Vectors – Transition Matrix – Orthogonal and Orthonormal Sets – Orthogonal and Orthonormal Basis – Gram-Schmidt orthogonolisation process – Inner product spaces – Examples.

Module IV: Fourier Transforms **(14 hours)**

Fourier Integral theorem (Proof not required) – Fourier Sine and Cosine integral representations – Fourier Transforms – Fourier Sine and Cosine Transforms – Properties of Fourier Transforms.

UNIT 1
Functions of a Complex Variable

1.1. INTRODUCTION

A complex number z is an ordered pair (x, y) of real numbers and is written as

$$z = x + iy, \quad \text{where } i = \sqrt{-1}.$$

The real numbers x and y are called the real and imaginary parts of z. In the Argand's diagram, the complex number z is represented by the point $P(x, y)$. If (r, θ) are the polar coordinates of P, then $r = \sqrt{x^2 + y^2}$ is called the modulus of z and is denoted by $|z|$. Also $\theta = \tan^{-1} \dfrac{y}{x}$ is called the argument of z and is denoted by arg. z. Every non-zero complex number z can be expressed as

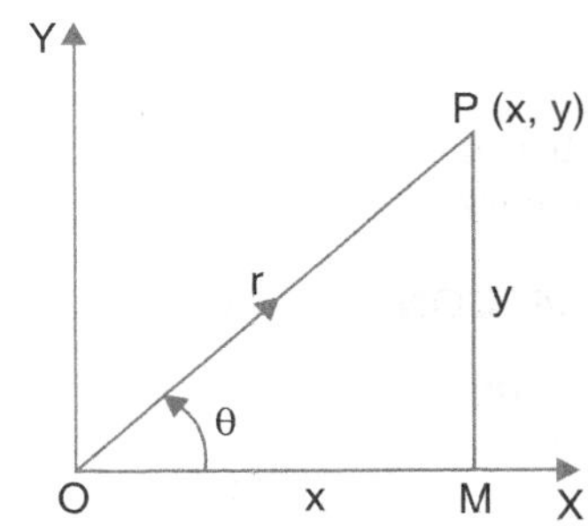

$$z = r(\cos\theta + i\sin\theta) = re^{i\theta}$$

If $z = x + iy$, then the complex number $x - iy$ is called the conjugate of the complex number z and is denoted by $\bar{z}$.

Clearly, $\quad |\bar{z}| = |z|, |z|^2 = z\bar{z},$

$$R(z) = \frac{z + \bar{z}}{2}, \quad I(z) = \frac{z - \bar{z}}{2i}.$$

1.2. FUNCTIONS OF A COMPLEX VARIABLE

If x and y are real variables, then $z = x + iy$ is called a **complex variable.** If corresponding to each value of a complex variable $z(= x + iy)$ in a given region R, there correspond one or more values of another complex variable $w\ (= u + iv)$, then w is called a function of the complex variable z and is denoted by

$$w = f(z) = u + iv$$

For example, if $\quad w = z^2, \quad$ where $z = x + iy$ and $w = f(z) = u + iv$

then $\quad u + iv = (x + iy)^2 = (x^2 - y^2) + i(2xy)$

$\Rightarrow \quad u = x^2 - y^2 \quad \text{and} \quad v = 2xy$

Thus u and v, the real and imaginary parts of w, are functions of the real variables x and y.

$\therefore \quad w = f(z) = u(x, y) + iv(x, y)$

If to each value of z, there corresponds one and only one value of w, then w is called a *single-valued function* of z. If to each value of z, there correspond more than one values of w, then w is called a *multi-valued function of z*.

To represent $w = f(z)$ graphically, we take two Argand diagrams : one to represent the point z and the other to represent w. The former diagram is called the xoy-plane or the z-plane and the latter uov-plane or the w-plane.

1.3. LIMIT OF f(z)

A function $f(z)$ tends to the limit l as z tends to z_0 *along any path,* if to each positive arbitrary number ε, however small, there corresponds a positive number δ, such that

$$|f(z) - l| < \varepsilon \quad \text{whenever} \quad 0 < |z - z_0| < \delta$$

i.e., $\quad l - \varepsilon < f(z) < l + \varepsilon$

whenever $\quad z_0 - \delta < z < z_0 + \delta, z \neq z_0$

and we write $\quad \underset{z \to z_0}{\text{Lt}} f(z) = l.$

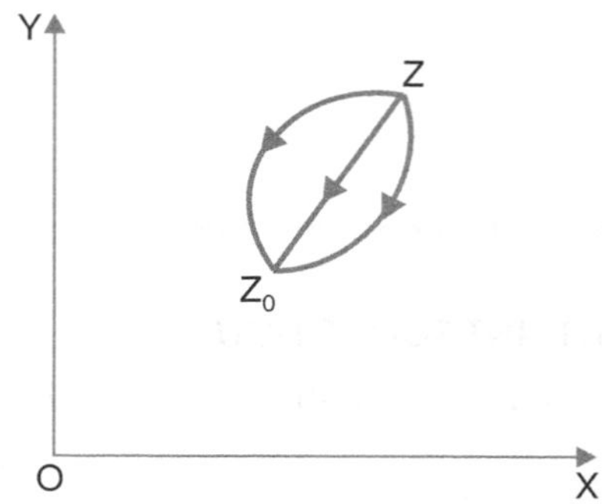

Note. In real variables, $x \to x_0$ implies that x approaches x_0 along the number line, either from left or from right. In complex variables, $z \to z_0$ implies that z approaches z_0 along any path, straight or curved, since the two points representing z and z_0 in a complex plane can be joined by an infinite number of curves.

1.4. CONTINUITY OF f(z)

A single-valued function $f(z)$ is said to be continuous at a point $z = z_0$ if $\underset{z \to z_0}{\text{Lt}} f(z) = f(z_0)$.

A function $f(z)$ is said to be continuous in a region R of the z-plane if it is continuous at every point of the region.

1.5. DERIVATIVE OF f(z)

Let $w = f(z)$ be a single-valued function of the variable $z(= x + iy)$, then the derivative or differential co-efficient of $w = f(z)$ is defined as

$$\frac{dw}{dz} = f'(z) = \underset{\delta z \to 0}{\text{Lt}} \frac{f(z + \delta z) - f(z)}{\delta z}$$

provided the limit exists, independent of the manner in which $\delta z \to 0$.

1.6. ANALYTIC FUNCTION

If a single-valued function $f(z)$ possesses a unique derivative at every point of a region R, then $f(z)$ is called an **analytic function** or a **regular function** or a **holomorphic function** of z in R.

A point where the function ceases to be analytic is called a **singular point.**

1.7. NECESSARY AND SUFFICIENT CONDITIONS FOR f(z) TO BE ANALYTIC

The necessary and sufficient conditions for the function

$$w = f(z) = u(x, y) + iv(x, y)$$

to be analytic in a region R, are

(*i*) $\dfrac{\partial u}{\partial x}, \dfrac{\partial u}{\partial y}, \dfrac{\partial v}{\partial x}, \dfrac{\partial v}{\partial y}$ *are continuous functions of x and y in the region R.*

(ii) $\dfrac{\partial u}{\partial x} = \dfrac{\partial v}{\partial y}, \dfrac{\partial u}{\partial y} = -\dfrac{\partial v}{\partial x}$.

The conditions in (ii) are known as ***Cauchy-Riemann equations*** *or briefly* ***C-R equations.*** (C.U. June 2007, Dec. 2007)

Proof. (*a*) **Necessary Condition.** Let $w = f(z) = u(x, y) + iv(x, y)$ be analytic in a region R, then $\dfrac{dw}{dz} = f'(z)$ exists uniquely at every point of that region.

Let δx and δy be the increments in x and y respectively. Let δu, δv and δz be the corresponding increments in u, v and z respectively. Then,

$$f'(z) = \underset{\delta z \to 0}{\text{Lt}} \frac{f(z+\delta z) - f(z)}{\delta z} = \underset{\delta z \to 0}{\text{Lt}} \frac{(u+\delta u) + i(v+\delta v) - (u+iv)}{\delta z}$$

$$= \underset{\delta z \to 0}{\text{Lt}} \left(\frac{\delta u}{\delta z} + i\frac{\delta v}{\delta z}\right) \qquad ...(1)$$

Since the function $w = f(z)$ is analytic in the region R, the limit (1) must exist independent of the manner in which $\delta z \to 0$, *i.e.*, along whichever path δx and $\delta y \to 0$.

First, let $\delta z \to 0$ along a line parallel to x-axis so that $\delta y = 0$ and $\delta z = \delta x$.

[since $z = x + iy$, $z + \delta z = (x + \delta x) + i(y + \delta y)$ and $\delta z = \delta x + i\delta y$]

$$\therefore \quad \text{From (1)}, \quad f'(z) = \underset{\delta x \to 0}{\text{Lt}} \left(\frac{\delta u}{\delta x} + i\frac{\delta v}{\delta x}\right) = \frac{\partial u}{\partial x} + i\frac{\partial v}{\partial x} \qquad ...(2)$$

Now, let $\delta z \to 0$ along a line parallel to y-axis so that $\delta x = 0$ and $\delta z = i\,\delta y$.

$$\therefore \quad \text{From (1)}, \quad f'(z) = \underset{\delta y \to 0}{\text{Lt}} \left(\frac{\delta u}{i\delta y} + i\frac{\delta v}{i\delta y}\right) = \frac{1}{i}\frac{\partial u}{\partial y} + \frac{\partial v}{\partial y}$$

$$= \frac{\partial v}{\partial y} - i\frac{\partial u}{\partial y} \qquad ...(3) \qquad \left|\ \because \frac{1}{i} = -i\right.$$

From (2) and (3), we have $\dfrac{\partial u}{\partial x} + i\dfrac{\partial v}{\partial x} = \dfrac{\partial v}{\partial y} - i\dfrac{\partial u}{\partial y}$

Equating the real and imaginary parts, $\dfrac{\partial u}{\partial x} = \dfrac{\partial v}{\partial y}$ and $\dfrac{\partial u}{\partial y} = -\dfrac{\partial v}{\partial x}$.

Hence the necessary condition for f(z) to be analytic is that the C-R equations must be satisfied.

(*b*) **Sufficient Condition.** Let $f(z) = u + iv$ be a single-valued function possessing partial derivatives $\dfrac{\partial u}{\partial x}, \dfrac{\partial u}{\partial y}, \dfrac{\partial v}{\partial x}, \dfrac{\partial v}{\partial y}$ at each point of a region R and satisfying C-R equations.

i.e., $$\frac{\partial u}{\partial x} = \frac{\partial v}{\partial y} \quad \text{and} \quad \frac{\partial u}{\partial y} = -\frac{\partial v}{\partial x}.$$

We shall show that $f(z)$ is analytic, *i.e.*, $f'(z)$ exists at every point of the region R.

By Taylor's theorem for functions of two variables, we have, on omitting second and higher degree terms of δx and δy.

$$f(z + \delta z) = u(x + \delta x, y + \delta y) + iv(x + \delta x, y + \delta y)$$

$$= \left[u(x, y) + \left(\frac{\partial u}{\partial x}\delta x + \frac{\partial u}{\partial y}\delta y\right)\right] + i\left[v(x, y) + \left(\frac{\partial v}{\partial x}\delta x + \frac{\partial v}{\partial y}\delta y\right)\right]$$

$$= [u(x, y) + iv(x, y)] + \left(\frac{\partial u}{\partial x} + i\frac{\partial v}{\partial x}\right)\delta x + \left(\frac{\partial u}{\partial y} + i\frac{\partial v}{\partial y}\right)\delta y$$

$$= f(z) + \left(\frac{\partial u}{\partial x} + i\frac{\partial v}{\partial x}\right)\delta x + \left(\frac{\partial u}{\partial y} + i\frac{\partial v}{\partial y}\right)\delta y$$

or $$f(z + \delta z) - f(z) = \left(\frac{\partial u}{\partial x} + i\frac{\partial v}{\partial x}\right)\delta x + \left(\frac{\partial u}{\partial y} + i\frac{\partial v}{\partial y}\right)\delta y$$

$$= \left(\frac{\partial u}{\partial x} + i\frac{\partial v}{\partial x}\right)\delta x + \left(-\frac{\partial v}{\partial x} + i\frac{\partial u}{\partial x}\right)\delta y \qquad | \text{ Using C-R equations}$$

$$= \left(\frac{\partial u}{\partial x} + i\frac{\partial v}{\partial x}\right)\delta x + \left(\frac{\partial u}{\partial x} + i\frac{\partial v}{\partial x}\right)i\delta y \qquad | \because \; -1 = i^2$$

$$= \left(\frac{\partial u}{\partial x} + i\frac{\partial v}{\partial x}\right)(\delta x + i\delta y) = \left(\frac{\partial u}{\partial x} + i\frac{\partial v}{\partial x}\right)\delta z \qquad | \because \; \delta x + i\delta y = \delta z$$

$\Rightarrow$ $$\frac{f(z+\delta z) - f(z)}{\delta z} = \frac{\partial u}{\partial x} + i\frac{\partial v}{\partial x}$$

$\therefore$ $$f'(z) = \underset{\delta z \to 0}{\text{Lt}} \frac{f(z+\delta z) - f(z)}{\delta z} = \frac{\partial u}{\partial x} + i\frac{\partial v}{\partial x}$$

Thus $f'(z)$ exists, because $\frac{\partial u}{\partial x}, \frac{\partial v}{\partial x}$ exist.

Hence $f(z)$ is analytic.

Note 1. The real and imaginary parts of an analytic function are called **conjugate functions.** Thus, if $f(z) = u(x, y) + iv(x, y)$ is an analytic function, then $u(x, y)$ and $v(x, y)$ are conjugate functions. The relation between two conjugate functions is given by C-R equations.

Note 2. When a function $f(z)$ is known to be analytic, it can be differentiated in the ordinary way as if z is a real variable.

Thus, $f(z) = z^2 \Rightarrow f'(z) = 2z$

$f(z) = \sin z \Rightarrow f'(z) = \cos z$ etc.

1.8. CAUCHY-RIEMANN EQUATIONS IN POLAR COORDINATES

(*C.U. June 2006, June 2007, Dec. 2007*)

Let (r, θ) be the polar coordinates of the point whose cartesian coordinates are (x, y), then

$$x = r\cos\theta, y = r\sin\theta,$$

$$z = x + iy = r(\cos\theta + i\sin\theta) = re^{i\theta}$$

$\therefore$ $$u + iv = f(z) = f(re^{i\theta}) \qquad ...(1)$$

Differentiating (1) partially w.r.t. r, we have

$$\frac{\partial u}{\partial r} + i\frac{\partial v}{\partial r} = f'(re^{i\theta}) \, . \, e^{i\theta} \qquad ...(2)$$

Differentiating (1) partially w.r.t. θ, we have

$$\frac{\partial u}{\partial \theta} + i\frac{\partial v}{\partial \theta} = f'(re^{i\theta}) \cdot ire^{i\theta} = ir\left(\frac{\partial u}{\partial r} + i\frac{\partial v}{\partial r}\right) \quad | \text{ Using (2)}$$

$$= -r\frac{\partial v}{\partial r} + ir\frac{\partial u}{\partial r}$$

Equating real and imaginary parts, we get

$$\frac{\partial u}{\partial \theta} = -r\frac{\partial v}{\partial r} \quad \text{and} \quad \frac{\partial v}{\partial \theta} = r\frac{\partial u}{\partial r}$$

or $\frac{\partial u}{\partial r} = \frac{1}{r}\frac{\partial v}{\partial \theta}$ and $\frac{\partial v}{\partial r} = -\frac{1}{r}\frac{\partial u}{\partial \theta}$ which is the polar form of C-R equations.

1.9. HARMONIC FUNCTIONS

Any solution of the Laplace's equation, $\frac{\partial^2 \phi}{\partial x^2} + \frac{\partial^2 \phi}{\partial y^2} = 0$ is called a harmonic function.

Let $f(z) = u + iv$ be analytic in some region of the z-plane, then u and v satisfy C-R equations.

$$\therefore \quad \frac{\partial u}{\partial x} = \frac{\partial v}{\partial y} \quad ...(1)$$

and

$$\frac{\partial u}{\partial y} = -\frac{\partial v}{\partial x} \quad ...(2)$$

Differentiating (1) partially w.r.t. x and (2) w.r.t. y, we get

$$\frac{\partial^2 u}{\partial x^2} = \frac{\partial^2 v}{\partial x \partial y} \quad ...(3)$$

and

$$\frac{\partial^2 u}{\partial y^2} = -\frac{\partial^2 v}{\partial y \partial x} \quad ...(4)$$

Assuming $\frac{\partial^2 v}{\partial x \partial y} = \frac{\partial^2 v}{\partial y \partial x}$ and adding (3) and (4), we get

$$\frac{\partial^2 u}{\partial x^2} + \frac{\partial^2 u}{\partial y^2} = 0 \quad ...(5)$$

Now, differentiating (1) partially w.r.t. y and (2) w.r.t. x, we get

$$\frac{\partial^2 u}{\partial y \partial x} = \frac{\partial^2 v}{\partial y^2} \quad ...(6)$$

and

$$\frac{\partial^2 u}{\partial x \partial y} = -\frac{\partial^2 v}{\partial x^2} \quad ...(7)$$

Assuming $\frac{\partial^2 u}{\partial y \partial x} = \frac{\partial^2 u}{\partial x \partial y}$ and subtracting (7) from (6), we get

$$\frac{\partial^2 v}{\partial x^2} + \frac{\partial^2 v}{\partial y^2} = 0 \quad ...(8)$$

Equations (5) and (8) show that the real and imaginary parts u and v of an analytic function satisfy the Laplace's equation.

Hence u and v are known as harmonic functions.

1.10. ORTHOGONAL SYSTEM

Every analytic function $f(z) = u + iv$ defines two families of curves $u(x, y) = c_1$ and $v(x, y) = c_2$, which form an orthogonal system.

Consider the two families of curves

$$u(x, y) = c_1 \quad \ldots(1)$$

and

$$v(x, y) = c_2 \quad \ldots(2)$$

Differentiating (1) w.r.t. x, we get

$$\frac{\partial u}{\partial x} + \frac{\partial u}{\partial y} \cdot \frac{dy}{dx} = 0 \quad \text{or} \quad \frac{dy}{dx} = -\frac{\frac{\partial u}{\partial x}}{\frac{\partial u}{\partial y}} = m_1 \text{ (say)}$$

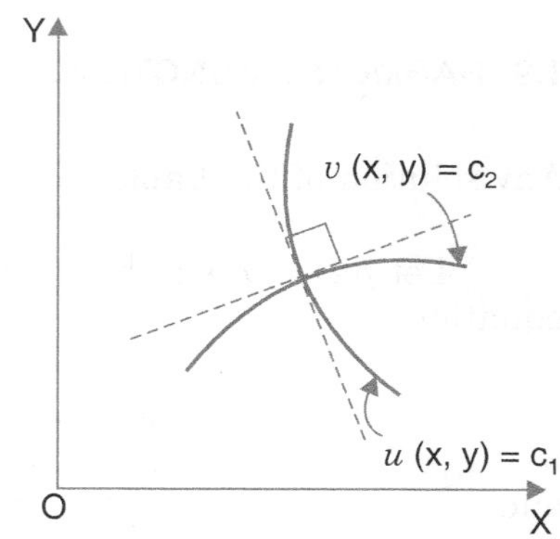

Similarly, from (2), we get $\dfrac{dy}{dx} = -\dfrac{\frac{\partial v}{\partial x}}{\frac{\partial v}{\partial y}} = m_2$ (say)

$$\therefore \qquad m_1 m_2 = \frac{\frac{\partial u}{\partial x} \cdot \frac{\partial v}{\partial x}}{\frac{\partial u}{\partial y} \cdot \frac{\partial v}{\partial y}} \quad \ldots(3)$$

Since $f(z)$ is analytic, u and v satisfy C-R equations

i.e.,

$$\frac{\partial u}{\partial x} = \frac{\partial v}{\partial y} \quad \text{and} \quad \frac{\partial u}{\partial y} = -\frac{\partial v}{\partial x}$$

$$\therefore \text{ From (3),} \qquad m_1 m_2 = \frac{\frac{\partial v}{\partial y} \cdot \frac{\partial v}{\partial x}}{-\frac{\partial v}{\partial x} \cdot \frac{\partial v}{\partial y}} = -1$$

Thus the product of the slopes of the curves (1) and (2) is – 1. Hence the curves intersect at right angles, *i.e.,* they form an orthogonal system.

1.11. APPLICATION OF ANALYTIC FUNCTIONS TO FLOW PROBLEMS

Since the real and imaginary parts of an analytic function satisfy the Laplace's equation in two variables, these conjugate functions provide solutions to a number of field and flow problems.

For example, consider the two dimensional irrotational motion of an incompressible fluid, in planes parallel to xy-plane.

Let V be the velocity of a fluid particle, then it can be expressed as

$$\mathrm{V} = v_x \hat{i} + v_y \hat{j} \quad \ldots(1)$$

Since the motion is irrotational, there exists a scalar function $\phi(x, y)$, such that

$$V = \nabla\phi(x, y) = \frac{\partial \phi}{\partial x}\hat{i} + \frac{\partial \phi}{\partial y}\hat{j} \qquad \text{...(2)}$$

From (1) and (2), we have $v_x = \dfrac{\partial \phi}{\partial x}$ and $v_y = \dfrac{\partial \phi}{\partial y}$ ...(3)

The scalar function $\phi(x, y)$, which gives the velocity components, is called the **velocity potential function** or simply the **velocity potential.**

Also the fluid being incompressible, div V = 0

$$\Rightarrow \quad \left(\hat{i}\frac{\partial}{\partial x} + \hat{j}\frac{\partial}{\partial y}\right)(v_x\hat{i} + v_y\hat{j}) = 0$$

$$\Rightarrow \quad \frac{\partial v_x}{\partial x} + \frac{\partial v_y}{\partial y} = 0 \qquad \text{...(4)}$$

Substituting the values of v_x and v_y from (3) in (4), we get

$$\frac{\partial}{\partial x}\left(\frac{\partial \phi}{\partial x}\right) + \frac{\partial}{\partial y}\left(\frac{\partial \phi}{\partial y}\right) = 0 \quad \text{or} \quad \frac{\partial^2 \phi}{\partial x^2} + \frac{\partial^2 \phi}{\partial y^2} = 0$$

Thus the function ϕ is harmonic and can be treated as real part of an analytic function

$$w = f(z) = \phi(x, y) + i\,\psi(x, y)$$

For interpretation of conjugate function $\psi(x, y)$, the slope at any point of the curve $\psi(x, y) = c'$ is given by

$$\frac{dy}{dx} = -\frac{\dfrac{\partial \psi}{\partial x}}{\dfrac{\partial \psi}{\partial y}} = \frac{\dfrac{\partial \phi}{\partial y}}{\dfrac{\partial \phi}{\partial x}} \qquad \text{[By C-R equations]}$$

$$= \frac{v_y}{v_x} \qquad \text{[By (3)]}$$

This shows that the resultant velocity $\sqrt{v_x^2 + v_y^2}$ of the fluid particle is along the tangent to the curve $\psi(x, y) = c'$ *i.e.*, the fluid particles move along this curve. Such curves are known as *stream lines* and $\psi(x, y)$ is called the *stream function*. The curves represented by $\phi(x, y) = c$ are called *equipotential lines*.

Since $\phi(x, y)$ and $\psi(x, y)$ are conjugate functions of analytic function $w = f(z)$, the equipotential lines $\phi(x, y) = c$ and the stream lines $\phi(x, y) = c'$, intersect each other orthogonally.

Now,

$$\frac{dw}{dz} = \frac{\partial \phi}{\partial x} + i\frac{\partial \psi}{\partial x}$$

$$= \frac{\partial \phi}{\partial x} - i\frac{\partial \phi}{\partial y} \qquad \text{[By C-R equations]}$$

$$= v_x - iv_y \qquad \text{[By (3)]}$$

$\therefore$ The magnitude of resultant velocity $= \left|\dfrac{dw}{dz}\right| = \sqrt{v_x^2 + v_y^2}$

The function $w = f(z)$ which fully represents the flow pattern is called the *complex potential*.

In the study of electrostatics and gravitational fields, the curves $\phi(x, y) = c$ and $\psi(x, y) = c'$ are called *equipotential lines* and *lines of force* respectively. In heat flow problems, the curves $\phi(x, y) = c$ and $\psi(x, y) = c'$ are known as *isothermals* and *heat flow lines* respectively.

ILLUSTRATIVE EXAMPLES

Example 1. *Find p such that the function f(z) expressed in polar coordinates as $f(z) = r^2 \cos 2\theta + ir^2 \sin p\theta$ is analytic.*

Sol. Let $f(z) = u + iv$, then $u = r^2 \cos 2\theta,\ v = r^2 \sin p\theta$

$$\frac{\partial u}{\partial r} = 2r \cos 2\theta, \quad \frac{\partial v}{\partial r} = 2r \sin p\theta$$

$$\frac{\partial u}{\partial \theta} = -2r^2 \sin 2\theta, \quad \frac{\partial v}{\partial \theta} = pr^2 \cos p\theta$$

For $f(z)$ to be analytic, $\quad \dfrac{\partial u}{\partial r} = \dfrac{1}{r}\dfrac{\partial v}{\partial \theta}$ and $\dfrac{\partial v}{\partial r} = -\dfrac{1}{r}\dfrac{\partial u}{\partial \theta}$

$\therefore \quad 2r \cos 2\theta = pr \cos p\theta$ and $2r \sin p\theta = 2r \sin 2\theta$

Both these equations are satisfied if $p = 2$.

Note. For a function $f(z)$ to be analytic, the first order partial derivatives of u and v must be continuous in addition to C-R equations.

Example 2. *Show that the function $f(z) = \sqrt{|xy|}$ is not regular at the origin, although Cauchy-Riemann equations are satisfied.* (C.U. Dec. 2009)

Sol. Let $\quad f(z) = u(x, y) + iv(x, y) = \sqrt{|xy|}$, then $u(x, y) = \sqrt{|xy|},\ v(x, y) = 0$

At the origin (0, 0), we have

$$\frac{\partial u}{\partial x} = \underset{x \to 0}{\text{Lt}} \frac{u(x, 0) - u(0, 0)}{x} = \underset{x \to 0}{\text{Lt}} \frac{0 - 0}{x} = 0$$

$$\frac{\partial u}{\partial y} = \underset{y \to 0}{\text{Lt}} \frac{u(0, y) - u(0, 0)}{y} = \underset{y \to 0}{\text{Lt}} \frac{0 - 0}{y} = 0$$

$$\frac{\partial v}{\partial x} = \underset{x \to 0}{\text{Lt}} \frac{v(x, 0) - v(0, 0)}{x} = \underset{x \to 0}{\text{Lt}} \frac{0 - 0}{x} = 0$$

$$\frac{\partial v}{\partial y} = \underset{y \to 0}{\text{Lt}} \frac{v(0, y) - v(0, 0)}{y} = \underset{y \to 0}{\text{Lt}} \frac{0 - 0}{y} = 0$$

Clearly, $\quad \dfrac{\partial u}{\partial x} = \dfrac{\partial v}{\partial y},\ \dfrac{\partial u}{\partial y} = -\dfrac{\partial v}{\partial x}$

Hence C-R equations are satisfied at the origin.

Now $\quad f'(0) = \underset{z \to 0}{\text{Lt}} \dfrac{f(z) - f(0)}{z} = \underset{z \to 0}{\text{Lt}} \dfrac{\sqrt{|xy|} - 0}{x + iy}$

If $z \to 0$ along the line $y = mx$, we get

$$f'(0) = \underset{x \to 0}{\text{Lt}} \frac{\sqrt{|mx^2|}}{x(1 + im)} = \underset{x \to 0}{\text{Lt}} \frac{\sqrt{|m|}}{1 + im}$$

Now this limit is not unique since it depends on m. Therefore, $f'(0)$ does not exist. Hence the function $f(z)$ is not regular at the origin.

Example 3. *Prove that the function $f(z)$ defined by*

$$f(z) = \frac{x^3(1+i) - y^3(1-i)}{x^2+y^2}, \; z \neq 0 \text{ and } f(0) = 0$$

is continuous and the Cauchy-Riemann equations are satisfied at the origin, yet $f'(0)$ does not exist.

Sol. Here, $$f(z) = \frac{(x^3 - y^3) + i(x^3 + y^3)}{x^2+y^2}, \; z \neq 0$$

Let $$f(z) = u + iv = \frac{x^3 - y^3}{x^2+y^2} + i\frac{x^3 + y^3}{x^2+y^2},$$

then $$u = \frac{x^3 - y^3}{x^2+y^2}, \; v = \frac{x^3 + y^3}{x^2+y^2}$$

Since $z \neq 0 \;\Rightarrow\; x \neq 0, y \neq 0$

$\therefore$ u and v are rational functions of x and y with non-zero denominators. Thus, u, v and hence $f(z)$ *are continuous functions when $z \neq 0$.* To test them for continuity at $z = 0$, on changing u, v to polar coordinates by putting $x = r\cos\theta$, $y = r\sin\theta$, we get

$$u = r(\cos^3\theta - \sin^3\theta) \text{ and } v = r(\cos^3\theta + \sin^3\theta)$$

When $z \to 0$, $r \to 0$

$$\therefore \quad \underset{z\to 0}{\text{Lt}}\, u = \underset{r\to 0}{\text{Lt}}\, r(\cos^3\theta - \sin^3\theta) = 0$$

Similarly, $$\underset{z\to 0}{\text{Lt}}\, v = 0$$

$$\therefore \quad \underset{r\to 0}{\text{Lt}}\, f(z) = 0 = f(0)$$

$\Rightarrow$ $f(z)$ is continuous at $z = 0$.

Hence $f(z)$ is continuous for all values of z.

At the origin $(0, 0)$, we have

$$\frac{\partial u}{\partial x} = \underset{x\to 0}{\text{Lt}} \frac{u(x,0) - u(0,0)}{x} = \underset{x\to 0}{\text{Lt}} \frac{x-0}{x} = 1$$

$$\frac{\partial u}{\partial y} = \underset{y\to 0}{\text{Lt}} \frac{u(0,y) - u(0,0)}{y} = \underset{y\to 0}{\text{Lt}} \frac{-y-0}{y} = -1$$

$$\frac{\partial v}{\partial x} = \underset{x\to 0}{\text{Lt}} \frac{v(x,0) - v(0,0)}{x} = \underset{x\to 0}{\text{Lt}} \frac{x-0}{x} = 1$$

$$\frac{\partial v}{\partial y} = \underset{y\to 0}{\text{Lt}} \frac{v(0,y) - v(0,0)}{y} = \underset{y\to 0}{\text{Lt}} \frac{y-0}{y} = 1$$

$$\therefore \quad \frac{\partial u}{\partial x} = \frac{\partial v}{\partial y} \text{ and } \frac{\partial u}{\partial y} = -\frac{\partial v}{\partial x}$$

Hence C-R equations are satisfied at the origin.

Now, $$f'(0) = \underset{z\to 0}{\text{Lt}} \frac{f(z) - f(0)}{z} = \underset{z\to 0}{\text{Lt}} \frac{(x^3 - y^3) + i(x^3 + y^3) - 0}{(x^2+y^2)(x+iy)}$$

Let $z \to 0$ along the line $y = x$, then

$$f'(0) = \lim_{x \to 0} \frac{0 + 2ix^3}{2x^3(1+i)} = \frac{i}{1+i} = \frac{i(1-i)}{2} = \frac{1+i}{2} \quad ...(1)$$

Also, let $z \to 0$ along the x-axis (*i.e.*, $y = 0$), then

$$f'(0) = \lim_{x \to 0} \frac{x^3 + ix^3}{x^3} = 1 + i \quad ...(2)$$

Since the limits (1) and (2) are different, $f'(0)$ does not exist.

Example 4. *Prove that the function sinh z is analytic and find its derivative.*

Sol. Here $f(z) = u + iv = \sinh z = \sinh (x + iy) = \sinh x \cos y + i \cosh x \sin y$

$\therefore$ $u = \sinh x \cos y$ and $v = \cosh x \sin y$

$$\frac{\partial u}{\partial x} = \cosh x \cos y, \quad \frac{\partial u}{\partial y} = - \sinh x \sin y$$

$$\frac{\partial v}{\partial x} = \sinh x \sin y, \quad \frac{\partial v}{\partial y} = \cosh x \cos y$$

$$\therefore \quad \frac{\partial u}{\partial x} = \frac{\partial v}{\partial y} \quad \text{and} \quad \frac{\partial u}{\partial y} = -\frac{\partial v}{\partial x}$$

Thus C-R equations are satisfied.

Since $\sinh x$, $\cosh x$, $\sin y$ and $\cos y$ are continuous functions, $\frac{\partial u}{\partial x}, \frac{\partial u}{\partial y}, \frac{\partial v}{\partial x}$ and $\frac{\partial v}{\partial y}$ are also continuous functions satisfying C-R equations.

Hence $f(z)$ is analytic everywhere.

Now $$f'(z) = \frac{\partial u}{\partial x} + i\frac{\partial v}{\partial x}$$

$$= \cosh x \cos y + i \sinh x \sin y = \cosh (x + iy) = \cosh z.$$

Example 5. *Determine the analytic function whose real part is $e^{2x} (x \cos 2y - y \sin 2y)$.*

Sol. Let $f(z) = u + iv$ be the analytic function,

where $u = e^{2x} (x \cos 2y - y \sin 2y)$

$$\therefore \quad \frac{\partial u}{\partial x} = 2e^{2x} (x \cos 2y - y \sin 2y) + e^{2x} \cos 2y$$

$$= e^{2x} (2x \cos 2y - 2y \sin 2y + \cos 2y) \quad ...(1)$$

$$\frac{\partial u}{\partial y} = e^{2x} (- 2x \sin 2y - \sin 2y - 2y \cos 2y)$$

$$= - e^{2x}(2x \sin 2y + \sin 2y + 2y \cos 2y) \quad ...(2)$$

Since $f(z)$ is analytic, u and v must satisfy C-R equations

$$\frac{\partial u}{\partial x} = \frac{\partial v}{\partial y} \quad \text{and} \quad \frac{\partial u}{\partial y} = -\frac{\partial v}{\partial x}$$

Now $$\frac{\partial v}{\partial y} = \frac{\partial u}{\partial x} = e^{2x} (2x \cos 2y - 2y \sin 2y + \cos 2y)$$

Integrating w.r.t. y, treating x as constant, we get

$$v = e^{2x}\left[2x.\frac{\sin 2y}{2} - \left\{2y\left(-\frac{\cos 2y}{2}\right) - (2)\left(-\frac{\sin 2y}{4}\right)\right\} + \frac{\sin 2y}{2}\right] + \phi(x)$$

$$= e^{2x}(x \sin 2y + y \cos 2y) + \phi(x) \qquad ...(3)$$

where $\phi(x)$ is an arbitrary function of x.

$$\therefore \qquad \frac{\partial v}{\partial x} = 2e^{2x}(x \sin 2y + y \cos 2y) + e^{2x}(\sin 2y) + \phi'(x)$$

$$= e^{2x}(2x \sin 2y + \sin 2y + 2y \cos 2y) + \phi'(x)$$

But $$\frac{\partial v}{\partial x} = -\frac{\partial u}{\partial y} = e^{2x}(2x \sin 2y + \sin 2y + 2y \cos 2y) \qquad \text{[From (2)]}$$

$\therefore \qquad \phi'(x) = 0$

$\Rightarrow \qquad \phi(x) = c$, an arbitrary constant.

$\therefore$ From (3), $v = e^{2x}(x \sin 2y + y \cos 2y) + c$

$$f(z) = u + iv = e^{2x}(x \cos 2y - y \sin 2y) + ie^{2x}(x \sin 2y + y \cos 2y) + ic$$

$$= e^{2x}[(x + iy)\cos 2y + i(x + iy)\sin 2y] + c'$$

$$= (x + iy)\,e^{2x}(\cos 2y + i \sin 2y) + c'$$

$$= ze^{2z}\,.\,e^{2iy} + c' = ze^{2(x + iy)} + c' = ze^{2z} + c'.$$

(Milne Thomson's Method)

This method determines the analytic function $f(z)$ when u or v is given.

Since $z = x + iy,\ \bar{z} = x - iy$ so that $x = \dfrac{z + \bar{z}}{2},\ y = \dfrac{z - \bar{z}}{2i}$

Let $$f(z) = u(x, y) + iv\,(x, y) \qquad ...(1)$$

$$= u\left(\frac{z + \bar{z}}{2}, \frac{z - \bar{z}}{2i}\right) + iv\left(\frac{z + \bar{z}}{2}, \frac{z - \bar{z}}{2i}\right)$$

Considering this as an identity in the two independent variables z, $\bar{z}$ and putting $\bar{z} = z$, we get

$$f(z) = u(z, 0) + iv\,(z, 0)$$

which is the same as (1) if we replace x by z and y by 0.

Now $f(z) = u + iv$

$$\Rightarrow \qquad f'(z) = \frac{\partial u}{\partial x} + i\frac{\partial v}{\partial x} = \frac{\partial u}{\partial x} - i\frac{\partial u}{\partial y} \qquad \text{[C-R equations]}$$

$$= e^{2x}(2x \cos 2y - 2y \sin 2y + \cos 2y) + ie^{2x}(2x \sin 2y + \sin 2y + 2y \cos 2y)$$

On replacing x by z and y by 0 on R.H.S., we get $f'(z) = e^{2z}(2z + 1)$

Integrating w.r.t. z, we have $f(z) = (2z + 1)\dfrac{e^{2z}}{2} - 2.\dfrac{e^{2z}}{4} + c = ze^{2z} + c.$

Example 6. *Determine the analytic function $w = u + iv$, if $v = \log (x^2 + y^2) + x - 2y$.*

Sol. Here $v = \log (x^2 + y^2) + x - 2y$

$$\therefore \quad \frac{\partial v}{\partial x} = \frac{2x}{x^2 + y^2} + 1$$

$$\frac{\partial v}{\partial y} = \frac{2y}{x^2 + y^2} - 2$$

Since $w = u + iv$

$$\frac{dw}{dz} = \frac{\partial u}{\partial x} + i\frac{\partial v}{\partial x} = \frac{\partial v}{\partial y} + i\frac{\partial v}{\partial x} \quad \text{[C-R equations]}$$

$$= \left(\frac{2y}{x^2 + y^2} - 2\right) + i\left(\frac{2x}{x^2 + y^2} + 1\right)$$

Replacing x by z and y by 0, we get $\frac{dw}{dz} = -2 + i\left(\frac{2}{z} + 1\right) = (i - 2) + \frac{2i}{z}$

Integrating w.r.t. z, we have $w = (i - 2)z + 2i \log z + c.$

Example 7. *Show that the function $u = e^{-2xy} \sin (x^2 - y^2)$ is harmonic. Find the conjugate function v and express $u + iv$ as an analytic function of z.* (C.U. Dec. 2006, 2009)

Sol. Here $u = e^{-2xy} \sin (x^2 - y^2)$

$$\therefore \quad \frac{\partial u}{\partial x} = -2y\, e^{-2xy} \sin (x^2 - y^2) + 2x\, e^{-2xy} \cos (x^2 - y^2)$$

$$\frac{\partial^2 u}{\partial x^2} = 4y^2 e^{-2xy} \sin (x^2 - y^2) - 4xy\, e^{-2xy} \cos (x^2 - y^2) + 2e^{-2xy} \cos (x^2 - y^2)$$
$$- 4xy\, e^{-2xy} \cos (x^2 - y^2) - 4x^2 e^{-2xy} \sin (x^2 - y^2) \quad ...(1)$$

$$\frac{\partial u}{\partial y} = -2x\, e^{-2xy} \sin (x^2 - y^2) - 2y\, e^{-2xy} \cos (x^2 - y^2)$$

$$\frac{\partial^2 u}{\partial y^2} = 4x^2 e^{-2xy} \sin (x^2 - y^2) + 4xy\, e^{-2xy} \cos (x^2 - y^2) - 2e^{-2xy} \cos (x^2 - y^2)$$
$$+ 4xy\, e^{-2xy} \cos (x^2 - y^2) - 4y^2 e^{-2xy} \sin (x^2 - y^2) \quad ...(2)$$

Adding (1) and (2), we get

$$\frac{\partial^2 u}{\partial x^2} + \frac{\partial^2 u}{\partial y^2} = 0$$ which proves that u is harmonic.

Now, let $f(z) = u + iv$

then $$f'(z) = \frac{\partial u}{\partial x} + i\frac{\partial v}{\partial x} = \frac{\partial u}{\partial x} - i\frac{\partial u}{\partial y} \quad \text{[C-R equations]}$$

$$= [-2y\, e^{-2xy} \sin (x^2 - y^2) + 2x\, e^{-2xy} \cos (x^2 - y^2)]$$
$$+ i\, [2x\, e^{-2xy} \sin (x^2 - y^2) + 2y\, e^{-2xy} \cos (x^2 - y^2)]$$

Replacing x by z and y by 0, we get

$$f'(z) = 2z \cos z^2 + 2iz \sin z^2 = 2z (\cos z^2 + i \sin z^2) = 2z e^{iz^2}$$

Integrating w.r.t. z, we have

$$f(z) = -i\, e^{iz^2} + C \text{ (C = A + iB is a complex constant)}$$

which expresses $u + iv$ as an analytic function of z.

Since $$u + iv = -ie^{iz^2} + C = -ie^{i(x+iy)^2} + C$$
$$= -ie^{i(x^2-y^2+2ixy)} + C = -ie^{-2xy} \cdot e^{i(x^2-y^2)} + C$$
$$= -ie^{-2xy}[\cos(x^2 - y^2) + i \sin(x^2 - y^2)] + C$$
$$= e^{-2xy} \sin(x^2 - y^2) + i[-e^{-2xy} \cos(x^2 - y^2)] + C$$

$\therefore$ $$v = -e^{-2xy} \cos(x^2 - y^2) + B.$$

Example 8. *An electrostatic field in the xy-plane is given by the potential function* $\phi = 3x^2y - y^3$, *find the stream function.*

Sol. Let $\psi(x, y)$ be a stream function.

By C-R equations $$\frac{\partial \psi}{\partial x} = -\frac{\partial \phi}{\partial y} = -3x^2 + 3y^2 \quad \text{...(1)}$$

$$\frac{\partial \psi}{\partial y} = \frac{\partial \phi}{\partial x} = 6xy \quad \text{...(2)}$$

Integrating (1) w.r.t.x, treating y as constant, we get

$$\psi = -x^3 + 3xy^2 + F(y)$$

so that $$\frac{\partial \psi}{\partial y} = 6xy + F'(y) \quad \text{...(3)}$$

From (2) and (3), $6xy + F'(y) = 6xy$ or $F'(y) = 0$ $\therefore$ $F(y) = c$

Hence $$\psi = -x^3 + 3xy^2 + c.$$

Example 9. *If* $u - v = (x - y)(x^2 + 4xy + y^2)$ *and* $f(z) = u + iv$ *is an analytic function of* $z = x + iy$, *find* $f(z)$ *in terms of* z.

Sol. Here $$f(z) = u + iv$$

$\therefore$ $$i f(z) = iu + v$$

Adding $$(1 + i) f(z) = (u - v) + i(u + v)$$

Let $(1 + i) f(z) = F(z)$, $u - v = U$, $u + v = V$, then

$$F(z) = U + iV$$

Now $$U = u - v = (x - y)(x^2 + 4xy + y^2)$$

$\Rightarrow$ $$\frac{\partial U}{\partial x} = x^2 + 4xy + y^2 + (x - y)(2x + 4y) = 3x^2 + 6xy - 3y^2$$

and $$\frac{\partial U}{\partial y} = -(x^2 + 4xy + y^2) + (x - y)(4x + 2y) = 3x^2 - 6xy - 3y^2$$

$\therefore$ $$F'(z) = \frac{\partial U}{\partial x} + i\frac{\partial V}{\partial x} = \frac{\partial U}{\partial x} - i\frac{\partial U}{\partial y} \quad \text{[C-R equations]}$$
$$= (3x^2 + 6xy - 3y^2) - i(3x^2 - 6xy - 3y^2)$$

Replacing x by z and y by 0, we get

$$F'(z) = 3z^2 - 3iz^2 = 3(1 - i)z^2$$

Integrating both sides,

$$F(z) = (1 - i) z^3 + c$$

$\Rightarrow \quad (1 + i) f(z) = (1 - i) z^3 + c$

$$f(z) = \frac{1-i}{1+i} z^3 + \frac{c}{1+i} = \frac{(1-i)^2}{1-i^2} z^3 + \frac{c}{1+i}$$

Hence $\quad f(z) = - iz^3 + A.$

Example 10. *If f(z) is a regular function of z, prove that*

$$\left(\frac{\partial^2}{\partial x^2} + \frac{\partial^2}{\partial y^2}\right) |f(z)|^2 = 4 \, |f'(z)|^2. \quad \textit{(C.U. June 2007, Dec. 2006, 08, 09)}$$

Sol. Let $f(z) = u + iv$ so that $|f(z)| = \sqrt{u^2 + v^2}$

or $\quad |f(z)|^2 = u^2 + v^2 = \phi(x, y)$ (say)

$$\therefore \quad \frac{\partial \phi}{\partial x} = 2u \frac{\partial u}{\partial x} + 2v \frac{\partial v}{\partial x}$$

$$\frac{\partial^2 \phi}{\partial x^2} = 2\left[u \frac{\partial^2 u}{\partial x^2} + \left(\frac{\partial u}{\partial x}\right)^2 + v \frac{\partial^2 v}{\partial x^2} + \left(\frac{\partial v}{\partial x}\right)^2\right]$$

Similarly, $$\frac{\partial^2 \phi}{\partial y^2} = 2\left[u \frac{\partial^2 u}{\partial y^2} + \left(\frac{\partial u}{\partial y}\right)^2 + v \frac{\partial^2 v}{\partial y^2} + \left(\frac{\partial v}{\partial y}\right)^2\right]$$

Adding, we get

$$\frac{\partial^2 \phi}{\partial x^2} + \frac{\partial^2 \phi}{\partial y^2} = 2\left[u\left(\frac{\partial^2 u}{\partial x^2} + \frac{\partial^2 u}{\partial y^2}\right) + \left(\frac{\partial u}{\partial x}\right)^2 + \left(\frac{\partial u}{\partial y}\right)^2 + v\left(\frac{\partial^2 v}{\partial x^2} + \frac{\partial^2 v}{\partial y^2}\right) + \left(\frac{\partial v}{\partial x}\right)^2 + \left(\frac{\partial v}{\partial y}\right)^2\right] \quad ...(1)$$

Since $f(z) = u + iv$ is a regular function of z, u and v satisfy C-R equations and Laplace's equation.

$$\therefore \quad \frac{\partial u}{\partial x} = \frac{\partial v}{\partial y}, \frac{\partial u}{\partial y} = -\frac{\partial v}{\partial x} \quad \text{and} \quad \frac{\partial^2 u}{\partial x^2} + \frac{\partial^2 u}{\partial y^2} = 0 = \frac{\partial^2 v}{\partial x^2} + \frac{\partial^2 v}{\partial y^2}$$

$\therefore$ From (1), we get

$$\frac{\partial^2 \phi}{\partial x^2} + \frac{\partial^2 \phi}{\partial y^2} = 2\left[0 + \left(\frac{\partial u}{\partial x}\right)^2 + \left(\frac{\partial v}{\partial x}\right)^2 + 0 + \left(\frac{\partial v}{\partial x}\right)^2 + \left(\frac{\partial u}{\partial x}\right)^2\right]$$

$$= 4\left[\left(\frac{\partial u}{\partial x}\right)^2 + \left(\frac{\partial v}{\partial x}\right)^2\right] \quad ...(2)$$

Now $\quad f(z) = u + iv$

$$\therefore \quad f'(z) = \frac{\partial u}{\partial x} + i \frac{\partial v}{\partial x} \quad \text{and} \quad |f'(z)|^2 = \left(\frac{\partial u}{\partial x}\right)^2 + \left(\frac{\partial v}{\partial x}\right)^2$$

From (2), we get

$$\left(\frac{\partial^2}{\partial x^2} + \frac{\partial^2}{\partial y^2}\right) \phi = 4 \, |f'(z)|^2 \quad \text{or} \quad \left(\frac{\partial^2}{\partial x^2} + \frac{\partial^2}{\partial y^2}\right) |f(z)|^2 = 4 \, |f'(z)|^2.$$

TEST YOUR KNOWLEDGE

1. Determine a, b, c, d so that the function $f(z) = (x^2 + axy + by^2) + i(cx^2 + dxy + y^2)$ is analytic.
2. Determine p such that the function $f(z) = \frac{1}{2}\log(x^2 + y^2) + i\tan^{-1}\frac{px}{y}$ be an analytic function.
3. Show that the polar form of Cauchy-Riemann equations are $\frac{\partial u}{\partial r} = \frac{1}{r}\frac{\partial v}{\partial \theta}, \frac{\partial v}{\partial r} = -\frac{1}{r}\frac{\partial u}{\partial \theta}$.

   Deduce that $\frac{\partial^2 u}{\partial r^2} + \frac{1}{r}\frac{\partial u}{\partial r} + \frac{1}{r^2}\frac{\partial^2 u}{\partial \theta^2} = 0$.
4. If $f(z) = \frac{x^3 y(y - ix)}{x^6 + y^2}, z \neq 0, f(0) = 0$, prove that $\frac{f(z) - f(0)}{z} \to 0$ as $z \to 0$ along any radius vector but not as $z \to 0$ in any manner.
5. Show that the function $f(z)$ defined by $f(z) = \frac{x^3 y^5 (x + iy)}{x^6 + y^{10}}$, $z \neq 0$, $f(0) = 0$, is not analytic at the origin even though it satisfies Cauchy-Riemann equations at the origin.
6. Determine which of the following functions are analytic:

   (i) e^z (ii) $\sin z$ (iii) $\cosh z$

   (iv) $\frac{1}{z}$ (v) $\frac{x + iy}{x^2 + y^2}$ (vi) $\frac{1}{2}\log(x^2 + y^2) + i\tan^{-1}\frac{y}{x}$.
7. Show that $|z|^2$ is not analytic at any point.
8. Show that $u + iv = \frac{x - iy}{x - iy + a}$ where $a \neq 0$, is not an analytic function of $z = x + iy$ whereas $u - iv$ is such a function.
9. Determine the analytic function whose real part is

   (i) $x^3 - 3xy^2 + 3x^2 - 3y^2 + 1$ *(C.U. June 2007, 09)* (ii) $\log\sqrt{x^2 + y^2}$

   (iii) $e^x(x\cos y - y\sin y)$ (iv) $\cos x\cosh y$

   (v) $e^{-x}(x\sin y - y\cos y)$ (vi) $\frac{\sin 2x}{\cosh 2y - \cos 2x}$.
10. Find the regular function whose imaginary part is

    (i) $\frac{x - y}{x^2 + y^2}$ (ii) $3x^2y - y^3$ *(June 2009, 11)* (iii) $\cos x\cosh y$

    (iv) $\sinh x\cos y$. (v) $e^{-x}(x\sin y - y\cos y)$ *(C.U. June 2010)*
11. Prove that $u = x^2 - y^2 - 2xy - 2x + 3y$ is harmonic. Find a function v such that $f(z) = u + iv$ is analytic. Also express $f(z)$ in terms of z.
12. An electrostatic field in the xy-plane is given by the potential function $\phi = x^2 - y^2$, find the stream function.
13. If $w = \phi + i\psi$ represents the complex potential for an electric field and $\psi = x^2 - y^2 + \frac{x}{x^2 + y^2}$, determine the function ϕ. *(C.U. Dec. 2008)*

14. If the potential function is $\log (x^2 + y^2)$, find the flux function and the complex potential function.

15. In a two dimensional fluid flow, the stream function is $\psi = \tan^{-1}\left(\frac{y}{x}\right)$, find the velocity potential ϕ.

16. If $f(z) = u + iv$ is an analytic function, find $f(z)$ if

(*i*) $u - v = e^x (\cos y - \sin y)$ (*C.U. Dec. 2006*) (*ii*) $u + v = \frac{x}{x^2 + y^2}$, when $f(1) = 1$

(*iii*) $u - v = \frac{\cos x + \sin x - e^{-y}}{2 \cos x - e^y - e^{-y}}$, when $f\left(\frac{\pi}{2}\right) = 0$. (*C.U. Oct. 2011*)

17. If $f(z)$ is an analytic function of z, prove that

(*i*) $\left(\frac{\partial^2}{\partial x^2} + \frac{\partial^2}{\partial y^2}\right) \log | f'(z) | = 0$ (*C.U. June 2007, Dec. 2006*)

(*ii*) $\left(\frac{\partial^2}{\partial x^2} + \frac{\partial^2}{\partial y^2}\right) | \mathrm{R} f(z) |^2 = 2 | f'(z) |^2$.

Answers

1. $a = 2, b = -1, c = -1, d = 2$ **2.** $p = -1$

6. (*i*), (*ii*), (*iii*), (*iv*) except when $z = 0$, (*v*) except when $z = 0$

9. (*i*) $z^3 + 3z^2 + 1 + c$ (*ii*) $\log z + c$ (*iii*) $z e^z + c$

(*iv*) $\cos z + c$ (*v*) $ize^{-z} + 6i$ (*vi*) $\cot z + c$

10. (*i*) $\frac{1+i}{z} + c$ (*ii*) $z^3 + c$ (*iii*) $\sin x \sinh y + c$

(*iv*) $-\cosh x \sin y + c$ (*v*) $-ze^{-z} + c$

11. $v = x^2 - y^2 + 2xy - 2y - 3x + 6$, $f(z) = (1 + i)z^2 - (2 + 3i)z + i6$

12. $\psi = 2xy + c$ **13.** $-2xy + \frac{x}{x^2 + y^2} + c$ **14.** $2 \tan^{-1}\left(\frac{y}{x}\right)$, $2 \log z + c$

15. $\frac{1}{2} \log (x^2 + y^2) + c$ **16.** (*i*) $e^z + c$ (*ii*) $\frac{1}{1-i}\left(\frac{1}{z} - 1\right)$

(*iii*) $\frac{1}{2}\left(1 - \cot \frac{z}{2}\right)$.

1.12. TRANSFORMATION OR MAPPING

We know that the real function $y = f(x)$ can be represented graphically by a curve in the xy-plane. Also, the real function $z = f(x, y)$ can be represented by a surface in three dimensional space. However, this method of graphical representation fails in the case of complex functions because a complex function $w = f(z)$ *i.e.*, $u + iv = f(x + iy)$ involves four real variables, two independent variables x, y and two dependent variables u, v. Thus a four dimensional region is required to represent it graphically in the cartesian fashion. As it is not possible, we choose, two complex planes and call them z-plane and w-plane. In the z-plane, we plot the point $z = x + iy$ and in the w-plane, we plot the corresponding point $w = u + iv$. Thus the function $w = f(z)$ defines a correspondence between points of these two planes. If the point z describes some curve C in the z-plane, the point w will move along a corresponding curve C′ in the w-plane, since to each (x, y) there corresponds a point (u, v). *The function $w = f(z)$ thus defines a mapping or transformation of the z-plane into the w-plane.*

For example, consider the transformation $w = z + (1 - i)$. Let us determine the region D′ of the w-plane corresponding to the rectangular region D in the z-plane bounded by $x = 0$, $y = 0$, $x = 1$ and $y = 2$.

Since $w = z + (1 - i)$, we have

$$u + iv = (x + iy) + (1 - i) = (x + 1) + i(y - 1)$$

Thus $u = x + 1$ and $v = y - 1$

Hence the lines $x = 0$, $y = 0$, $x = 1$ and $y = 2$ in the z-plane are mapped onto the lines $u = 1$, $v = -1$, $u = 2$ and $v = 1$ in the w-plane. The regions D and D′ are shown shaded in the figure.

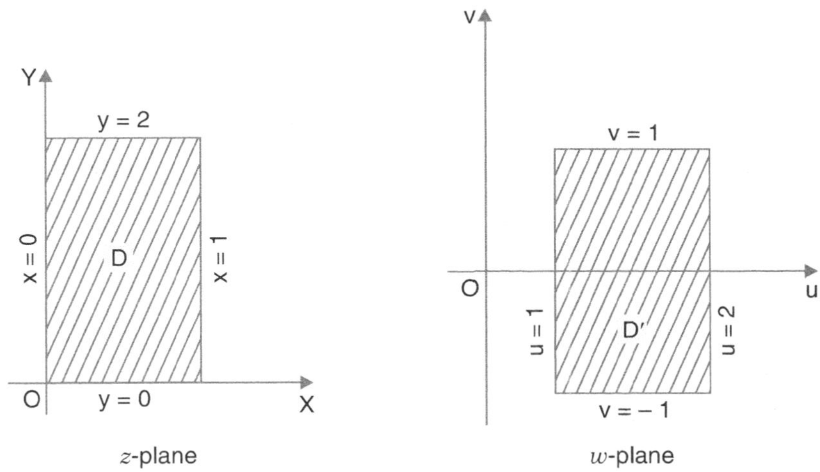

1.13. CONFORMAL TRANSFORMATION

Suppose two curves C_1, C_2 in the z-plane intersect at the point P and the corresponding curves C_1', C_2' in the w-plane intersect at P′ under the transformation $w = f(z)$. *If the angle of intersection of the curves at P is the same as the angle of intersection of the curves at P′, both in magnitude and sense, then the transformation is said to be conformal at P.*

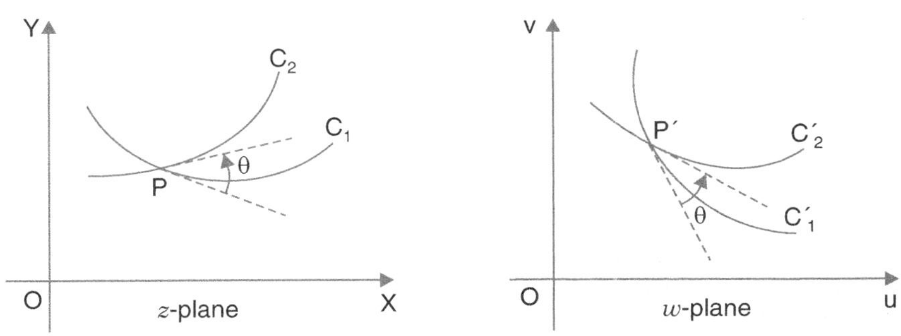

Definition. A transformation which preserves angles both in magnitude and sense between every pair of curves through a point is said to be **conformal** at the point. If a transformation preserve angles in magnitude alone is called **isogonal.**

The conditions under which the transformation $w = f(z)$ is conformal are given by the following theorem.

1.14. THEOREM

If $f(z)$ is analytic and $f'(z) \neq 0$ in a region R of the z-plane, then the mapping $w = f(z)$ is conformal at all points of R.

Proof. Let P(z) be a point in the region R of the z-plane and P′(w) the corresponding point in the region R′ of the w-plane. Suppose P moves on a curve C and P′ moves on the corresponding curve C′. Let Q($z + \delta z$) be a neighbouring point on C and Q′ ($w + \delta w$) the corresponding point on C′ so that $\overrightarrow{PQ} = \delta z$ and $\overrightarrow{P'Q'} = \delta w$.

Then δz is a complex number whose modulus r is the length PQ and amplitude θ is the angle which PQ makes with the x-axis.

$$\therefore \qquad \delta z = re^{i\theta}$$

Similarly, $\delta w = r'e^{i\theta'}$, where r' is the modulus and θ' is the amplitude of δw.

$$\therefore \qquad \frac{\delta w}{\delta z} = \frac{r'}{r} e^{i(\theta' - \theta)}$$

Let the tangent to C at P make an angle α with x-axis and the tangent to C′ at P′ make an angle α' with u-axis, then as $\delta z \to 0$, $\theta \to \alpha$ and $\theta' \to \alpha'$.

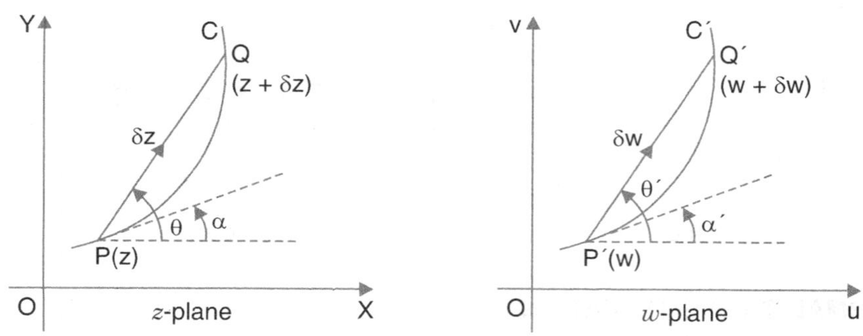

$$\therefore \qquad f'(z) = \frac{dw}{dz} = \underset{\delta z \to 0}{\text{Lt}} \frac{\delta w}{\delta z} = \underset{\delta z \to 0}{\text{Lt}} \left(\frac{r'}{r}\right) e^{i(\theta' - \theta)} \qquad \ldots(1)$$

Since $f'(z) \neq 0$, let $f'(z) = \rho e^{i\phi}$, then $\rho = |\, f'(z) \,|$ and ϕ = amplitude of $f'(z)$.

$$\therefore \text{ From (1),} \qquad \rho e^{i\phi} = \underset{\delta z \to 0}{\text{Lt}} \left(\frac{r'}{r}\right) e^{i(\theta' - \theta)}$$

Thus
$$\rho = \underset{\delta z \to 0}{\text{Lt}} \frac{r'}{r} \qquad \ldots(2)$$

and
$$\phi = \underset{\delta z \to 0}{\text{Lt}} (\theta' - \theta) = \alpha' - \alpha \qquad \ldots(3)$$

Now let C_1 be another curve through P in the z-plane and C_1' the corresponding curve through P′ in the w-plane. If the tangent to C_1 at P makes an angle β with x-axis and the tangent to C_1' at P′ makes an angle β' with u-axis, then as in (3),

$$\phi = \beta' - \beta \qquad \ldots(4)$$

From (3) and (4), $\alpha' - \alpha = \beta' - \beta$ or $\beta - \alpha = \beta' - \alpha' = \gamma$

Thus angle between the curves before and after the mapping is preserved in magnitude and sense. Hence the mapping by the analytic function $w = f(z)$ is conformal at each point where $f'(z) \neq 0$.

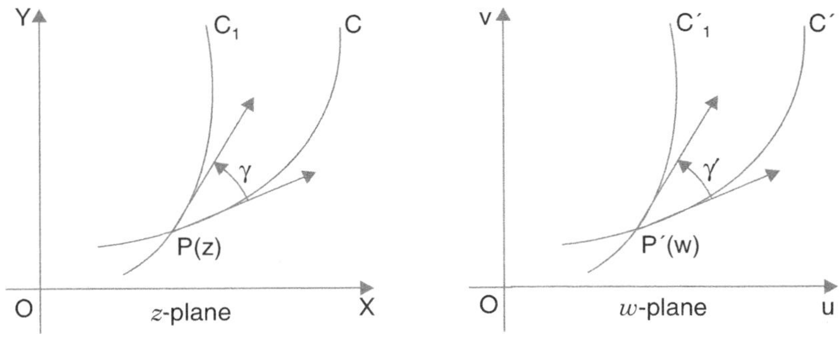

Note 1. A point at which $f'(z) = 0$ is called a **critical point** of the transformation.

Note 2. From (2), $$\rho = \underset{\delta z \to 0}{\text{Lt}} \frac{r'}{r}$$

It follows that under the conformal transformation $w = f(z)$, the lengths of arcs through P are magnified in the ratio $\rho : 1$, where $\rho = | f'(z) |$. Thus an infinitesimal length in the z-plane is magnified by the factor $| f'(z) |$ in the w-plane and consequently infinitesimal areas in the z-plane are magnified by the factor $| f'(z) |^2$ in the w-plane.

Note 3. From (3), $\alpha' = \alpha + \phi$ shows that the tangent to the curve C at P is rotated through an angle $\phi = \text{amp } [f'(z)]$ under the given transformation.

Note 4. A harmonic function remains harmonic under a conformal transformation.

Example. *For the conformal transformation $w = z^2$, show that*

(i) the co-efficient of magnification at $z = 1 + i$ is $2\sqrt{2}$.

(ii) the angle of rotation at $z = 1 + i$ is $\frac{\pi}{4}$.

Sol. Here $$f(z) = w = z^2$$

$$\therefore \quad f'(z) = 2z \quad \text{and} \quad f'(1 + i) = 2 + 2i$$

$\therefore$ The co-efficient of magnification at $z = 1 + i$ is $| f'(1 + i) | = \sqrt{4 + 4} = 2\sqrt{2}$

The angle of rotation at $z = 1 + i$ is amp. $[f'(1 + i)] = \tan^{-1} \frac{2}{2} = \frac{\pi}{4}$.

1.15. SOME STANDARD TRANSFORMATIONS

1. Translation: w = z + c, where c is a complex constant.

Let $z = x + iy$, $\quad c = a + ib$ and $w = u + iv$

then the transformation becomes $u + iv = (x + iy) + (a + ib) = (x + a) + i(y + b)$

so that $u = x + a$ and $v = y + b$

Thus the transformation is a mere translation of the axes and preserves the shape and size.

For example, the rectangle OMPN in z-plane is transformed to rectangle O′M′P′N′ in the w-plane under the transformation $w = z + (1 + 2i)$.

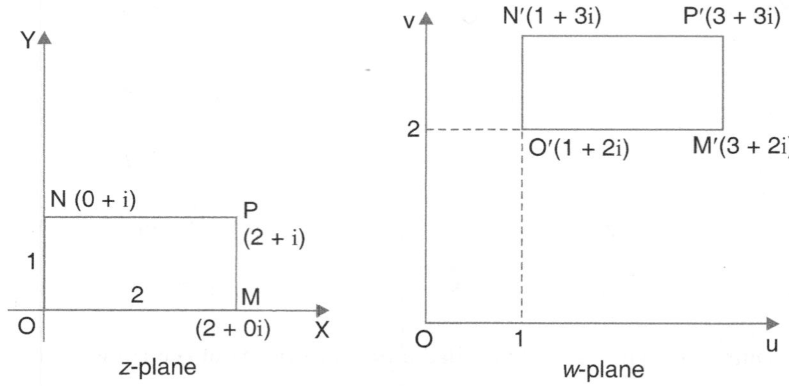

2. Rotation and Magnification: w = cz, where c is complex constant.

Let $$c = pe^{i\alpha},\ z = re^{i\theta} \quad \text{and} \quad w = Re^{i\phi}$$

then the transformation becomes $$Re^{i\phi} = \rho re^{i(\theta + \alpha)}$$

so that $$R = \rho r \quad \text{and} \quad \phi = \theta + \alpha$$

Thus the transformation maps a point (r, θ) in the z-plane into a point P′ $(\rho r, \theta + \alpha)$ in the w-plane. Hence the transformation consists of magnification of the radius vector of P by $\rho = |\, c \,|$ and its rotation through an angle $\alpha = \text{amp}\,(c)$. It maps figures in the z-plane into geometrically similar figures in the w-plane.

For example, the square OMPN in z-plane is transformed to square OM′P′N′ in w-plane under the mapping $w = (1 + i)z$.

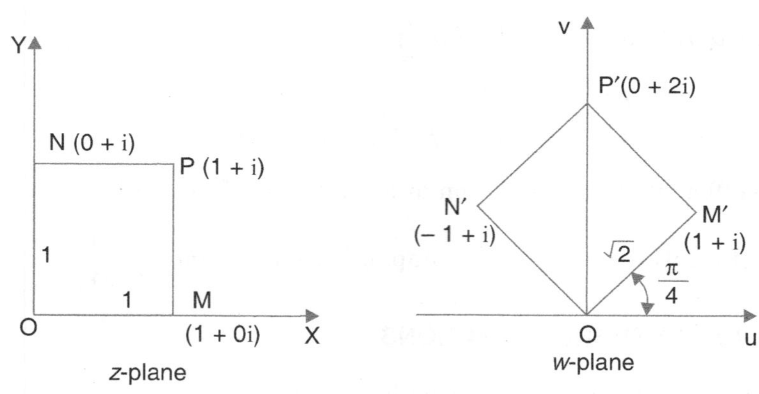

Here $$c = 1 + i = \sqrt{2}\left(\cos\frac{\pi}{4} + i\sin\frac{\pi}{4}\right) = \sqrt{2}\, e^{i\frac{\pi}{4}} \quad \text{so that} \quad w = \sqrt{2}\, re^{i\left(\theta + \frac{\pi}{4}\right)}.$$

3. Inversion: $\mathbf{w = \dfrac{1}{z}}$

Let $$z = re^{i\theta} \quad \text{and} \quad w = Re^{i\phi}$$

then the transformation becomes $Re^{i\phi} = \dfrac{1}{r}e^{-i\theta}$ so that $R = \dfrac{1}{r}$ and $\phi = -\,\theta$.

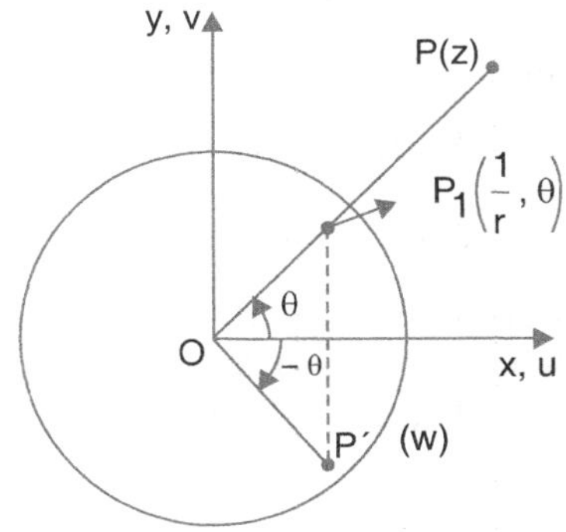

Thus under the transformation $w = \frac{1}{z}$, a point $P(r, \theta)$ in z-plane is mapped into the point $P\left(\frac{1}{r}, -\theta\right)$.

Consider the w-plane superposed on the z-plane. If P is (r, θ) and P_1 is $\left(\frac{1}{r}, \theta\right)$, then

$$OP_1 = \frac{1}{r} = \frac{1}{OP} \quad \textit{i.e.,}\ OP \,.\, OP_1 = 1$$

so that P_1 is inverse of P w.r.t. the unit circle with centre O.

[*The inverse of a point P w.r.t. a circle having centre O and radius k is defined as the point Q on OP such that OP . OQ =* k^2]

The reflection P′ of P_1 in the real axis represents $w = \frac{1}{z}$. Thus the transformation $w = \frac{1}{z}$ is an inversion of z w.r.t. the unit circle $|z| = 1$ followed by reflection of the inverse into the real axis.

Obviously, the transformation $w = \frac{1}{z}$ maps the interior of the unit circle $|z| = 1$ into the exterior of the unit circle $|w| = 1$ and the exterior of $|z| = 1$ into the interior of $|w| = 1$.

However, the origin $z = 0$ is mapped to the point $w = \infty$, called the *point at infinity*.

This transformation maps a circle in z-plane to a circle in w-plane or to a straight line if the circle in z-plane passes through the origin. (C.U. June 2006, 09)

The general equation of any circle in the z-plane is

$$x^2 + y^2 + 2gx + 2fy + c = 0 \qquad \text{...(1)}$$

Let $w = u + iv = \frac{1}{z}$, then $z = \frac{1}{w}$ or $x + iy = \frac{1}{u + iv} = \frac{u - iv}{u^2 + v^2}$

so that $$x = \frac{u}{u^2 + v^2} \quad \text{and} \quad y = \frac{-v}{u^2 + v^2}$$

Substituting the values of x and y in (1), we get

$$\frac{u^2}{(u^2 + v^2)^2} + \frac{v^2}{(u^2 + v^2)^2} + \frac{2gu}{u^2 + v^2} - \frac{2fv}{u^2 + v^2} + c = 0$$

or $$\frac{u^2 + v^2}{(u^2 + v^2)^2} + \frac{2gu}{u^2 + v^2} - \frac{2fv}{u^2 + v^2} + c = 0$$

or $$\frac{1}{u^2 + v^2} + \frac{2gu}{u^2 + v^2} - \frac{2fv}{u^2 + v^2} + c = 0$$

or $$c(u^2 + v^2) + 2gu - 2fv + 1 = 0 \qquad \text{...(2)}$$

If $c \neq 0$, the circle (1) does not pass through the origin and equation (2) represents a circle in the w-plane.

If $c = 0$, the circle (1) passes through the origin and equation (2) reduces to $2gu - 2fv + 1 = 0$ which is a straight line in the w-plane.

Regarding a straight line as a circle of infinite radius, we can say that the transformation $w = \frac{1}{z}$ maps circles into circles.

4. Bilinear Transformation:

A transformation of the form $$w = \frac{az+b}{cz+d} \quad ...(1)$$

where a, b, c, d are complex constants and $ad - bc \neq 0$ is called a **bilinear** or **Mobius transformation** or **linear fractional transformation.**

The transformation given by (1) is conformal, since

$$\frac{dw}{dz} = \frac{ad-bc}{(cz+d)^2} \neq 0$$

The inverse mapping of (1) is $z = \frac{-dw+b}{cw-a}$ ...(2)

which is also a bilinear transformation.

The transformation (1) can be written as

$$cwz + wd - az - b = 0$$

which is linear both in w and z and hence the name bilinear transformation.

From (1), we observe that each point in the z-plane except the point $z = -\frac{d}{c}$ maps into a unique point in the w-plane. Similarly, from (2), we observe that each point in the w-plane except the point $w = \frac{a}{c}$ maps into a unique point in the z-plane. Considering the two exceptional points as points at infinity in respective planes, we can say that there is one to one correspondence between all points in the two planes.

Every bilinear transformation $w = \frac{az+b}{cz+d}$, $ad - bc \neq 0$ is the combination of basic transformations

(*i*) translation: $w = z + c$ (*ii*) rotation and magnification: $w = cz$

(*iii*) inversion: $w = \frac{1}{z}$

By actual division, we have $$w = \frac{a}{c} + \frac{bc-ad}{c^2} \cdot \frac{1}{z+\frac{d}{c}}$$

Taking $w_1 = z + \frac{d}{c}$, $w_2 = \frac{1}{w_1}$, $w_3 = \frac{bc-ad}{c^2} w_2$, we get $w = \frac{a}{c} + w_3$

Thus, by these transformations, we successively pass from z-plane to w_1-plane, from w_1-plane to w_2-plane, from w_2-plane to w_3-plane and finally from w_3-plane to w-plane.

Since each of these auxiliary transformations maps circles into circles, hence a *bilinear transformation also maps circles into circles.*

Note 1. *The cross-ratio is invariant under a bilinear transformation.* (*C.U. Dec. 2006*)

Thus if w_1, w_2, w_3 and w_4 are the respective images of four distinct points z_1, z_2, z_3 and z_4, then

$$\frac{(w_1-w_3)(w_2-w_4)}{(w_1-w_4)(w_2-w_3)} = \frac{(z_1-z_3)(z_2-z_4)}{(z_1-z_4)(z_2-z_3)}.$$

Note 2. In the bilinear transformation $w = \dfrac{az+b}{cz+d}$, $ad - bc \neq 0$ dividing the numerator and denominator of the right hand side by one of the four constants, we observe that there are only three independent constants. Hence *three independent conditions are required to determine a bilinear transformation.*

ILLUSTRATIVE EXAMPLES

Example 11. *Consider the transformation $w = z\, e^{i\pi/4}$ and determine the region in the w-plane corresponding to the triangular region bounded by the lines $x = 0$, $y = 0$ and $x + y = 1$ in the z-plane.*

Sol. The given transformation is

$$w = u + iv = \left(\cos\frac{\pi}{4} + i\sin\frac{\pi}{4}\right)(x + iy)$$

$$= \frac{1}{\sqrt{2}}(1 + i)(x + iy) = \frac{1}{\sqrt{2}}[(x - y) + i(x + y)]$$

$$\therefore \qquad u = \frac{1}{\sqrt{2}}(x - y) \quad \text{and} \quad v = \frac{1}{\sqrt{2}}(x + y)$$

The line $x = 0$ maps into $u = -\dfrac{1}{\sqrt{2}}y$, $v = \dfrac{1}{\sqrt{2}}y$ or into $v = -u$.

The line $y = 0$ maps into $u = \dfrac{1}{\sqrt{2}}x$, $u = \dfrac{1}{\sqrt{2}}x$

or into $v = u$

The line $x + y = 1$ maps into $v = \dfrac{1}{\sqrt{2}}$.

The two regions are shown shaded in the figure.

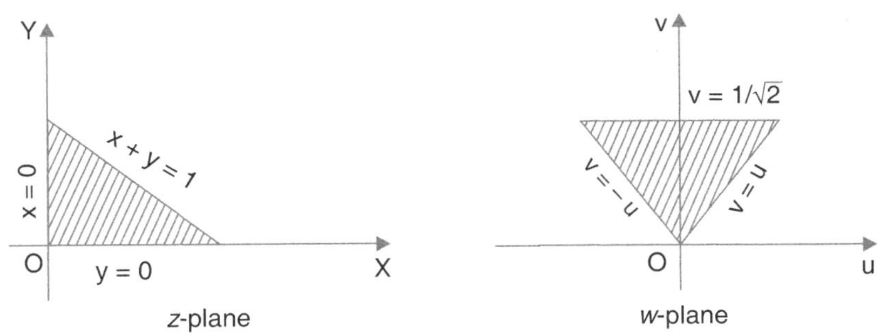

Example 12. *Under the transformation $w = \dfrac{1}{z}$, find the image of $|z - 2i| = 2$.*

Sol. The given transformation is

$$w = \frac{1}{z} \quad \text{or} \quad z = \frac{1}{w} \quad \text{or} \quad x + iy = \frac{1}{u + iv} = \frac{u - iv}{u^2 + v^2}$$

so that $$x = \frac{u}{u^2 + v^2} \quad \text{and} \quad y = -\frac{v}{u^2 + v^2} \qquad \ldots(1)$$

The given curve is $| z - 2i | = 2$ or $| x + i(y - 2) | = 2$

or $x^2 + (y - 2)^2 = 4$ or $x^2 + y^2 - 4y = 0$ ...(2)

which is a circle in the z-plane with centre (0, 2) and radius 2.

Substituting the values of x and y from (1) in (2), we get

$$\frac{u^2}{(u^2+v^2)^2} + \frac{v^2}{(u^2+v^2)^2} + \frac{4v}{u^2+v^2} = 0 \quad \text{or} \quad \frac{u^2+v^2}{(u^2+v^2)^2} + \frac{4v}{u^2+v^2} = 0$$

or $1 + 4v = 0$, a straight line which is the required image of the given curve.

Example 13. *Find the image of the infinite strip* $\frac{1}{4} \le y \le \frac{1}{2}$ *under the transformation* $w = \frac{1}{z}$. *Also show the regions graphically.*

Sol. The given transformation is

$$w = \frac{1}{z} \quad \text{or} \quad z = \frac{1}{w} \quad \text{or} \quad x + iy = \frac{1}{u+iv} = \frac{u - iv}{u^2+v^2}$$

so that $$x = \frac{u}{u^2+v^2} \quad \text{and} \quad y = \frac{-v}{u^2+v^2}$$

If $y = \frac{1}{4}$, then $\frac{-v}{u^2+v^2} = \frac{1}{4}$

or $u^2 + v^2 + 4v = 0$ or $u^2 + (v + 2)^2 = 4$

If $y = \frac{1}{2}$, then $\frac{-v}{u^2+v^2} = \frac{1}{2}$ or $u^2 + v^2 + 2v = 0$ or $u^2 + (v + 1)^2 = 1$

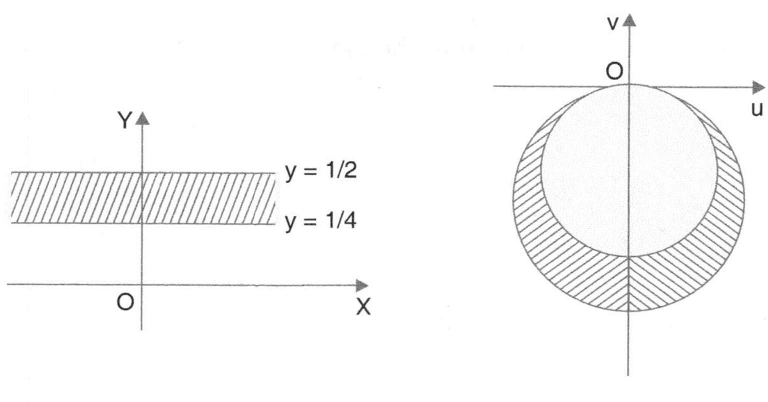

Hence the infinite strip $\frac{1}{4} \le y \le \frac{1}{2}$ is transformed into the region between the two circles

$u^2 + (v + 2)^2 = 4$, centre (0, – 2), radius 2

and $u^2 + (v + 1)^2 = 1$, centre (0, – 1), radius 1.

Example 14. *Show that the transformation* $w = \frac{2z+3}{z-4}$ *maps the circle* $x^2 + y^2 - 4x = 0$ *onto the straight line* $4u + 3 = 0$.

Sol. The given transformation is $\qquad w = \dfrac{2z+3}{z-4}$

The inverse transformation is $\qquad z = \dfrac{4w+3}{w-2}$ ...(1)

Now the equation $x^2 + y^2 - 4x = 0$ can be written as $z\bar{z} - 2(z + \bar{z}) = 0$

Substituting for z and $\bar{z}$ from (1), we get

$$\frac{4w+3}{w-2}\cdot\frac{4\bar{w}+3}{\bar{w}-2} - 2\left(\frac{4w+3}{w-2}+\frac{4\bar{w}+3}{\bar{w}-2}\right) = 0$$

or $\quad 16w\bar{w} + 12w + 12\bar{w} + 9 - 2\,(4w\bar{w} + 3\bar{w} - 8w - 6 + 4w\bar{w} + 3w - 8\bar{w} - 6) = 0$

or $\quad 22(w + \bar{w}) + 33 = 0 \quad$ or $\quad 22(2u) + 33 = 0 \quad$ or $\quad 4u + 3 = 0.$

Example 15. *Show that the transformation $w = z^2$ maps the circle $|z - 1| = 1$ into the cardioid $\rho = 2(1 + \cos\phi)$, where $w = \rho e^{i\phi}$ in the w-plane.*

Sol. Let $z = re^{i\theta}$, then $w = z^2 \Rightarrow \rho e^{i\phi} = r^2e^{2i\theta}$

so that $\qquad \rho = r^2 \quad$ and $\quad \phi = 2\theta$ ...(1)

Now the equation of circle in the z-plane is

$|z - 1| = 1 \quad$ or $\quad |x + iy - 1| = 1$

or $\quad |(x - 1) + iy| = 1 \quad$ or $\quad (x - 1)^2 + y^2 = 1$

or $\quad x^2 + y^2 - 2x = 0 \quad$ or $\quad r^2 - 2r\cos\theta = 0 \quad [\because\ z = x + iy = re^{i\theta} = r(\cos\theta + i\sin\theta)]$

or $\quad r = 2\cos\theta \quad$ or $\quad r^2 = 4\cos^2\theta$

or $\quad r^2 = 2(1 + \cos 2\theta) \quad$ or $\quad \rho = 2(1 + \cos\phi)$ [Using (1)]

$\therefore$ The circle $|z - 1| = 1$ in z-plane transforms into the cardioid $\rho = 2(1 + \cos\phi)$ in w plane.

Example 16. *Determine the region of the w-plane into which the first quadrant of z-plane is mapped by the transformation $w = z^2$.*

Sol. Proceeding as in example 5, $\phi = 2\theta$

For the first quadrant in z-plane, $0 < \theta < \dfrac{\pi}{2} \Rightarrow 0 < \phi < \pi$

Hence the first quadrant of z-plane is mapped into the upper half of w-plane.

Example 17. *Determine the region of the w-plane into which the region $\frac{1}{2} \le x \le 1$ and $\frac{1}{2} \le y \le 1$ is mapped by the transformation $w = z^2$.* (C.U. June 2007)

Sol. The given transformation is $\qquad w = z^2 \quad$ or $\quad u + iv = (x + iy)^2 = (x^2 - y^2) + 2ixy$

so that $\qquad u = x^2 - y^2 \quad$ and $\quad v = 2xy$

When $x = \frac{1}{2}$, we have $\qquad u = \frac{1}{4} - y^2 \quad$ and $\quad v = y \quad$ so that $v^2 = -(u - \frac{1}{4})$

[a left-handed parabola with vertex $(\frac{1}{4}, 0)$ and latus rectum 1]

When $\quad x = 1$, we have $u = 1 - y^2 \quad$ and $\quad v = 2y \quad$ so that $v^2 = -4(u - 1)$

[a left-handed parabola with vertex (1, 0) and latus rectum 4]

When $\quad y = \frac{1}{2}$, we have $u = x^2 - \frac{1}{4}$ and $v = x \quad$ so that $v^2 = u + \frac{1}{4}$

[a right-handed parabola with vertex $(-\frac{1}{4}, 0)$ and latus rectum 1]

When $\quad y = 1$, we have $u = x^2 - 1$ and $v = 2x \quad$ so that $v^2 = 4(u + 1)$

[a right-handed parabola with vertex (– 1, 0) and latus rectum 4]

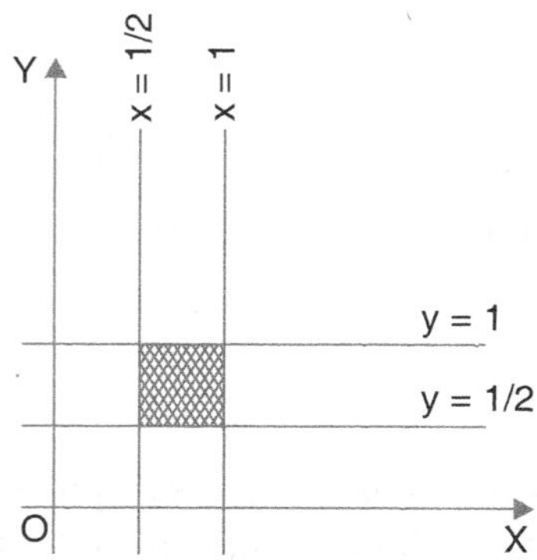

z-plane

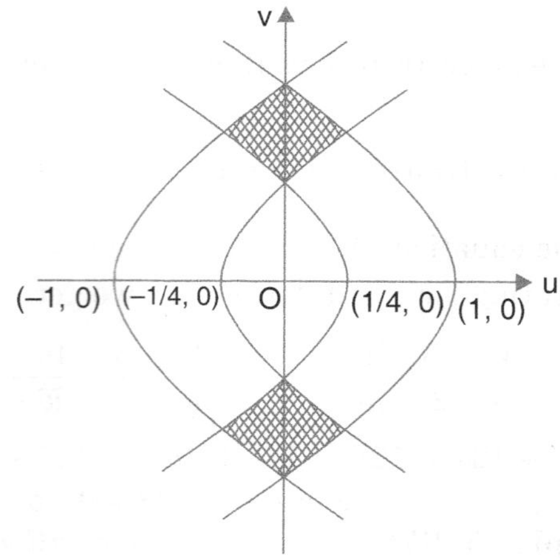

w-plane

Thus the rectangular region bounded by the lines $x = \frac{1}{2}$, $x = 1$ and $y = \frac{1}{2}$, $y = 1$ maps into the region bounded by the parabolas

$$v^2 = -\left(u - \tfrac{1}{4}\right),\ v^2 = -4(u - 1) \quad \text{and} \quad v^2 = u + \tfrac{1}{4},\ v^2 = 4(u + 1).$$

Example 18. *Show that the transformation $w = z + \dfrac{1}{z}$ maps the circle $|z| = c$ into the ellipse $u = \left(c + \dfrac{1}{c}\right)\cos\theta$, $v = \left(c - \dfrac{1}{c}\right)\sin\theta$. Discuss the case when $c = 1$.*

Sol. A point on the circle $|z| = c$ can be written as $z = ce^{i\theta}$

$\therefore$
$$w = z + \frac{1}{z} \text{ becomes } u + iv = ce^{i\theta} + \frac{1}{c}e^{-i\theta}$$

or
$$u + iv = c(\cos\theta + i\sin\theta) + \frac{1}{c}(\cos\theta - i\sin\theta) = \left(c + \frac{1}{c}\right)\cos\theta + i\left(c - \frac{1}{c}\right)\sin\theta$$

$\therefore$
$$u = \left(c + \frac{1}{c}\right)\cos\theta \quad \text{and} \quad v = \left(c - \frac{1}{c}\right)\sin\theta$$

which are the parametric equations of an ellipse.

When $c = 1$, we have $u = 2\cos\theta$ and $v = 0$

Since $|\cos\theta| \le 1$, we get $-2 \le u \le 2$ and $v = 0$

$\therefore$ The transformation gives a segment of the u-axis of length 4.

Example 19. *Discuss the transformation $w = e^z$ and show that it transforms the region between the real axis and a line parallel to real axis at $y = \pi$ into the upper half of the w-plane.*

(C.U. June 2006)

Sol. Let $w = Re^{i\phi}$, then the given transformation becomes

$$Re^{i\phi} = e^{x+iy} = e^x \cdot e^{iy} \text{ so that } R = e^x \text{ and } \phi = y$$

The real axis *i.e.*, $y = 0$ maps into the positive u-axis $\phi = 0$ in the w-plane.

The line $y = \pi$ maps into the negative u-axis $\phi = \pi$ in the w-plane.

Thus the region between the lines $y = 0$ and $y = \pi$ maps into the upper half of w-plane.

Note. The region between the lines $y = 0$ and $y = -\pi$ maps into the lower half of w-plane.

The region between the lines $y = c$ and $y = c + 2\pi$ maps into the whole of the w-plane, since e^z is periodic with period $2\pi i$.

The imaginary axis $x = 0$ maps into a unit circle $R = e^0 = 1$ in the w-plane.

Example 20(*a*). *Discuss the transformation $w = \sin z$.* (C.U. June 2006)

Sol. The given transformation is

$$w = u + iv = \sin(x + iy)$$

or $$u + iv = \sin x \cosh y + i \cos x \sinh y$$

so that $$u = \sin x \cosh y$$

and $$v = \cos x \sinh y \quad ...(1)$$

Eliminating y from equation (1), we get

$$\frac{u^2}{\sin^2 x} - \frac{v^2}{\cos^2 x} = 1 \qquad [\because \cosh^2 y - \sinh^2 y = 1]$$

Thus the straight lines $x = c$ in the z-plane are mapped into confocal hyperbolas in the w-plane.

Eliminating x from equation (1), we get $\dfrac{u^2}{\cosh^2 y} + \dfrac{v^2}{\sinh^2 y} = 1$

Thus the straight lines $y = c$ in the z-plane are mapped into confocal ellipses.

The lines $x = 0$ and $y = 0$ map into the lines $u = 0$ and $v = 0$ respectively in the w-plane.

Example 20(*b*). *Discuss the transformation $w = \cos z$.*

Sol. $w = \cos z = \sin\left(z + \dfrac{\pi}{2}\right)$. Hence the transformation is the combination of (i) $z = z + \dfrac{\pi}{2}$ and (ii) $w = \sin z$. Transformation (i) shift S every point in the z-plane to the right through the distance $\pi/2$. So the transformation $w = \cos z$ is same as that in example 20(a), with the above shifting.

Example 21. *Find the bilinear transformation which maps the points $z = 1, i, -1$ into the points $w = i, 0, -i$.*

Hence find the image of $|z| < 1$. (C.U. June 2007, Dec. 2010)

Sol. Let the required bilinear transformation be $w = \dfrac{az + b}{cz + d}$ ...(1)

Substituting the corresponding values of w and z in (1), we get

$$i = \frac{a + b}{c + d}, \quad 0 = \frac{ai + b}{ci + d}, \quad -i = \frac{-a + b}{-c + d}$$

These equations can be written as

$$(a + b) - i(c + d) = 0 \quad ...(2)$$

$$b + ia = 0 \quad ...(3)$$

and $$(-a + b) + i(-c + d) = 0 \quad ...(4)$$

From (3), $$b = -ia$$

Adding (2) and (4), $$2b - 2ic = 0 \text{ or } c = \frac{b}{i} = -a \qquad [\text{Using (3)}]$$

Subtracting (4) from (2), $$2a - 2id = 0 \text{ or } d = \frac{a}{i} = -ia$$

Substituting for b, c, d in (1), we get $w = \dfrac{az - ia}{-az - ia}$ or $w = \dfrac{i - z}{i + z}$ ...(5)

which is the required bilinear transformation.

Now, from (5), $z = i\dfrac{1-w}{1+w}$

$\therefore$ $|z| < 1$ is mapped into the region

$$\left| i\frac{1-w}{1+w} \right| < 1 \quad \text{or} \quad \frac{|i||1-w|}{|1+w|} < 1$$

or $|1 - w| < |1 + w|$ $\qquad | \because \ |i| = 1$

or $|1 - u - iv| < |1 + u + iv|$ or $(1 - u)^2 + v^2 < (1 + u)^2 + v^2$

or $u > 0$.

Hence the interior of the circle $x^2 + y^2 = 1$ in the z-plane is mapped into the entire half of the w-plane to the right of the imaginary axis.

TEST YOUR KNOWLEDGE

1. What is the region of the w-plane into which the rectangular region in the z-plane bounded by the lines $x = 0, y = 0, x = 1$ and $y = 2$ is mapped under the transformation $w = z + (2 - i)$?
2. Find the image of the triangle with vertices at $i, 1 + i, 1 - i$ in the z-plane under the transformation $w = 3z + 4 - 2i$.
3. Determine the region in the w-plane in which the rectangle bounded by the lines $x = 0, y = 0, x = 2$ and $y = 3$ is mapped under the transformation $w = \sqrt{2}\, e^{i\pi/4} \,.\, z$.
4. Consider the transformation $w = 2z$ and determine the region D′ of the w-plane into which the triangular region D enclosed by the lines $x = 0, y = 0, x + y = 1$ in the z-plane is mapped under this transformation.
5. Find the image of the semi-infinite strip $x > 0, 0 < y < 2$ under the transformation $w = iz + 1$. Show the region graphically. *(C.U. Oct. 2011)*
6. Find the image of the circle $|z| = 2$ under the transformation $w = z + 3 + 2i$.
7. Find the image of the following curves under the mapping $w = \dfrac{1}{z}$

   (*i*) the line $y - x + 1 = 0$ *(C.U. Dec. 2010)* (*ii*) the circle $|z - 3| = 5$.

   (*iii*) $|z + 2| = 2$. *(C.U. Dec. 2008)*
8. Show that the image of the hyperbola $x^2 - y^2 = 1$ under the transformation $w = \dfrac{1}{z}$ is the lemniscate $\rho^2 = \cos 2\phi$, where $w = \rho e^{i\phi}$.
9. Show that the map of the real axis of the z-plane on the w-plane by the transformation $w = \dfrac{1}{z+i}$ is a circle and find its centre and radius.
10. Prove that $w = \dfrac{z}{i - z}$ maps the upper half of the z-plane into the upper half of the w-plane.
11. Under the transformation $w = \dfrac{z - i}{1 - iz}$, find the map of the circle $|z| = 1$ in the w-plane.

12. Show that the transformation $w = i\dfrac{1-z}{1+z}$ transforms the circle $|z| = 1$ into the real axis of w-plane and the interior of the circle $|z| < 1$ into the upper half of the w-plane.
(C.U. June 2010)

13. Show that under the transformation $w = \dfrac{z-i}{z+i}$, real axis in the z-plane is mapped into the circle $|w| = 1$. What portion of the z-plane corresponds to the interior of the circle?

14. Under the transformation $w = z^2$, obtain the map in the w-plane of the square with vertices (0, 0), (2, 0), (2, 2), (0, 2) in the z-plane.

15. Find the images of the straight lines $x = 0, y = 0, x = 1$ and $y = 1$ under the transformation $w = z^2$.

16. Determine the region of the w-plane into which the triangle formed by $x = 1, y = 1$ and $x + y = 1$ is mapped under the transformation $w = z^2$.

17. Show that the transformation $w = \sqrt{z}$ maps the domain in the z-plane to the right of the line $x = a$ into the interior of a hyperbola in the w-plane.

18. Show that the map of the circle $|z| = 2$ under the transformation $w + 2i = z + \dfrac{1}{z}$ is an ellipse, find its axes and centre.

19. Show that the transformation $w = z + \dfrac{1}{z}$ converts the straight line $\arg z = \alpha\left(|\alpha| < \dfrac{\pi}{2}\right)$ into a branch of the hyperbola of eccentricity $\sec\alpha$.

20. Show that the transformation $w = z + \dfrac{a^2 - b^2}{4z}$ transforms the circle $|z| = \dfrac{1}{2}(a + b)$ in the z-plane into an ellipse of semi-axes a, b in the w-plane.

21. If $w = z + \dfrac{a^2}{z}$, prove that, when z describes the circle $x^2 + y^2 = a^2$, w describes a straight line and find its length. Also prove that if z describes the circle $x^2 + y^2 = b^2$, where $b > a$, w describes an ellipse.

22. Show that the transformation $w = \cosh z$ maps the lines parallel to x-axis and lines parallel to y-axis into confocal central conics. What physical problems can we study with the help of this transformation?

23. Find the bilinear transformation which maps:
(*a*) the points $z = 1, -i, -1$ into the points $w = i, 0, -i$.
(*b*) the points $z = 1, i, -1$ into the points $w = 0, 1, \infty$. *(C.U. June 2006)*
(*c*) the points $z = 0, -i, -1$ into the points $w = i, 1, 0$. Find the image of the line $y = mx$ under this transformation. *(C.U. Dec. 2008)*
(*d*) the points $z = 0, -1, \infty$ into the points $w = -1, -2-i, i$. *(C.U. June 2005)*

Answers

1. Rectangular region bounded by the lines $u = 2, v = -1, u = 3, v = 1$.
2. A triangle with vertices $(4, -1)$, $(7, 1)$ and $(7, -3)$.
3. Rectangular region bounded by the lines $v = -u, v = u, u + v = 4, v - u = 6$.
4. A triangular region bounded by the lines $u = 0, v = 0, u + v = 2$.
5. $-1 < u < 1, v > 0$
6. $(u-3)^2 + (v-2)^2 = 4$

7. (*i*) $u^2 + v^2 - u - v = 0$ (*ii*) $\left| w + \frac{3}{16} \right| = \frac{5}{16}$ (*iii*) $1 + 4u = 0$

9. $\left(0, -\frac{1}{2}\right); \frac{1}{2}$ **11.** $v = 0$ **13.** $y > 0$

14. (0, 0), (4, 0), (0, 8), (– 4, 0) ; an isosceles triangle

15. Negative real axis, positive real axis, $v^2 = 4(1 - u)$, $v^2 = 4(1 + u)$

16. Region bounded by the parabolas $v^2 = 4(1 \pm u)$, $u^2 = 1 - 2v$ **18.** $\frac{5}{2}, \frac{3}{2}$; (0, 0)

23. (*a*) $w = \frac{z + i}{z - i}$ (*b*) $w = \frac{i(1 - z)}{1 + z}$ (*c*) $w = \frac{i(1 + z)}{1 - z}$; $m(u^2 + v^2) + 2u - m = 0$

(*d*) $\frac{iz - 2}{z + 2}$.

1.16. COMPLEX INTEGRATION

Let $f(z)$ be a continuous function of the complex variable $z = x + iy$ defined at all points of a curve C having end points A and B. Divide the curve C into n parts at the points

$$A = P_0(z_0), P_1(z_1), ..., P_i(z_i), ..., P_n(z_n) = B.$$

Let $\delta z_i = z_i - z_{i-1}$ and ξ_i be any point on the arc $P_{i-1} P_i$. Then the limit of the sum

$$\sum_{i=1}^{n} f(\xi_i)\, \delta z_i$$

as $n \to \infty$ and each $\delta z_i \to 0$, if it exists, is called the **line integral of f(z)** along the curve C. It is denoted by

$$\int_C f(z)\, dz$$

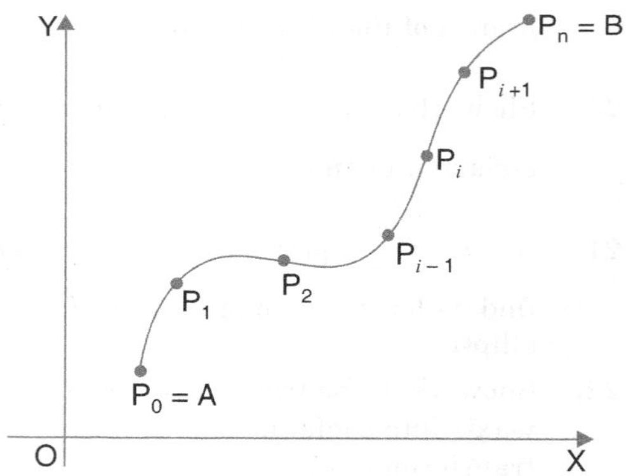

In case the points P_0 and P_n coincide so that C is a closed curve, then this integral is called **contour integral** and is denoted by $\oint_C f(z)\, dz$.

If $f(z) = u(x, y) + iv(x, y)$, then since $dz = dx + idy$, we have

$$\int_C f(z)\, dz = \int_C (u + iv)(dx + idy)$$

$$= \int_C (udx - vdy) + i \int_C (vdx + udy)$$

which shows that the evaluation of the line integral of a complex function can be reduced to the evaluation of two line integrals of real functions.

Moreover, the value of the integral depends on the path of integration unless the integrand is analytic. When the same path of integration is used in each integral, then

$$\int_a^b f(z)\, dz = -\int_b^a f(z)\, dz$$

If C is a point on the arc joining a and b, then

$$\int_a^b f(z)\,dz = \int_a^c f(z)\,d(z) + \int_c^b f(z)\,dz.$$

ILLUSTRATIVE EXAMPLES

Example 22. *Evaluate* $\int_0^{1+i} (x - y + ix^2)\,dz$

(a) along the straight line from $z = 0$ *to* $z = 1 + i$

(b) along the real axis from $z = 0$ *to* $z = 1$ *and then along a line parallel to imaginary axis from* $z = 1$ *to* $z = 1 + i$.

(c) along the imaginary axis from $z = 0$ *to* $z = i$ *and then along a line parallel to real axis from* $z = i$ *to* $z = 1 + i$.

Sol. (*a*) Along the straight line OP joining O($z = 0$) and P($z = 1 + i$), $y = x$, $dy = dx$ and x varies from 0 to 1.

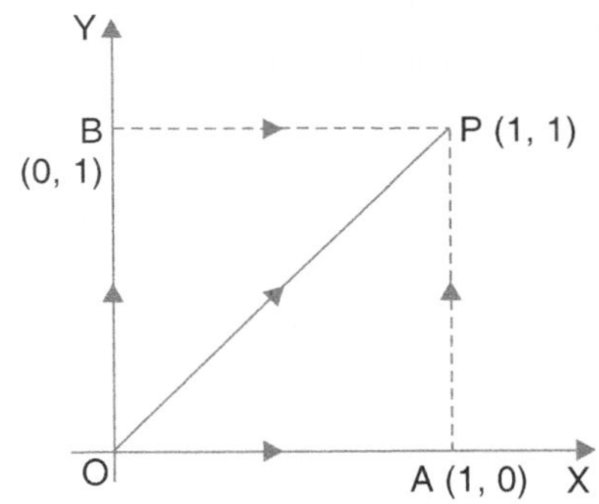

$$\therefore \quad \int_0^{1+i} (x - y + ix^2)\,dz = \int_0^{1+i} (x - y + ix^2)(dx + idy)$$

$$= \int_0^1 (x - x + ix^2)(dx + idx) = \int_0^1 ix^2(1+i)\,dx$$

$$= (-1 + i)\int_0^1 x^2\,dx = (-1+i)\left[\frac{x^3}{3}\right]_0^1$$

$$= (-1 + i)\left(\frac{1}{3}\right) = -\frac{1}{3} + \frac{1}{3}i.$$

(*b*) Along the path OAP where A is $z = 1$

$$\int_0^{1+i} (x - y + ix^2)dz = \int_{OA} (x - y + ix^2)dz + \int_{AP} (x - y + ix^2)\,dz \qquad ...(1)$$

Now along OA, $y = 0$, $dz = dx$ and x varies from 0 to 1.

$$\therefore \quad \int_{OA} (x - y + ix^2)dz = \int_0^1 (x + ix^2)dx = \left[\frac{x^2}{2} + i\frac{x^3}{3}\right]_0^1 = \frac{1}{2} + \frac{1}{3}i$$

Also, along AP, $x = 1$, $dz = idy$ and y varies from 0 to 1

$$\therefore \quad \int_{AP} (x - y + ix^2)\,dz = \int_0^1 (1 - y + i)\,idy = \left[(-1+i)y - i\frac{y^2}{2}\right]_0^1$$

$$= -1 + i - \frac{1}{2}i = -1 + \frac{1}{2}i$$

Hence, from (1),

$$\int_0^{1+i} (x - y + ix^2)\,dz = \left(\frac{1}{2} + \frac{1}{3}i\right) + \left(-1 + \frac{1}{2}i\right) = -\frac{1}{2} + \frac{5}{6}i.$$

(*c*) Along the path OBP where B is $z = i$

$$\int_0^{1+i} (x - y + ix^2)\,dz = \int_{OB} (x - y + ix^2)dz + \int_{BP} (x - y + ix^2)\,dz \qquad ...(2)$$

Now along OB, $x = 0$, $dz = idy$ and y varies from 0 to 1

$$\therefore \quad \int_{OB} (x - y + ix^2)\,dz = \int_0^1 (-y)\,i\,dy = -i\left[\frac{y^2}{2}\right]_0^1 = -\frac{1}{2}i$$

Also, along BP, $y = 1$, $dz = dx$ and x varies from 0 to 1

$$\therefore \quad \int_{BP} (x - y + ix^2)\,dz = \int_0^1 (x - 1 + ix^2)\,dx = \left[\frac{x^2}{2} - x + i\frac{x^3}{3}\right]_0^1 = -\frac{1}{2} + \frac{1}{3}i$$

Hence, from (2), $\int_0^{1+i} (x - y + ix^2)\,dz = -\frac{1}{2}i + \left(-\frac{1}{2} + \frac{1}{3}i\right) = -\frac{1}{2} - \frac{1}{6}i.$

Note. The values of the integral are different along the three different paths. But if the integrand is an analytic function, in a simply connected region, the integral is independent of the path.

Example 23. *Evaluate* $\int_0^{1+i} (x^2 - iy)\,dz$ *along the paths*

(*a*) $y = x$ (*b*) $y = x^2$.

Sol. (*a*) Along the line $y = x$,

$$dy = dx \quad \text{so that} \quad dz = dx + idx = (1 + i)\,dx$$

$$\therefore \quad \int_0^{1+i} (x^2 - iy)\,dz = \int_0^1 (x^2 - ix)(1 + i)\,dx$$

$$= (1 + i)\left[\frac{x^3}{3} - i\frac{x^2}{2}\right]_0^1 = (1 + i)\left(\frac{1}{3} - \frac{1}{2}i\right)$$

$$= \frac{(1 + i)(2 - 3i)}{6} = \frac{5}{6} - \frac{1}{6}i.$$

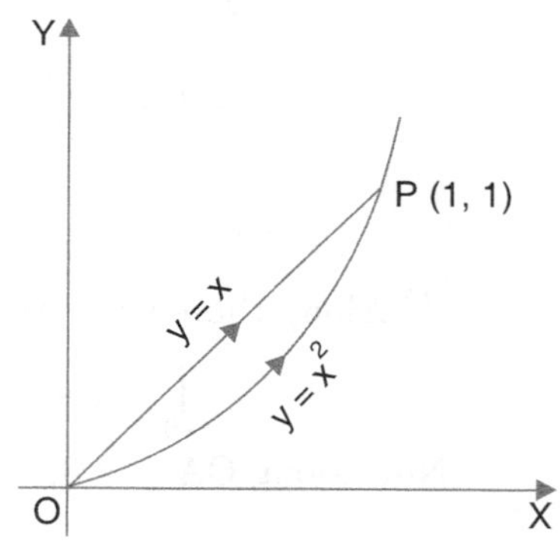

(*b*) Along the parabola $y = x^2$, $dy = 2x\,dx$ so that

$$dz = dx + 2ix\,dx = (1 + 2ix)\,dx$$

and x varies from 0 to 1.

$$\therefore \quad \int_0^{1+i} (x^2 - iy)\,dz = \int_0^1 (x^2 - ix^2)(1 + 2ix)\,dx$$

$$= (1 - i)\int_0^1 x^2(1 + 2ix)\,dx = (1 - i)\left[\frac{x^3}{3} + i\frac{x^4}{2}\right]_0^1$$

$$= (1 - i)\left(\frac{1}{3} + \frac{1}{2}i\right) = \frac{(1 - i)(2 + 3i)}{6} = \frac{5}{6} + \frac{1}{6}i.$$

Example 24. *Evaluate* $\int_0^{2+i} (\bar{z})^2\,dz$*, along*

(*a*) *the real axis to 2 and then vertically to* $2 + i$.

(*b*) *along the line* $2y = x$.

Sol. $(\bar{z})^2 = (x - iy)^2 = (x^2 - y^2) - 2ixy$

(*a*) Along the path OAP where A is (2, 0) and P is (2, 1).

$$\int_0^{2+i} (\bar{z})^2\,dz = \int_{OA} (x^2 - y^2 - 2ixy)\,dz + \int_{AP} (x^2 - y^2 - 2ixy)\,dz \qquad \text{...(1)}$$

Now, along OA, $y = 0$, $dz = dx$ and x varies from 0 to 2

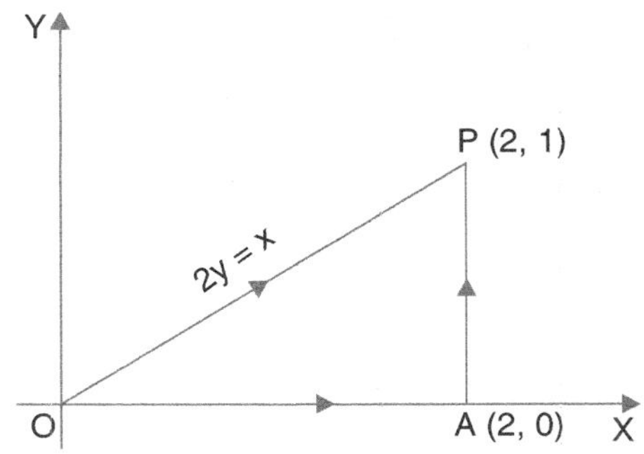

$$\therefore \int_{OA} (x^2 - y^2 - 2ixy)\, dz = \int_0^2 x^2\, dx = \left[\frac{x^3}{3}\right]_0^2 = \frac{8}{3}$$

Also, along AP, $x = 2$, $dz = idy$ and y varies from 0 to 1

$$\therefore \int_{AP} (x^2 - y^2 - 2ixy)\, dz$$

$$= \int_0^1 (4 - y^2 - 4iy)\, idy$$

$$= \left[4iy - i\frac{y^3}{3} + 2y^2\right]_0^1 = 4i - \frac{1}{3}i + 2 = 2 + \frac{11}{3}i$$

Hence from (1), we have $\displaystyle\int_0^{2+i} (\bar{z})^2\, dz = \frac{8}{3} + 2 + \frac{11}{3}i = \frac{14}{3} + \frac{11}{3}i.$

(*b*) Along the line OP, $2y = x$, $dx = 2dy$

so that $dz = 2dy + i\, dy = (2 + i)\, dy$

and y varies from 0 to 1.

$$\therefore \int_0^{2+i} (\bar{z})^2\, dz = \int_0^{2+i} (x^2 - y^2 - 2ixy)\, dz = \int_0^1 (4y^2 - y^2 - 4iy^2)(2 + i)\, dy$$

$$= (2 + i)(3 - 4i) \int_0^1 y^2\, dy = (10 - 5i)\left[\frac{y^3}{3}\right]_0^1 = \frac{10}{3} - \frac{5}{3}i.$$

Example 25. *Integrate $f(z) = x^2 + ixy$ from A(1, 1) to B(2, 4) along the curve $x = t$, $y = t^2$.*

Sol. Equations of the path of integration are $x = t$, $y = t^2$

$\therefore \quad dx = dt, \quad dy = 2t\, dt$

At A(1, 1), $t = 1$ and at B(2, 4), $t = 2$

$$\therefore \int_A^B f(z)\, dz = \int_A^B (x^2 + ixy)(dx + idy) = \int_1^2 (t^2 + it^3)(dt + 2it\, dt)$$

$$= \int_1^2 (t^2 - 2t^4)\, dt + i\int_1^2 3t^3\, dt = \left[\frac{t^3}{3} - \frac{2t^5}{5}\right]_1^2 + i\left[\frac{3t^4}{4}\right]_1^2$$

$$= \left(\frac{8}{3} - \frac{64}{5}\right) - \left(\frac{1}{3} - \frac{2}{5}\right) + i\left(12 - \frac{3}{4}\right) = -\frac{151}{5} + \frac{45}{4}i.$$

Example 26. *Prove that*

(*i*) $\displaystyle\oint_C \frac{dz}{z - a} = 2\pi i$

(*ii*) $\displaystyle\oint_C (z - a)^n\, dz = 0$ *[n is an integer* $\neq -1$*] where C is the circle* $|\, z - a\,| = r$.

Sol. The equation of the circle C is

$$|\, z - a\,| = r \quad \text{or} \quad z - a = re^{i\theta}$$

where θ varies from 0 to 2π as z describes C once in the anti-clockwise direction. $dz = ire^{i\theta}\, d\theta$.

(*i*) $$\oint_C \frac{dz}{z-a} = \int_0^{2\pi} \frac{ire^{i\theta}\, d\theta}{re^{i\theta}} = i\int_0^{2\pi} d\theta = 2\pi i$$

(*ii*) $$\oint_C (z-a)^n\, dz = \int_0^{2\pi} r^n e^{ni\theta} \,.\, ire^{i\theta}\, d\theta$$

$$= ir^{n+1} \int_0^{2\pi} e^{i(n+1)\theta}\, d\theta$$

$$= ir^{n+1} \left[\frac{e^{i(n+1)\theta}}{i(n+1)}\right]_0^{2\pi} \qquad [\because \ n \neq -1]$$

$$= \frac{r^{n+1}}{n+1} [e^{i2(n+1)\pi} - 1]$$

$$= 0. \qquad [\because \ e^{i2(n+1)\pi} = \cos 2(n+1)\pi + i \sin 2(n+1)\pi = 1 + i0 = 1]$$

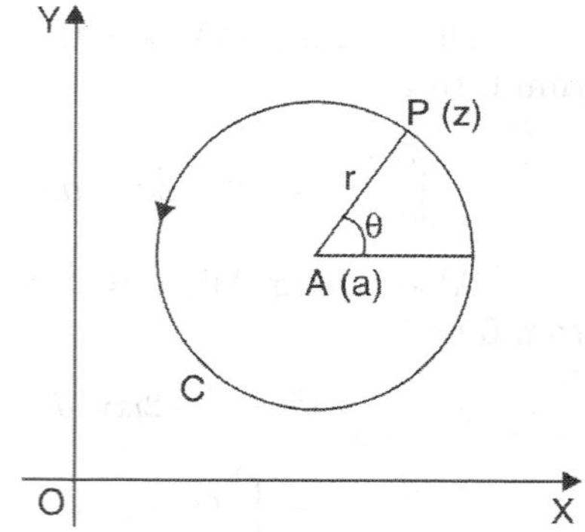

TEST YOUR KNOWLEDGE

1. Evaluate $\int_0^{3+i} z^2\, dz$, along

(*a*) the line $y = \frac{x}{3}$ (*b*) the real axis to 3 and then vertically to $3 + i$

(*c*) the parabola $x = 3y^2$.

2. Evaluate $\int_{1-i}^{2+i} (2x + iy + 1)\, dz$, along
(*a*) the straight line joining $(1 - i)$ to $(2 + i)$. (*b*) the curve $x = t + 1$, $y = 2t^2 - 1$.

3. Evaluate $\int_0^{4+2i} \bar{z}\, dz$, along the curve given by $z = t^2 + it$.

4. Evaluate $\oint_C |z|^2\, dz$, around the square with vertices at (0, 0), (1, 0), (1, 1) and (0, 1).

5. Show that $\oint_C (z+1)\, dz = 0$, where C is the boundary of the square whose vertices are at the points $z = 0$, $z = 1$, $z = 1 + i$ and $z = i$.

6. Evaluate $\oint_C (y - x - 3x^2 i)\, dz$, where C is the straight line from $z = 0$ to $z = 1 + i$.

7. Evaluate $\oint_C (z - z^2)\, dz$ where C is the upper half of the circle $|z| = 1$.

8. Prove that $\int_C \frac{1}{z}\, dz = -\pi i$ or πi according as C is the semi-circular arc $|z| = 1$ from $z = -1$ to $z = 1$ above or below the real axis.

9. Evaluate $\oint_C |z|\, dz$, where C is the left half of the unit circle $|z| = 1$ from $z = -i$ to $z = i$.

10. Evaluate $\oint_C \log z\, dz$, where C is the unit circle $|z| = 1$.

11. Evaluate $\oint_C x^2\, dx + y^3 dy$ along $y = x^3$ from (1, 1) to (2, 8). *(C.U. June 2006)*

Answers

1. (*a*) $6 + \frac{26}{3}i$ (*b*) $6 + \frac{26}{3}i$ (*c*) $6 + \frac{26}{3}i$

2. (*a*) $4 + 8i$ (*b*) $4 + \frac{25}{3}i$ **3.** $10 - \frac{8}{3}i$ **4.** $-1 + i$

6. $1 - i$ **7.** $\frac{2}{3}$ **9.** $2i$ **10.** 0

11. 1026.

1.17. SIMPLY AND MULTIPLY CONNECTED REGIONS

A curve is called *simple closed curve* if it does not cross itself (Fig. 1). A curve which crosses itself is called a *multiple curve* (Fig. 2).

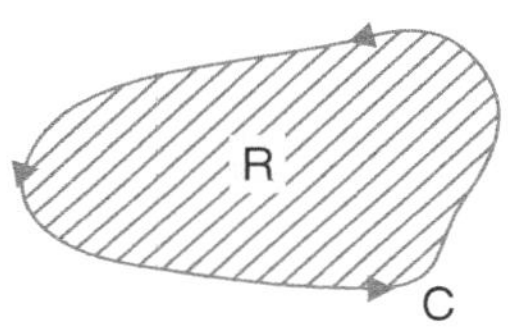

Fig. 1

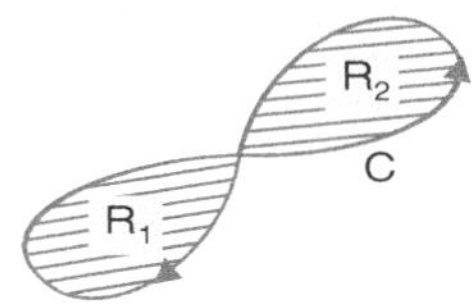

Fig. 2

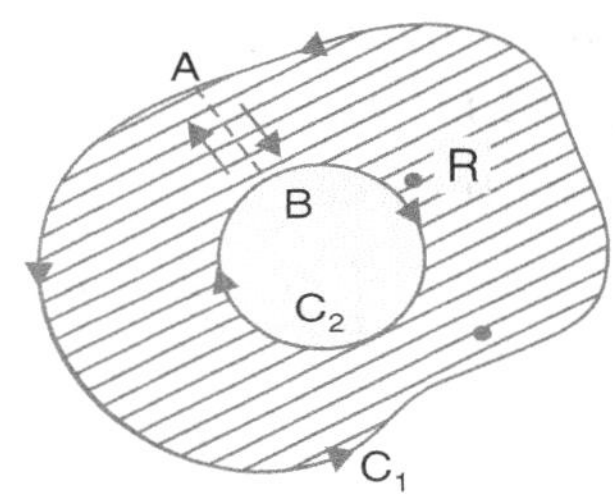

Fig. 3

A region is called *simply connected* if every closed curve in the region encloses points of the region only, *i.e.*, every closed curve lying in it can be contracted indefinitely without passing out of it. A region which is not simply connected is called a *multiply connected* region. In plain terms, a simply connected region is one which has no holes. Figure 3 shows a multiply connected region R enclosed between two separate curves C_1 and C_2. (There can be more than two separate curves). We can convert a multiply connected region into a simply connected one, by giving it one or more cuts (*e.g.*, along the dotted line AB).

1.18. CAUCHY'S INTEGRAL THEOREM

Statement. *If f(z) is an analytic function and f '(z) is continuous at each point within and on a simple closed curve C, then*

$$\oint_C f(z)dz = 0.$$

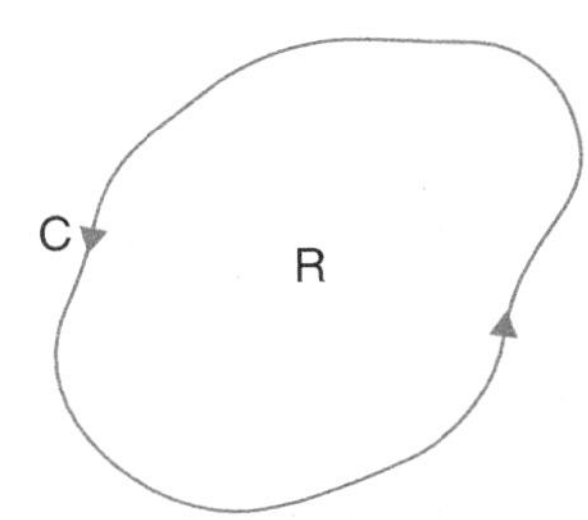

Proof. Let R be the region bounded by the curve C.

Let $\qquad f(z) = u(x, y) + iv(x, y)$, then

$$\oint_C f(z)dz = \oint_C (u + iv)(dx + idy)$$

$$= \oint_C (udx - vdy) + i\oint_C (vdx + udy) \qquad ...(1)$$

Since $f'(z)$ is continuous, the partial derivatives $\frac{\partial u}{\partial x}, \frac{\partial u}{\partial y}, \frac{\partial v}{\partial x}, \frac{\partial v}{\partial y}$ are also continuous in R. Hence, by Green's Theorem, we have

$$\oint_C f(z)dz = \iint_R \left(-\frac{\partial v}{\partial x} - \frac{\partial u}{\partial y}\right) dx\,dy + i \iint_R \left(\frac{\partial u}{\partial x} - \frac{\partial v}{\partial y}\right) dx\,dy \qquad \ldots(2)$$

Now $f(z)$ being analytic at each point of the region R, by Cauchy-Riemann equations, we have

$$\frac{\partial u}{\partial x} = \frac{\partial v}{\partial y} \quad \text{and} \quad \frac{\partial u}{\partial y} = -\frac{\partial v}{\partial x}$$

Thus, the integrals of the two double integrals in (2) vanish.

Hence, $\oint_C f(z)dz = 0.$

Cor. 1. *If f(z) is analytic in a region R and P and Q are two points in R, then* $\int_P^Q f(z)dz$ *is independent of the path joining P and Q and lying entirely in R.*

Let PAQ and PBQ be any two paths joining P and Q.

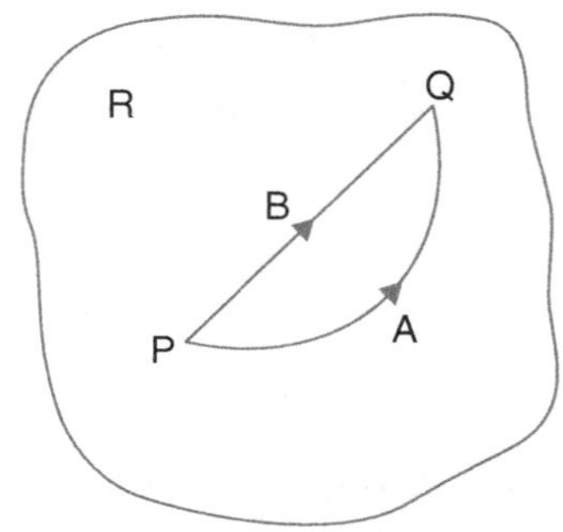

By Cauchy's theorem,

$$\int_{PAQBP} f(z)dz = 0$$

$$\Rightarrow \quad \int_{PAQ} f(z)dz + \int_{QBP} f(z)dz = 0$$

$$\Rightarrow \quad \int_{PAQ} f(z)dz - \int_{PBQ} f(z)dz = 0$$

Hence $\int_{PAQ} f(z)dz = \int_{PBQ} f(z)dz$.

Cor. 2. *If f(z) is analytic in the region bounded by two simple closed curves* C_1 *and* C_2*, then*

$$\oint_C f(z)dz = \oint_{C_1} f(z)dz$$

Let AB be a cross-cut joining the curves C and C_1, then the doubly connected region becomes simply connected.

By Cauchy's theorem, $\int_{APQABDEBA} f(z)\ dz = 0$

$$\Rightarrow \quad \int_{APQA} f(z)dz + \int_{AB} f(z)dz + \int_{BDEB} f(z)dz + \int_{BA} f(z)dz = 0$$

$$\Rightarrow \quad \oint_C f(z)dz + \int_{AB} f(z)dz - \int_{BEDB} f(z)dz - \int_{AB} f(z)dz = 0$$

$$\Rightarrow \quad \oint_C f(z)dz - \oint_{C_1} f(z)dz = 0$$

(integrals around a closed curve are taken positive when the curve is traversed in counter-clockwise direction)

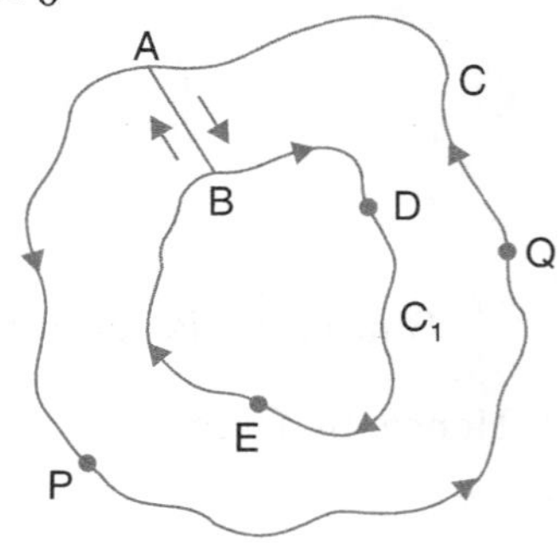

Hence, $\oint_C f(z)dz = \oint_{C_1} f(z)dz$

The theorem can be extended.

If a closed curve C contains non-intersecting closed curves $C_1, C_2, \ldots, C_n$, then by introducing cross-cuts, it can be shown that

$$\oint_C f(z)\,dz = \oint_{C_1} f(z)\,dz + \oint_{C_2} f(z)\,dz + \ldots\ldots + \oint_{C_n} f(z)\,dz.$$

1.19. CAUCHY'S INTEGRAL FORMULA

Statement. *If $f(z)$ is analytic within and on a closed curve C and a is any point within C, then*

$$f(a) = \frac{1}{2\pi i}\oint_C \frac{f(z)}{z-a}\,dz.$$

Proof. Consider the function $\frac{f(z)}{z-a}$, which is analytic at every point within C except at $z = a$.

Draw a circle C_1 with a as centre and radius ρ such that C_1 lies entirely inside C.

Thus $\frac{f(z)}{z-a}$ is analytic in the region between C and C_1.

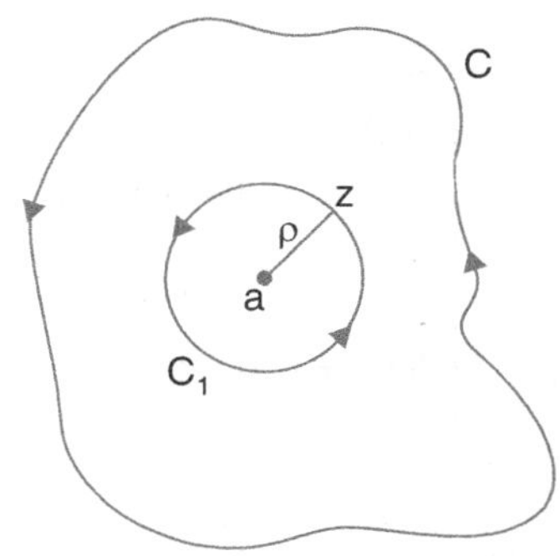

∴ By Cauchy's theorem, we have

$$\oint_C \frac{f(z)}{z-a}\,dz = \oint_{C_1} \frac{f(z)}{z-a}\,dz \qquad \ldots(1)$$

Now, the equation of circle C_1 is

$$|z-a| = \rho \quad \text{or} \quad z-a = \rho e^{i\theta}$$

so that $$dz = i\rho e^{i\theta}\,d\theta$$

$$\oint_{C_1} \frac{f(z)}{z-a}\,dz = \int_0^{2\pi} \frac{f(a+\rho e^{i\theta})}{\rho e^{i\theta}}\,.\,i\rho e^{i\theta}\,d\theta = i\int_0^{2\pi} f(a+\rho e^{i\theta})\,d\theta$$

Hence, by (1), we have

$$\oint_C \frac{f(z)}{z-a}\,dz = i\int_0^{2\pi} f(a+\rho e^{i\theta})\,d\theta \qquad \ldots(2)$$

In the limiting form, as the circle C_1 shrinks to the point a, *i.e.,* $\rho \to 0$, then from (2),

$$\oint_C \frac{f(z)}{z-a}\,dz = i\int_0^{2\pi} f(a)\,d\theta = i\,f(a)\int_0^{2\pi} d\theta = 2\pi i\,f(a)$$

Hence, $$f(a) = \frac{1}{2\pi i}\oint_C \frac{f(z)}{z-a}\,dz$$

which is the required Cauchy's integral formula.

Cor. By Cauchy's integral formula, we have

$$f(a) = \frac{1}{2\pi i}\oint_C \frac{f(z)}{z-a} \qquad \ldots(1)$$

where a is any point within C, it may be treated as a parameter.

Differentiating both sides of (1) w.r.t. a,

$$f'(a) = \frac{1}{2\pi i}\oint_C \frac{\partial}{\partial a}\left[\frac{f(z)}{z-a}\right]dz = \frac{1}{2\pi i}\oint_C \frac{f(z)}{(z-a)^2}\,dz$$

Similarly, $$f''(a) = \frac{2\,!}{2\pi i}\oint_C \frac{f(z)}{(z-a)^3}\,dz$$

$$f'''(a) = \frac{3\,!}{2\pi i}\oint_C \frac{f(z)}{(z-a)^4}\,dz$$

and in general, $$f^n(a) = \frac{n\,!}{2\pi i}\oint_C \frac{f(z)}{(z-a)^{n+1}}\,dz.$$

Thus, *if a function of a complex variable has a first derivative in a simply connected region, all its higher derivatives exist in that region. This property is not exhibited by the functions of real variables.*

ILLUSTRATIVE EXAMPLES

Example 27. *Evaluate* $\oint_C (x^2 - y^2 + 2ixy)\,dz$, *where C is the contour* $|\,z\,| = 1$.

Sol. $f(z) = x^2 - y^2 + 2ixy = (x + iy)^2 = z^2$ is analytic everywhere within and on $|\,z\,| = 1$.

∴ By Cauchy's integral theorem,

$$\oint_C f(z)\,dz = 0.$$

Example 28. *Evaluate* $\int_C (3z^2 + 4z + 1)\,dz$, *where C is the arc of the cycloid* $x = a(\theta - \sin\theta)$, $y = a(1 - \cos\theta)$ *between* $(0, 0)$ *and* $(2\pi a, 0)$.

Sol. Here, $f(z) = 3z^2 + 4z + 1$ is analytic everywhere so that the integral is independent of the path of integration and depends only on the end points $z_1 = 0 + i0$ and $z_2 = 2\pi a + i0$.

$$\therefore \quad \int_C (3z^2 + 4z + 1)\,dz = \int_0^{2\pi a} (3z^2 + 4z + 1)\,dz = \left[z^3 + 2z^2 + z\right]_0^{2\pi a}$$

$$= 8\pi^3 a^3 + 8\pi^2 a^2 + 2\pi a$$

$$= 2\pi a\,(4\pi^2 a^2 + 4\pi a + 1).$$

Example 29. *Evaluate* $\oint_C \frac{e^{-z}}{z+1}\,dz$, *where C is the circle*

(*a*) $|\,z\,| = 2$ (*b*) $|\,z\,| = \frac{1}{2}$.

Sol. $f(z) = e^{-z}$ is an analytic function.

(*a*) The point $a = -1$ lies inside the circle $|\,z\,| = 2$.

∴ By Cauchy's integral formula,

$$\frac{1}{2\pi i}\oint_C \frac{f(z)}{z-(-1)}\,dz = f(-1) \quad \Rightarrow \quad \oint_C \frac{e^{-z}}{z+1}\,dz = 2\pi i e.$$

(*b*) The point $a = -1$ lies outside the circle $|\,z\,| = \frac{1}{2}$.

∴ The function $\frac{e^{-z}}{z+1}$ is analytic within and on C.

By Cauchy's integral theorem, we have $\oint_C \frac{e^{-z}}{z+1}\,dz = 0.$

Example 30. *Evaluate* $\oint_C \frac{\cos \pi z^2}{(z-1)(z-2)} dz$, *where C is the circle* $|z| = 3$.

Sol. The integrand has singularities where

$$(z-1)(z-2) = 0 \quad i.e., \quad \text{at } z = 1 \quad \text{and} \quad z = 2.$$

Both these points lie within the circle $|z| = 3$

$f(z) = \cos \pi z^2$ is an analytic function.

Also $$\frac{1}{(z-1)(z-2)} = -\frac{1}{z-1} + \frac{1}{z-2}$$

$$\therefore \quad \oint_C \frac{\cos \pi z^2}{(z-1)(z-2)} dz = -\oint_C \frac{\cos \pi z^2}{z-1} dz + \oint_C \frac{\cos \pi z^2}{z-2} dz \quad \text{...(1)}$$

$$= -2\pi i\, f(1) + 2\pi i\, f(2) \quad \text{where} \quad f(z) = \cos \pi z^2$$

$$= -2\pi i \cos \pi + 2\pi i \cos 4\pi = 2\pi i + 2\pi i = 4\pi i.$$

Example 31. *Evaluate* $\oint_C \frac{3z^2 + z}{z^2 - 1} dz$, *where C is the circle* $|z - 1| = 1$.

Sol. The integrand has singularities where $z^2 - 1 = 0$ *i.e.,* at $z = 1$ and $z = -1$.

The circle $|z - 1| = 1$ has centre at $z = 1$ and radius 1 and includes the point $z = 1$. $f(z) = 3z^2 + z$ is an analytic function.

Also $$\frac{1}{z^2-1} = \frac{1}{(z-1)(z+1)} = \frac{1}{2}\left(\frac{1}{z-1} - \frac{1}{z+1}\right)$$

$$\therefore \quad \oint_C \frac{3z^2+z}{z^2-1} dz = \frac{1}{2}\oint_C \frac{3z^2+z}{z-1} dz - \frac{1}{2}\oint_C \frac{3z^2+z}{z+1} dz \quad \text{...(1)}$$

By Cauchy's integral formula,

$$\oint_C \frac{3z^2+z}{z-1} dz = 2\pi i\, f(1), \quad \text{where } f(z) = 3z^2 + z$$

$$= 8\pi i$$

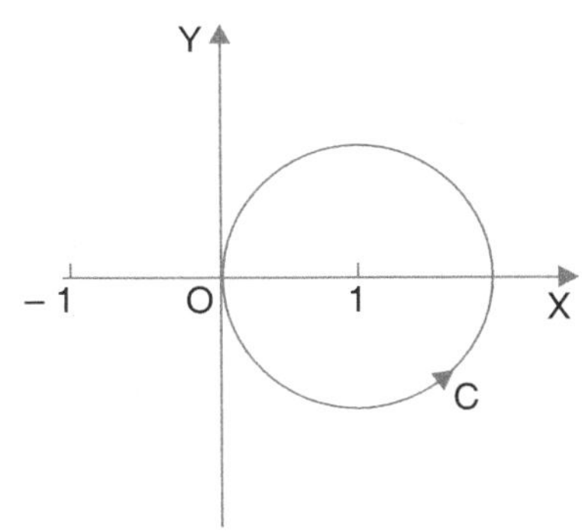

By Cauchy's integral theorem,

$$\oint_C \frac{3z^2+z}{z-1} dz = 0$$

$\therefore$ From (1), we have

$$\oint_C \frac{3z^2+z}{z^2-1} dz = 4\pi i.$$

Example 32. *Use Cauchy's integral formula to evaluate*

$$\oint_C \frac{e^{2z}}{(z+1)^4} dz, \text{ where C is the circle } |z| = 2.$$

Sol. The integrand has a singularity at $z = -1$ which lies within the circle $|z| = 2$.

Now $$f^n(a) = \frac{n!}{2\pi i} \oint_C \frac{f(z)}{(z-a)^{n+1}} dz \quad \text{...(1)}$$

Here $a = -1, \quad n + 1 = 4 \quad i.e., \quad n = 3, f(z) = e^{2z}$

$\therefore \quad f^n(z) = 2^n e^{2z}, f^3(a) = f^3(-1) = 2^3 e^{-2}$

From (1), we have $f^3(-1) = \dfrac{3!}{2\pi i} \oint_C \dfrac{e^{2z}}{(z+1)^4} dz \Rightarrow 8e^{-2} = \dfrac{3}{\pi i} \oint_C \dfrac{e^{2z}}{(z+1)^4} dz$

Hence $\oint_C \dfrac{e^{2z}}{(z+1)^4} dz = \dfrac{8\pi i}{3e^2}$.

Example 33. *If* $f(\xi) = \int_C \dfrac{3z^2 + 7z + 1}{z - \xi} dz$, *where C is the circle* $x^2 + y^2 = 4$, *find the values of* $f(3)$, $f'(1 - i)$ *and* $f''(1 - i)$.

Sol. The given circle C is $x^2 + y^2 = 4$ or $|z| = 2$.

The point $z = 3$ lies outside the circle $|z| = 2$ while $z = 1 - i$ and $z = 1 + i$ lie inside the circle.

Now $f(3) = \oint_C \dfrac{3z^2 + 7z + 1}{z - 3} dz$ and $\dfrac{3z^2 + 7z + 1}{z - 3}$ is analytic within and on C.

$\therefore$ By Cauchy's integral theorem, we have

$$\oint_C \frac{3z^2 + 7z + 1}{z - 3} dz = 0 \Rightarrow f(3) = 0.$$

Now let $\phi(z) = 3z^2 + 7z + 1$ which is analytic everywhere.

$\therefore$ By Cauchy's integral formula, we have

$$\phi(\xi) = \frac{1}{2\pi i} \oint_C \frac{\phi(z)}{z - \xi} dz, \quad \text{where } \xi \text{ is a point within C.}$$

$$\Rightarrow \quad 2\pi i \phi(\xi) = \oint_C \frac{3z^2 + 7z + 1}{z - \xi} dz = f(\xi)$$

$$\Rightarrow \quad f(\xi) = 2\pi i(3\xi^2 + 7\xi + 1) \Rightarrow f'(\xi) = 2\pi i(6\xi + 7)$$

$$\therefore \quad f'(1 - i) = 2\pi i[6(1 - i) + 7] = 2\pi i(13 - 6i) = 2\pi(6 + 13i)$$

Also $\quad f''(\xi) = 12\pi i$

$$\therefore \quad f''(1 - i) = 12\pi i.$$

TEST YOUR KNOWLEDGE

1. Evaluate $\oint_C \dfrac{z^2 + 5}{z - 3} dz$, where C is the circle

(*a*) $|z| = 4$ (*b*) $|z| = 1$.

2. Evaluate $\int_C \dfrac{e^z}{z - 2} dz$, where C is the circle

(*a*) $|z| = 3$ (*b*) $|z| = 1$.

3. Evaluate $\oint_C \dfrac{3z^2 + 7z + 1}{z + 1} dz$, where C is the circle

(*a*) $|z| = 1.5$ (*b*) $|z + i| = 1$. (*C.U. Dec. 2010*)

4. Evaluate $\oint_C \frac{\sin 3z}{z + \frac{\pi}{2}} dz$, where C is the circle $|z| = 5$.

5. Evaluate $\oint_C \frac{z^3 + z + 1}{z^2 - 3z + 2} dz$, where C is the ellipse $4x^2 + 9y^2 = 1$.

6. Evaluate $\oint_C \frac{\cos \pi z}{z^2 - 1} dz$ around a rectangle with vertices

(*a*) $2 \pm i, -2 \pm i$ (*b*) $-i, 2 - i, 2 + i, i$.

7. Evaluate $\oint_C \frac{\sin^2 z}{\left(z - \frac{\pi}{6}\right)^3} dz$, where C is the circle $|z| = 1$.

8. Evaluate $\oint_C \frac{z\,dz}{(z-1)(z-3)}$, where C is the circle

(*a*) $|z| = 3$ (*b*) $|z| = 3/2$.

9. Evaluate $\oint_C \frac{z + 4}{z^2 + 2z + 5} dz$, where C is the circle $|z| = 1$.

10. Evaluate $\oint_C \frac{\sin \pi z^2 + \cos \pi z^2}{(z-1)(z-2)} dz$, where C is the circle $|z| = 3$. *(C.U. June 2009, Oct. 2011)*

11. Evaluate $\oint_C \frac{e^z}{(z-1)(z-4)} dz$, where C is the circle $|z| = 2$.

12. Evaluate $\oint_C \frac{e^z}{z(z+1)} dz$, where C is the circle $|z| = \frac{1}{4}$.

13. Evaluate $\oint_C \frac{\cos z}{z - \pi} dz$, where C is the circle $|z - 1| = 3$.

14. Evaluate $\oint_C \frac{e^z}{(z+3)(z+2)} dz$, where C is the circle $|z - 1| = \frac{1}{2}$.

15. Let $P(z) = a + bz + cz^2$ and $\oint_C \frac{P(z)}{z} dz = \oint_C \frac{P(z)}{z^2} dz = \oint_C \frac{P(z)}{z^3} dz = 2\pi i$ where C is the circle $|z| = 1$. Evaluate P(*z*).

16. Evaluate $\oint_C \frac{e^{-z}}{z^2} dz$, where C is the circle $|z| = 1$.

17. Evaluate $\oint_C \frac{e^{-2z} dz}{(z+1)^3}$, where C is the circle $|z| = 2$.

18. If $f(\xi) = \oint_C \frac{4z^2 + z + 5}{z - \xi} dz$, where C is the ellipse $\frac{x^2}{4} + \frac{y^2}{9} = 1$, find $f(1), f(i), f'(-1)$ and $f''(-i)$.

(C.U. Dec. 2007)

Answers

1. (*a*) $28\pi i$ (*b*) 0	**2.** (*a*) $2\pi i\, e^2$ (*b*) 0	**3.** (*a*) $-6\pi i$ (*b*) 0	**4.** $2\pi i$
5. 0	**6.** (*a*) 0 (*b*) $-\pi i$	**7.** πi	**8.** (*a*) $2\pi i$ (*b*) $-\pi i$
9. 0	**10.** $4\pi i$	**11.** $-\frac{2}{3}\pi i e$	**12.** $2\pi i$

13. $-2\pi i$	**14.** 0	**15.** $1 + z + z^2$	**16.** $-2\pi i$
17. $4\pi ie^2$	**18.** $20\pi i$, $2\pi(i-1)$, $-14\pi i$, $16\pi i$.		

1.20. SERIES OF COMPLEX TERMS

A series of the form $(a_1 + ib_1) + (a_2 + ib_2) + ... + (a_n + ib_n) + ...$
where $a_1, b_1, a_2, b_2, ...$ are real numbers, is called a series of complex terms and can be expressed as

$$\sum_{n=1}^{\infty} a_n + i \sum_{n=1}^{\infty} b_n \qquad ...(1)$$

The series (1) is convergent if Σa_n and Σb_n both are convergent.

If the series Σa_n and Σb_n converge to a and b respectively, then the series (1) is said to converge to $a + ib$.

The necessary (not sufficient) condition for convergence of a series (1) is $\underset{n \to \infty}{\text{Lt}} (a_n + ib_n) = 0$.

The series (1) is said to be **absolutely convergent** if the series
$| a_1 + ib_1 | + | a_2 + ib_2 | + ... + | a_n + ib_n | + ...$ is convergent.

Since $| a_n | \le | a_n + ib_n |$ and $| b_n | \le | a_n + ib_n |$, we conclude that an absolutely convergent series is convergent. The converse is not true.

If the series of functions $u_1(z) + u_2(z) + ... + u_n(z) + ... = \sum_{n=1}^{\infty} u_n(z) \qquad ...(2)$

converges to $S(z)$ and $S_n(z)$ is its nth partial sum, then the series (2) is said to be **uniformly convergent** in a region R, if given any positive number ε, there exists a positive number N, depending on ε but not on z, such that for every z in R,

$$| S(z) - S_n(z) | < \varepsilon \text{ for all } n > N.$$

A series of the form

$$a_0 + a_1(z-a) + a_2(z-a)^2 + ... + a_n(z-a)^n + ... = \sum_{n=0}^{\infty} a_n (z-a)^n \qquad ...(3)$$

is called a **power series** in $(z - a)$.

If the series (3) is convergent for all values of z satisfying $| z - a | < R$, *i.e.*, for all values of z lying inside the circle with centre at $z = a$ and radius R, then this circle is called the **circle of convergence** and R is called the **radius of convergence.**

The power series (3) is uniformly convergent in a region R if there exists a series of positive terms ΣM_n such that $| a_n(z-a)^n | \le M_n$ for all values of z in the region R.

This is called **Wierstrass M-test** for uniform convergence of a power series.

1.21. TAYLOR'S SERIES

If f(z) is analytic inside a circle C with centre at a, then for all z inside C,

$$f(z) = f(a) + (z-a) f'(a) + \frac{(z-a)^2}{2!} f''(a) + ... + \frac{(z-a)^n}{n!} f^n(a) + ...$$

Proof. Let z be any point inside the circle C. Draw a circle C_1 with centre at a and radius smaller than that of C such that z is an interior point of C_1. Let w be any point on C_1, then

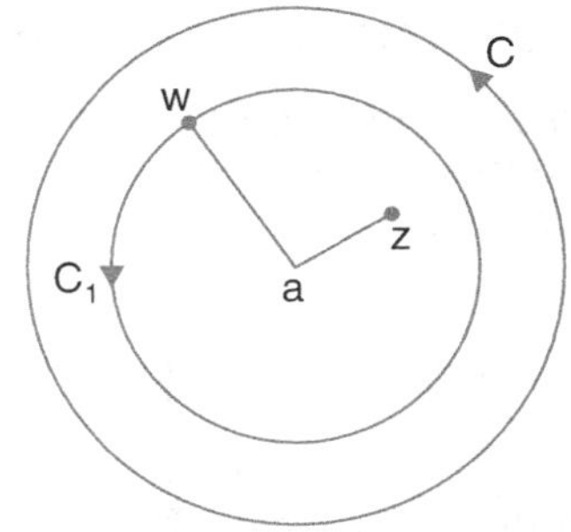

$$| z - a | < | z - w | \quad i.e., \left|\frac{z-a}{z-w}\right| < 1$$

Now, $$\frac{1}{w-z} = \frac{1}{(w-a)-(z-a)} = \frac{1}{w-a}\left[1-\frac{z-a}{w-a}\right]^{-1}$$

Expanding R.H.S. by binomial theorem as $\left|\frac{z-a}{w-a}\right| < 1$, we get

$$\frac{1}{w-z} = \frac{1}{w-a}\left[1+\frac{z-a}{w-a}+\left(\frac{z-a}{w-a}\right)^2+\ldots+\left(\frac{z-a}{w-a}\right)^n+\ldots\right] \quad \ldots(1)$$

This series converges uniformly since $\left|\frac{z-a}{w-a}\right| < 1$. Multiplying both sides of (1) by $\frac{1}{2\pi i} f(w)$ and integrating term by term w.r.t. w, over C_1, we get

$$\frac{1}{2\pi i}\oint_{C_1}\frac{f(w)}{w-z}dw = \frac{1}{2\pi i}\oint_{C_1}\frac{f(w)}{w-a}dw + \frac{z-a}{2\pi i}\oint_{C_1}\frac{f(w)}{(w-a)^2}dw + \frac{(z-a)^2}{2\pi i}\oint_{C_1}\frac{f(w)}{(w-a)^3}dw +$$
$$\ldots + \frac{(z-a)^n}{2\pi i}\oint_{C_1}\frac{f(w)}{(w-a)^{n+1}}dw + \ldots \quad \ldots(2)$$

Since $f(w)$ is analytic on and inside C_1, by Cauchy's formula,

$$\frac{1}{2\pi i}\oint_{C_1}\frac{f(w)}{w-z}dw = f(z)$$

Also $$f^n(a) = \frac{n!}{2\pi i}\oint_{C_1}\frac{f(w)}{(w-a)^{n+1}}dw \quad i.e., \quad \frac{1}{2\pi i}\oint_{C_1}\frac{f(w)}{(w-a)^{n+1}}dw = \frac{f^n(a)}{n!}$$

∴ From (2), we have

$$f(z) = f(a) + (z-a)f'(a) + \frac{(z-a)^2}{2!}f''(a) + \ldots + \frac{(z-a)^n}{n!}f^n(a) + \ldots \quad \ldots(3)$$

which is the required *Taylor's series* for $f(z)$ about $z = a$.

Cor. 1. Putting $z = a + h$ in (3), we get

$$f(a+h) = f(a) + hf'(a) + \frac{h^2}{2!}f''(a) + \ldots + \frac{h^n}{n!}f^n(a) + \ldots$$

Cor. 2. If $a = 0$, the series (3) becomes

$$f(z) = f(0) + zf'(0) + \frac{z^2}{2!}f''(0) + \ldots + \frac{z^n}{n!}f^n(0) + \ldots$$

This series is called **Maclaurin's series.**

1.22. LAURENT'S SERIES

If f(z) is analytic inside and on the boundary of the ring shaped region R bounded by two concentric circles C_1 and C_2 of radii r_1 and r_2 ($r_1 > r_2$) respectively having centre at a, then for all z in R,

$$f(z) = a_0 + a_1(z-a) + a_2(z-a)^2 + \ldots + a_{-1}(z-a)^{-1} + a_{-2}(z-a)^{-2} + \ldots$$

where $$a_n = \frac{1}{2\pi i}\oint_{C_1} \frac{f(w)}{(w-a)^{n+1}}\, dw \; ; \; n = 0, 1, 2, \ldots$$

and $$a_{-n} = \frac{1}{2\pi i}\oint_{C_2} \frac{f(w)}{(w-a)^{-n+1}}\, dw \; ; \; n = 1, 2, 3, \ldots$$

Proof. Let z be any point in the region R, then by Cauchy's integral formula for double connected region, we have

$$f(z) = \frac{1}{2\pi i}\oint_{C_1} \frac{f(w)}{w-z}\, dw - \frac{1}{2\pi i}\oint_{C_2} \frac{f(w)}{w-z}\, dw \qquad \ldots(1)$$

For the first integral in (1), w lies on C_2

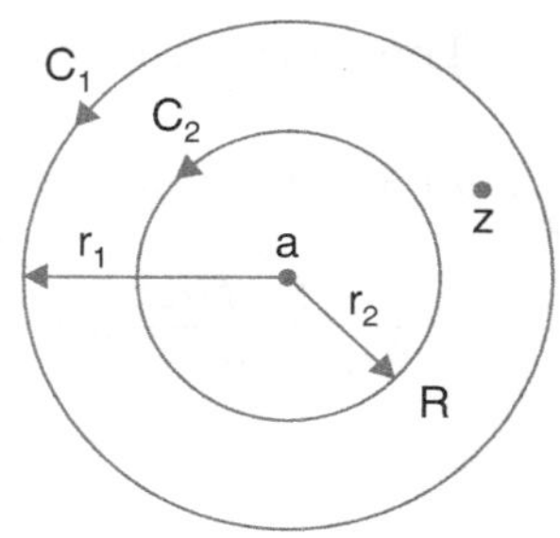

$$\therefore \qquad |z-a| < |w-a| \quad i.e., \quad \left|\frac{z-a}{w-a}\right| < 1$$

Now $$\frac{1}{w-a} = \frac{1}{(w-a)-(z-a)} = \frac{1}{w-a}\left(1 - \frac{z-a}{w-a}\right)^{-1}$$

$$= \frac{1}{w-a}\left[1 + \frac{z-a}{w-a} + \left(\frac{z-a}{w-a}\right)^2 + \ldots\right]$$

Multiplying both sides by $\frac{1}{2\pi i} f(w)$ and integrating term by term w.r.t. w, along the circle C_1, we get

$$\frac{1}{2\pi i}\oint_{C_1} \frac{f(w)}{w-z}\, dw = \frac{1}{2\pi i}\oint_{C_1} \frac{f(w)}{w-a}\, dw + \frac{z-a}{2\pi i}\oint_{C_1} \frac{f(w)}{(w-a)^2}\, dw + \frac{(z-a)^2}{2\pi i}\oint_{C_1} \frac{f(w)}{(w-a)^3}\, dw + \ldots$$

$$= a_0 + a_1(z-a) + a_2(z-a)^2 + \ldots$$

$$= \sum_{n=0}^{\infty} a_n (z-a)^n \quad \ldots(2) \quad \left[\because \; a_n = \frac{1}{2\pi i}\oint_{C_1} \frac{f(w)}{(w-a)^{n+1}}\, dw, n = 0, 1, 2, \ldots\right]$$

For the second integral in (1), w lies on C_2

$$\therefore \qquad |w-a| < |z-a| \quad i.e., \quad \left|\frac{w-a}{z-a}\right| < 1$$

Now $$\frac{1}{w-z} = \frac{1}{(w-a)-(z-a)} = -\frac{1}{z-a}\left(1 - \frac{w-a}{z-a}\right)^{-1}$$

$$= -\frac{1}{z-a}\left[1 + \frac{w-a}{z-a} + \left(\frac{w-a}{z-a}\right)^2 + \ldots.\right]$$

Multiplying both sides by $\frac{1}{2\pi i} f(w)$ and integrating term by term w.r.t. w, along the circle C_2, we get

$$-\frac{1}{2\pi i}\oint_{C_2}\frac{f(w)}{w-z}\,dw = \frac{1}{z-a}\cdot\frac{1}{2\pi i}\oint_{C_2} f(w)\,dw + \frac{1}{(z-a)^2}\cdot\frac{1}{2\pi i}\oint_{C_2}(w-a)\,f(w)\,dw$$

$$+\frac{1}{(z-a)^3}\cdot\frac{1}{2\pi i}\oint_{C_2}(w-a)^2 f(w)\,dw + \ldots$$

$$= a_{-1}(z-a)^{-1} + a_{-2}(z-a)^{-2} + a_{-3}(z-a)^{-3} + \ldots$$

$$= \sum_{n=1}^{\infty} a_{-n}(z-a)^{-n} \qquad \ldots(3)$$

$$\left[\because\ a_{-n} = \frac{1}{2\pi i}\oint_{C_2}\frac{f(w)}{(w-a)^{-n+1}}\,dw,\ n = 1, 2, 3, \ldots\right]$$

Substituting from (2) and (3) in (1), we get

$$f(z) = \sum_{n=0}^{\infty} a_n(z-a)^n + \sum_{n=1}^{\infty} a_{-n}(z-a)^{-n}$$

Note 1. In the statement of Laurent's series, $a_n = \frac{1}{2\pi i}\oint_{C_1}\frac{f(w)}{(w-a)^{n+1}}\,dw \neq \frac{f^n(a)}{n!}$ because $f(z)$ is not given to be analytic inside C_1.

Note 2. In case $f(z)$ is analytic inside C_1, then $a_{-n} = 0$ and $a_n = \frac{1}{2\pi i}\oint_{C_1}\frac{f(w)}{(w-a)^{n+1}}\,dw = \frac{f^n(a)}{n!}$ and Laurent's series reduces to Taylor's series.

Note 3. If C is any simple closed curve which lies in the ring-shaped region R and encloses the circle C_1, then

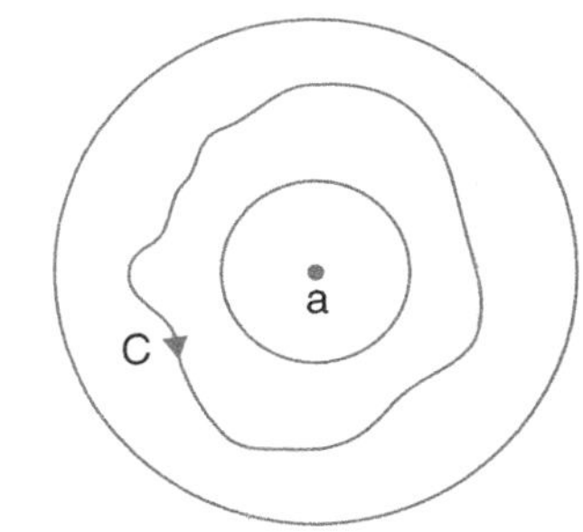

$$\oint_{C_1}\frac{f(w)}{(w-a)^{n+1}}\,dw = \oint_{C}\frac{f(w)}{(w-a)^{n+1}}\,dw$$

and
$$\oint_{C_2}\frac{f(w)}{(w-a)^{-n+1}}\,dw = \oint_{C}\frac{f(w)}{(w-a)^{-n+1}}\,dw$$

$\therefore$ Laurent's series can be written as

$$f(z) = \sum_{n=-\infty}^{\infty} a_n(z-a)^n, \quad \text{where } a_n = \frac{1}{2\pi i}\oint_{C}\frac{f(w)}{(w-a)^{n+1}}\,dw.$$

Note 4. The process of finding the co-efficient a_n by complex integration is complicated. In practice, we expand the function $f(z)$ by binomial theorem or by some other method to obtain Taylor's or Laurent's series.

ILLUSTRATIVE EXAMPLES

Example 34. *Expand* $\frac{1}{z^2 - 3z + 2}$ *in the region*

(*a*) $|z| < 1$ (*b*) $1 < |z| < 2$ (C.U. June, 2006, 07)

(*c*) $|z| > 2$ (*d*) $0 < |z - 1| < 1.$

Sol. Here $$f(z) = \frac{1}{z^2 - 3z + 2} = \frac{1}{(z-1)(z-2)} = \frac{1}{z-2} - \frac{1}{z-1} \quad \text{(Partial Fractions)}$$

(*a*) If $|z| < 1$, then $\left|\frac{z}{2}\right| < 1$

$$\therefore \quad f(z) = \frac{1}{-2\left(1 - \frac{z}{2}\right)} + \frac{1}{1-z}$$

[arranged suitably to make the binomial expansions valid]

$$= -\frac{1}{2}\left(1 - \frac{z}{2}\right)^{-1} + (1 - z)^{-1}$$

$$= -\frac{1}{2}\left(1 + \frac{z}{2} + \frac{z^2}{4} + \frac{z^3}{8} + \ldots\right) + (1 + z + z^2 + z^3 + \ldots)$$

(By binomial theorem)

$$= \frac{1}{2} + \frac{3z}{4} + \frac{7}{8}z^2 + \frac{15}{16}z^3 + \ldots$$

(*b*) If $1 < |z| < 2$, then $\left|\frac{1}{z}\right| < 1$ and $\left|\frac{z}{2}\right| < 1$

$$\therefore \quad f(z) = \frac{1}{-2\left(1 - \frac{z}{2}\right)} - \frac{1}{z\left(1 - \frac{1}{z}\right)} = -\frac{1}{2}\left(1 - \frac{z}{2}\right)^{-1} - \frac{1}{z}\left(1 - \frac{1}{z}\right)^{-1}$$

$$= -\frac{1}{2}\left(1 + \frac{z}{2} + \frac{z^2}{4} + \frac{z^3}{8} + \ldots\right) - \frac{1}{z}\left(1 + \frac{1}{z} + \frac{1}{z^2} + \frac{1}{z^3} + \ldots\right)$$

(By binomial theorem)

$$= -\frac{1}{2}\left(1 + \frac{z}{2} + \frac{z^2}{4} + \ldots\right) - (z^{-1} + z^{-2} + z^{-3} + \ldots)$$

(*c*) If $|z| > 2$, then $\left|\frac{2}{z}\right| < 1$ and $\left|\frac{1}{z}\right| < 1$

$$\therefore \quad f(z) = \frac{1}{z\left(1 - \frac{2}{z}\right)} - \frac{1}{z\left(1 - \frac{1}{z}\right)} = \frac{1}{z}\left(1 - \frac{2}{z}\right)^{-1} - \frac{1}{z}\left(1 - \frac{1}{z}\right)^{-1}$$

$$= \frac{1}{z}\left(1+\frac{2}{z}+\frac{4}{z^2}+\frac{8}{z^3}+\ldots\right)-\frac{1}{z}\left(1+\frac{1}{z}+\frac{1}{z^2}+\frac{1}{z^3}+\ldots\right)$$

(By binomial theorem)

$$= z^{-2} + 3z^{-3} + 7z^{-4} + \ldots$$

(*d*) For $0 < | z - 1 | < 1$, we have

$$f(z) = \frac{1}{(z-1)-1} - \frac{1}{z-1} = -\frac{1}{1-(z-1)} - \frac{1}{z-1} = -(z-1)^{-1} - [1-(z-1)]^{-1}$$

$$= -(z-1)^{-1} - [1 + (z-1) + (z-1)^2 + (z-1)^3 + \ldots].$$

Example 35. *Show that when* $| z + 1 | < 1$, $z^{-2} = 1 + \sum_{n=1}^{\infty} (n+1)(z+1)^n$.

Sol.

$$f(z) = z^{-2} = \frac{1}{z^2} = \frac{1}{[(z+1)-1]^2} = \frac{1}{[1-(z+1)]^2} = [1-(z+1)]^{-2}$$

$$= 1 + 2(z+1) + 3(z+1)^2 + 4(z+1)^3 + \ldots$$

[By binomial theorem, since $| z + 1 | < 1$]

$$= 1 + \sum_{n=1}^{\infty} (n+1)(z+1)^n.$$

Example 36. *Expand* $\cos z$ *in a Taylor's series about* $z = \frac{\pi}{4}$.

Sol. Here $f(z) = \cos z, f'(z) = -\sin z, f''(z) = -\cos z, f'''(z) = \sin z, \ldots$

$$\therefore \quad f\left(\frac{\pi}{4}\right) = \frac{1}{\sqrt{2}},\quad f'\left(\frac{\pi}{4}\right) = -\frac{1}{\sqrt{2}},\quad f''\left(\frac{\pi}{4}\right) = -\frac{1}{\sqrt{2}},\quad f'''\left(\frac{\pi}{4}\right) = \frac{1}{\sqrt{2}}, \ldots$$

Hence $\cos z = f(z)$

$$= f\left(\frac{\pi}{4}\right) + \left(z-\frac{\pi}{4}\right)f'\left(\frac{\pi}{4}\right) + \frac{\left(z-\frac{\pi}{4}\right)^2}{2!}f''\left(\frac{\pi}{4}\right) + \frac{\left(z-\frac{\pi}{4}\right)^3}{3!}f'''\left(\frac{\pi}{4}\right) + \ldots$$

$$= \frac{1}{\sqrt{2}}\left[1-\left(z-\frac{\pi}{4}\right)-\frac{1}{2!}\left(z-\frac{\pi}{4}\right)^2+\frac{1}{3!}\left(z-\frac{\pi}{4}\right)^3+\ldots\right].$$

Example 37. *Expand the function* $\frac{\sin z}{z-\pi}$ *about* $z = \pi$.

Sol. Putting $z - \pi = t$, we have

$$\frac{\sin z}{z-\pi} = \frac{\sin(\pi+t)}{t} = \frac{-\sin t}{t}$$

$$= -\frac{1}{t}\left(t-\frac{t^3}{3!}+\frac{t^5}{5!}\ldots\right) = -1+\frac{t^2}{3!}-\frac{t^4}{5!}+\ldots = -1+\frac{(z-\pi)^2}{3!}-\frac{(z-\pi)^4}{5!}+\ldots$$

Example 38. *Expand* $f(z) = \dfrac{z}{(z+1)(z+2)}$ *about* $z = -2$.

Sol. To expand $f(z)$ about $z = -2$, *i.e.*, in powers of $z + 2$, we put $z + 2 = t$.

$$\therefore \quad f(z) = \frac{z}{(z+1)(z+2)} = \frac{t-2}{(t-1)t} = \frac{2-t}{t(1-t)} = \frac{2-t}{t}(1-t)^{-1}$$

$$= \frac{2-t}{t}(1 + t + t^2 + t^3 + \ldots) \qquad \text{for } 0 < |t| < 1$$

$$= \frac{1}{t}(2 + t + t^2 + t^3 + \ldots) = \frac{2}{t} + 1 + t + t^2 + \ldots$$

$$= \frac{2}{z+2} + 1 + (z+2) + (z+2)^2 + \ldots \qquad \text{for } 0 < |z+2| < 1$$

which is the required Laurent's series.

TEST YOUR KNOWLEDGE

Expand the following functions as a Taylor's series:

1. $\log(1+z)$ about $z = 0$. (*C.U. June 2006*)

2. $\sin z$ about $z = \dfrac{\pi}{4}$.

3. $\dfrac{z}{(z+1)(z+2)}$ about $z = 2$.

Expand the following functions in Laurent's series:

4. $\dfrac{1}{z-2}$, for $|z| > 2$.

5. $\dfrac{1}{z^2 - 4z + 3}$, for $1 < |z| < 3$. (*C.U. June 2006*)

6. $\dfrac{1}{z(z-1)(z-2)}$, for $|z| > 2$.

7. (*a*) $\dfrac{z^2 - 1}{z^2 + 5z + 6}$ for $2 < |z| < 3$. (*C.U. June 2006*)

(*b*) $\dfrac{z^2 - 1}{(z+2)(z+3)}$, for $|z| > 3$. (*C.U. Dec. 2008*)

$\left[\textbf{Hint.} \text{ Put the function into partial fraction as } 1 + \dfrac{3}{z+2} - \dfrac{8}{z+3}\right].$

8. $\dfrac{1 - \cos z}{z^3}$, about $z = 0$.

9. $\dfrac{e^z}{(z-1)^2}$, about $z = 1$.

10. Expand $f(z) = \dfrac{(z-2)(z+2)}{(z+1)(z+4)}$ in the region:

(*a*) $|z| < 1$ (*b*) $1 < |z| < 4$ (*c*) $|z| > 4$.

11. $\dfrac{1}{(z-1)(z-2)}$, for $1 < |z| < 2$. (*C.U. June 2006*)

Answers

1. $z - \dfrac{z^2}{2} + \dfrac{z^3}{3} - \dfrac{z^4}{4} + \ldots$

2. $\dfrac{1}{\sqrt{2}}\left[1 + \left(z - \dfrac{\pi}{4}\right) - \dfrac{1}{2!}\left(z - \dfrac{\pi}{4}\right)^2 - \dfrac{1}{3!}\left(z - \dfrac{\pi}{4}\right)^3 + \ldots\right]$

3. $\left(\frac{1}{2}-\frac{1}{3}\right)-\left(\frac{1}{2^3}-\frac{1}{3^2}\right)(z-2)+\left(\frac{1}{2^5}-\frac{1}{3^3}\right)(z-2)^2-\ldots$

4. $\frac{1}{z}+\frac{2}{z^2}+\frac{2^2}{z^3}+\frac{2^3}{z^4}+\ldots$

5. $-\frac{1}{6}-\frac{1}{6}\sum_{n=1}^{\infty}\frac{z^n}{3^n}-\frac{1}{2}\sum_{n=1}^{\infty}z^{-n}$

6. $z^{-3}+3z^{-4}+7z^{-5}+\ldots+(2^{n-1}-1)z^{-(n+1)}+\ldots$

7. (*a*) $-\frac{5}{3}+\frac{3}{2}\left[1-\frac{2}{z}+\frac{4}{z^2}-\frac{8}{z^3}+\ldots\right]+\frac{8}{3}\left[\frac{z}{3}-\frac{z^2}{9}+\frac{z^2}{27}-\ldots\right]$

7. (*b*) $1+\frac{3}{z}\sum_{n=0}^{\infty}\left(-\frac{2}{z}\right)^n-\frac{8}{z}\sum_{n=0}^{\infty}\left(-\frac{3}{z}\right)^n$

8. $-\sum_{n=2}^{\infty}\frac{z^{2n-5}}{(2n-2)!}$

9. $e\left[(z-1)^{-2}+(z-1)^{-1}+\frac{1}{2!}+\frac{1}{3!}(z-1)+\frac{1}{4!}(z-1)^2+\ldots\right]$

10. (*a*) $-1+\sum_{n=1}^{\infty}(-1)^{n+1}(1+4^{-n})z^n$

(*b*) $\sum_{n=0}^{\infty}\frac{(-1)^{n+1}}{4^n}z^n+\sum_{n=1}^{\infty}(-1)^n z^{-n}$

(*c*) $1+\sum_{n=1}^{\infty}(-1)^n(1+4^n)z^{-n}$

11. $-z^{-4}-z^{-3}-z^{-2}-z^{-1}-\frac{1}{2}-\frac{z}{4}-\frac{z^2}{8}-\frac{z^3}{16}-\ldots$

1.23. SINGULAR POINTS, RESIDUES

A point at which a function $f(z)$ ceases to be analytic is called a *singular point* or *singularity* of $f(z)$.

For example, $z = 2$ is a singular point of $f(z) = \frac{1}{z-2}$.

A singular point $z = a$ of a function $f(z)$ is called an *isolated singular point* if there exists a circle with centre a which contains no other singular point of $f(z)$.

For example, $z = -1, 1$ are two isolated singular points of the function $f(z) = \frac{z}{z^2-1}$.

The function $f(z) = \frac{1}{\sin(\pi z)}$ has an infinite number of isolated singular points at $z = \pm 1, \pm 2, \ldots$

When $z = a$ is an isolated singular point of $f(z)$, we can expand $f(z)$ in a Laurent's series about $z = a$.

$$\text{Thus } f(z) = \sum_{n=0}^{\infty} a_n(z-a)^n + \sum_{n=1}^{\infty} a_{-n}(z-a)^{-n}$$

$$= \sum_{n=0}^{\infty} a_n(z-a)^n + [a_{-1}(z-a)^{-1} + a_{-2}(z-a)^{-2} + \ldots + a_{-m}(z-a)^{-m} + \ldots] \quad \ldots(1)$$

If the series with negative powers has a finite number of terms, say m, so that $a_{-m} \neq 0$; $a_{-m-1} = a_{-m-2} = \ldots = 0$, then $z = a$ is called a *pole of order m*. A pole of order one is called a *simple pole.*

If the series with negative powers does not terminate, *i.e.*, has an infinite number of terms, then $z = a$ is called an *essential singular point* of $f(z)$.

The co-efficient of $(z - a)^{-1}$ in the expansion of $f(z)$ about an isolated singularity $z = a$ is called the *residue* of $f(z)$ at $z = a$. Thus from equation (1), the residue of $f(z)$ at $z = a$ is a_{-1} and may be denoted by

$$a_{-1} = \text{Res } \{f(z), a\}$$

Since $$a_{-1} = \frac{1}{2\pi i} \oint_C f(z)\, dz$$

$$\therefore \quad \oint_C f(z)\, dz = 2\pi i a_{-1} = 2\pi i \text{ Res } \{f(z), a\}.$$

1.24. RESIDUE THEOREM

If $f(z)$ is analytic at all points inside and on a simple closed curve C, except at a finite number of isolated singular points within C, then

$$\oint_C f(z)\, dz = 2\pi i \text{ (sum of residues at singular points within C).}$$

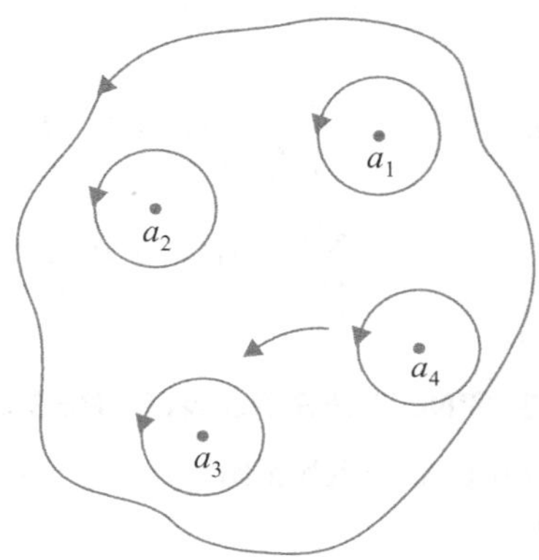

Proof. Around each of the isolated singular points $a_1, a_2, ..., a_n$ draw small non-intersecting circles $C_1, C_2, ..., C_n$ lying wholly inside C, with centres at $z = a_1, a_2, ..., a_n$ respectively.

Since $f(z)$ is analytic in the multiply connected region bounded by C, $C_1, C_2, ..., C_n$, we have by Cauchy's theorem for multiply connected region.

$$\oint_C f(z)\, dz = \oint_{C_1} f(z)\, dz + \oint_{C_2} f(z)\, dz + ... + \oint_{C_n} f(z)\, dz$$

$$= 2\pi i \,[\text{Res } \{(z), a_1\} + \text{Res } \{f(z), a_2\} + ... + \text{Res } \{f(z), a_n\}]$$

$$= 2\pi i \text{ (sum of residues at } a_1, a_2, ..., a_n).$$

1.25. CALCULATION OF RESIDUES

(1) *If $f(z)$ has a simple pole (i.e., pole of order 1) at $z = a$, then Res $\{f(z), a\} = \underset{z \to a}{Lt} (z - a) f(z)$.*

Since $z = a$ is a pole of order 1, the Laurent's series becomes

$$f(z) = a_0 + a_1(z - a) + a_2(z - a)^2 + ... + a_{-1}(z - a)^{-1}.$$

Multiplying both sides by $(z - a)$, we get

$$(z - a) f(z) = a_0(z - a) + a_1(z - a)^2 + a_2(z - a)^3 + ... + a_{-1}$$

$$\therefore \quad \underset{z \to a}{\text{Lt}} (z - a) f(z) = a_{-1} = \text{Res } \{f(z), a\}$$

(2) *If $f(z)$ has a pole of order m at $z = a$, then*

$$\textbf{Res } \{\mathbf{f(z), a}\} = \frac{1}{(m-1)!} \underset{z \to a}{\textbf{Lt}} \frac{d^{m-1}}{dz^{m-1}} [(z - a)^m f(z)]$$

Since $z = a$ is a pole of order m, the Laurent's series becomes

$$f(z) = a_0 + a_1(z - a) + a_2(z - a)^2 + ... + a_{-1}(z - a)^{-1} + a_{-2}(z - a)^{-2} + ... + a_{-m}(z - a)^{-m}$$

Multiplying both sides by $(z - a)^m$, we get

$$(z-a)^m f(z) = a_0(z-a)^m + a_1(z-a)^{m+1} + a_2(z-a)^{m+2} + \ldots$$
$$+ a_{-1}(z-a)^{m-1} + a_{-2}(z-a)^{m-2} + \ldots + a_{-m}$$

Differentiating both sides $(m - 1)$ times w.r.t. z and taking the limit as $z \to a$, we get

$$\underset{z \to a}{\text{Lt}} \frac{d^{m-1}}{dz^{m-1}} [(z-a)^m f(z)] = a_{-1} = (m-1)\,!$$

or
$$\frac{1}{(m-1)\,!} \underset{z \to a}{\text{Lt}} \frac{d^{m-1}}{dz^{m-1}} [(z-a)^m f(z)] = a_{-1} = \text{Res}\,\{f(z), a\}.$$

ILLUSTRATIVE EXAMPLES

Example 39. *Determine the poles of the function* $f(z) = \dfrac{z^2}{(z-1)^2(z+2)}$ *and the residue at each pole.* (C.U. June 2006, 07)

Sol. The function $f(z)$ has a pole of order 2 at $z = 1$ and a simple pole at $z = -2$.

Residue of $f(z)$ at $z = 1$ is

$$\underset{z \to 1}{\text{Lt}} \frac{d}{dz} [(z-1)^2 f(z)] = \underset{z \to 1}{\text{Lt}} \frac{d}{dz}\left(\frac{z^2}{z+2}\right)$$

$$= \underset{z \to 1}{\text{Lt}} \frac{(z+2)\,.\,2z - z^2\,.\,1}{(z+2)^2} = \underset{z \to 1}{\text{Lt}} \frac{z^2+4z}{(z+2)^2} = \frac{5}{9}$$

Residue of $f(z)$ at $z = -2$ is

$$= \underset{z \to -2}{\text{Lt}} [(z+2) f(z)] = \underset{z \to -2}{\text{Lt}} \frac{z^2}{(z-1)^2} = \frac{4}{9}.$$

Example 40. *Find the sum of the residues of the function* $f(z) = \dfrac{\sin z}{z \cos z}$ *at its poles inside the circle* $|\,z\,| = 2$.

Sol. The function $f(z)$ has simple poles at $z = 0, \pm \dfrac{\pi}{2}, \pm \dfrac{3\pi}{2}, \ldots$ Of these, $z = 0, \pm \dfrac{\pi}{2}$ lie inside $|\,z\,| = 2$.

Residue of $f(z)$ at $z = 0$ is $\underset{z \to 0}{\text{Lt}} [z\,.\,f(z)] = \underset{z \to 0}{\text{Lt}} \dfrac{\sin z}{\cos z} = 0$

Residue of $f(z)$ at $z = \dfrac{\pi}{2}$ is

$$\underset{z \to \frac{\pi}{2}}{\text{Lt}} \left(z - \frac{\pi}{2}\right) f(z) = \underset{z \to \frac{\pi}{2}}{\text{Lt}} \frac{\left(z - \frac{\pi}{2}\right)\sin z}{z \cos z} \qquad \Big|\ \text{Form } \frac{0}{0}$$

$$= \underset{z \to \frac{\pi}{2}}{\text{Lt}} \frac{\left(z - \frac{\pi}{2}\right)\cos z + \sin z}{\cos z - z \sin z} \qquad \text{[By L' Hospital's Rule]}$$

$$= \frac{1}{-\frac{\pi}{2}} = -\frac{2}{\pi}$$

Similarly, residue of $f(z)$ at $z = -\frac{\pi}{2}$ is $\frac{2}{\pi}$.

$\therefore$ Sum of residues $= 0 - \frac{2}{\pi} + \frac{2}{\pi} = 0.$

Example 41. *Evaluate* $\oint_C \frac{e^z}{(z+1)^2} dz$, *where C is the circle* $|z - 3| = 3$.

Sol. Here $f(z) = \frac{e^z}{(z+1)^2}$ has only one singular point $z = -1$ which is a pole of order 2 and it lies inside the circle $|z - 1| = 3$.

Residue of $f(z)$ at $z = -1$ is $\underset{z \to -1}{\text{Lt}} \frac{d}{dz} [(z+1)^2 f(z)] = \underset{z \to -1}{\text{Lt}} \frac{d}{dz}(e^z) = \underset{z \to -1}{\text{Lt}} e^z = e^{-1}$

$\therefore$ By residue theorem, we have $\oint_C \frac{e^z}{(z+1)^2} dz = 2\pi i(e^{-1}) = \frac{2\pi i}{e}$.

Example 42. *Evaluate* $\oint_C \frac{2z-1}{z(z+1)(z-3)} dz$, *where C is the circle* $|z| = 2$.

Sol. Here $f(z) = \frac{2z-1}{z(z+1)(z-3)}$ has three simple poles at $z = 0, -1, 3$ of which only $z = 0, -1$ lie inside the circle $|z| = 2$.

Residue of $f(z)$ at $z = 0$ is $\underset{z \to 0}{\text{Lt}}\ z f(z) = \underset{z \to 0}{\text{Lt}} \frac{2z-1}{(z+1)(z-3)} = \frac{1}{3}$

Residue of $f(z)$ at $z = -1$ is $\underset{z \to -1}{\text{Lt}} (z+1) f(z) = \underset{z \to -1}{\text{Lt}} \frac{2z-1}{z(z-3)} = -\frac{3}{4}$

$\therefore$ By residue theorem,

$$\oint_C \frac{2z-1}{z(z+1)(z-3)} dz = 2\pi i \text{ (sum of residues)}$$

$$= 2\pi i \left(\frac{1}{3} - \frac{3}{4}\right) = -\frac{5\pi i}{6}.$$

Example 43. *Evaluate* $\oint_C \frac{z-3}{z^2+2z+5} dz$, *where C is the circle*

(*i*) $|z| = 1$ (*ii*) $|z + 1 - i| = 2$ (*iii*) $|z + 1 + i| = 2$.

Sol. The poles of $f(z) = \frac{z-3}{z^2+2z+5}$ are given by

$$z^2 + 2z + 5 = 0 \quad i.e., \quad z = \frac{-2 \pm \sqrt{4-20}}{2} = -1 \pm 2i$$

(i) Both the poles lie outside the circle $| z | = 1$.

$\therefore$ By Cauchy's theorem, we have $\oint_C \frac{z-3}{z^2+2z+5}\, dz = 0$

(ii) Only the pole $z = -1 + 2i$ lies inside the circle $| z + 1 - i | = 2$.

Residue of $f(z)$ at $z = -1 + 2i$ is

$$\underset{z \to -1+2i}{\text{Lt}} (z + 1 - 2i) f(z) = \underset{z \to \alpha}{\text{Lt}} \frac{(z-\alpha)(z-3)}{z^2+2z+5}, \text{ where } \alpha = -1 + 2i \qquad \Big| \text{ Form } \frac{0}{0}$$

$$= \underset{z \to \alpha}{\text{Lt}} \frac{(z-\alpha)+(z-3)}{2z+2} \qquad | \text{ By L' Hospital's Rule}$$

$$= \frac{\alpha-3}{2\alpha+2} = \frac{-1+2i-3}{-2+4i+2} = \frac{i-2}{2i}$$

$\therefore$ By residue theorem, $\oint_C \frac{z-3}{z^2+2z+5}\, dz = 2\pi i\left(\frac{i-2}{2i}\right) = \pi(i-2)$.

(iii) Only the pole $z = -1 - 2i$ lies inside the circle $| z + 1 + i | = 2$

Residue of $f(z)$ at $z = -1 - 2i$ is

$$\underset{z \to -1-2i}{\text{Lt}} (z + 1 + 2i) f(z) = \underset{z \to \beta}{\text{Lt}} \frac{(z-\beta)(z-3)}{z^2+2z+5}, \text{ where } \beta = -1 - 2i \qquad \Big| \text{ Form } \frac{0}{0}$$

$$= \underset{z \to \beta}{\text{Lt}} \frac{(z-\beta)\,(z-3)}{2z+2} \qquad | \text{ By L' Hospital's Rule}$$

$$= \frac{\beta-3}{2\beta+2} = \frac{-4-2i}{-4i} = \frac{i+2}{2i}$$

$\therefore$ By residue theorem, $\oint_C \frac{z-3}{z^2+2z+5}\, dz = 2\pi i\left(\frac{i+2}{2i}\right) = \pi(i+2)$.

Example 44. *Evaluate* $\oint_C \frac{e^z}{\cos \pi z}$, *where C is the unit circle* $| z | = 1$. (C.U. Dec. 2010)

Sol. Here $f(z) = \frac{e^z}{\cos \pi z}$ has simple poles at $z = \pm \frac{1}{2}, \pm \frac{3}{2}, \pm \frac{5}{2}, \ldots$, of which only $z = \pm \frac{1}{2}$ lie inside the circle $| z | = 1$.

Residue of $f(z)$ at $z = \frac{1}{2}$ is

$$\underset{z \to \frac{1}{2}}{\text{Lt}} (z - \tfrac{1}{2}) f(z) = \underset{z \to \frac{1}{2}}{\text{Lt}} \frac{(z-\frac{1}{2})\, e^z}{\cos \pi z} \qquad \Big| \text{ Form } \frac{0}{0}$$

$$= \underset{z \to \frac{1}{2}}{\text{Lt}} \frac{(z-\frac{1}{2})\, e^z + e^z}{-\pi \sin \pi z} \qquad | \text{ By L' Hospital's Rule}$$

$$= \frac{e^{1/2}}{-\pi}.$$

Similarly, residue of $f(z)$ at $z = -\frac{1}{2}$ is $\frac{e^{-1/2}}{\pi}$.

$\therefore$ By residue theorem, $\oint_C \frac{e^z}{\cos \pi z} dz = 2\pi i$ (sum of residues)

$$= 2\pi i \left(-\frac{e^{1/2}}{\pi} + \frac{e^{-1/2}}{\pi} \right) = -4i \left(\frac{e^{1/2} - e^{-1/2}}{2} \right) = -4i \sinh \tfrac{1}{2}.$$

TEST YOUR KNOWLEDGE

Determine the poles of the following functions and the residue at each pole:

1. $\frac{2z+1}{z^2 - z - 2}$ **2.** $\frac{z+1}{z^2(z-2)}$ **3.** $\frac{z^2}{(z-1)(z-2)^2}$ **4.** $\frac{1-e^{2z}}{z^4}$

5. $\frac{e^z}{z^2 + \pi^2}$ **6.** $\frac{z}{\cos z}$ **7.**(*a*) $\frac{z^2 - 2z}{(z+1)^2 (z^2+4)}$ (*b*) $\frac{z}{z^2 - 3z + 2}$.

(C.U. Dec. 2008)

Find the residues at z = 0 of the following functions:

8. $z \cos \frac{1}{z}$ **9.** $\text{cosec}^2 z$ **10.** $\frac{1+e^z}{\sin z + z \cos z}$. *(C.U. June 2010)*

Evaluate the following integrals:

11. $\oint_C \frac{z^2 + 2z - 2}{z - 4} dz$, where C is a closed curve containing the point $z = 4$ in its interior.

12. $\oint_C \frac{1 - 2z}{z(z-1)(z-2)} dz$, where C is the circle $|z| = 1.5$.

13. $\oint_C \frac{z}{(z-1)(z-2)^2} dz$, where C is the circle $|z - 2| = \frac{1}{2}$. *(C.U. June 2007)*

14. $\oint_C \frac{12z - 7}{(z-1)^2 (2z+3)} dz$, where C is the circle $|z| = 2$.

15. $\oint_C \frac{\sin \pi z^2 + \cos \pi z^2}{(z-1)^2 (z-2)} dz$, where C is the circle $|z| = 3$. *(C.U. June 2009)*

16. $\oint_C \frac{z \sec z}{(1-z)^2} dz$, where C is the circle $|z| = 2$. *(C.U. June 2010)*

17. $\oint_C \frac{dz}{\sinh z}$, where C is the circle $|z| = 4$.

18. $\oint_C \tan z \, dz$, where C is the circle $|z| = 2$.

19. $\oint_C \frac{dz}{(z^2+4)^2}$, where C is the circle $|z - i| = 2$. *(C.U. June 2006)*

20. $\oint_C \frac{4 - 3z}{z(z-1)(z-2)} dz$, where C is $|z| = 1.5$. *(C.U. June 2006)*

Answers

1. $z = -1, 2 ; \frac{1}{3}, \frac{5}{3}$ **2.** $z = 0, 2 ; -\frac{3}{4}, \frac{3}{4}$ **3.** $z = 1, 2 ; 1, 0$ **4.** $z = 0 ; -\frac{4}{3}$

5. $z = \pm \pi i ; \pm \frac{i}{2\pi}$ **6.** $z = (2n+1)\frac{\pi}{2} ; (-1)^{n+1}(2n+1)\frac{\pi}{2}$, where n is an integer.

7. (*a*) $z = -1, \pm 2i ; -\frac{14}{25}, \frac{7 \pm i}{25}$ (*b*) $2, 1 ; 2, -1$ **8.** $-\frac{1}{2}$

9. 0 **10.** 1 **11.** $44\pi i$ **12.** $3\pi i$

13. $-2\pi i$ **14.** 0 **15.** $4\pi i(\pi + 1)$

16. $2\pi i \sec 1(1 + \tan 1)$ **17.** $-2\pi i$ **18.** $-4\pi i$. **19.** $\pi/6$

20. $2\pi i$.

1.26. APPLICATION OF RESIDUES TO EVALUATE REAL INTEGRALS

The residue theorem provides a simple and elegant method for evaluating many important definite integrals of real variables. Some of these are illustrated below:

(1) **Integrals of the type $\int_0^{2\pi} F(\cos\theta, \sin\theta)\, d\theta$,**

where $F(\cos\theta, \sin\theta)$ is a rational function of $\cos\theta$ and $\sin\theta$.

Such integrals can be reduced to complex line integrals by the substitution $z = e^{i\theta}$, so that

$$dz = ie^{i\theta}\, d\theta, \text{ i.e., } d\theta = \frac{dz}{iz}.$$

Also
$$\cos\theta = \frac{e^{i\theta} + e^{-i\theta}}{2} = \frac{1}{2}\left(z + \frac{1}{z}\right)$$

$$\sin\theta = \frac{e^{i\theta} + e^{-i\theta}}{2i} = \frac{1}{2i}\left(z - \frac{1}{z}\right).$$

As θ varies from 0 to 2π, z moves once round the unit circle in the anti-clockwise direction.

$$\therefore \quad \int_0^{2\pi} F(\cos\theta, \sin\theta)\, d\theta = \oint_C F\left(\frac{z + z^{-1}}{2}, \frac{z - z^{-1}}{2i}\right)\frac{dz}{iz}$$

where C is the unit circle $|z| = 1$.

The integral on the right can be evaluated by using the residue theorem.

ILLUSTRATIVE EXAMPLES

Example 45. *Evaluate* $\int_0^{2\pi} \frac{d\theta}{2 + \cos\theta}$. (C.U. June 2006)

Sol. Put $z = e^{i\theta}$ so that $\cos\theta = \frac{1}{2}\left(z + \frac{1}{z}\right)$ and $d\theta = \frac{dz}{iz}$

Then
$$\int_0^{2\pi} \frac{d\theta}{2 + \cos\theta} = \oint_C \frac{1}{2 + \frac{1}{2}\left(z + \frac{1}{z}\right)} \frac{dz}{iz} = \frac{2}{i}\oint_C \frac{1}{z^2 + 4z + 1}\, dz$$

where C is the circle $|z| = 1$.

The poles of the integrand are the roots of $z^2 + 4z + 1 = 0$, which are $z = -2 \pm \sqrt{3}$.

Of the two poles, only $z = -2 + \sqrt{3}$ lies inside the circle C.

Residue at $z = -2 + \sqrt{3}$ is

$$= \underset{z \to \alpha}{\text{Lt}} (z - \alpha) \frac{1}{z^2 + 4z + 1}, \quad \text{where } \alpha = -2 + \sqrt{3} \qquad \left| \text{Form } \frac{0}{0} \right.$$

$$= \underset{z \to \alpha}{\text{Lt}} \frac{1}{2z + 4} = \frac{1}{2\alpha + 4} = \frac{1}{2\sqrt{3}}$$

$\therefore$ By residue theorem, $\oint_C \frac{dz}{z^2 + 4z + 1} = 2\pi i \left(\frac{1}{2\sqrt{3}} \right) = \frac{\pi i}{\sqrt{3}}$

Hence $\int_0^{2\pi} \frac{d\theta}{2 + \cos\theta} = \frac{2}{i} \oint_C \frac{dz}{z^2 + 4z + 1} = \frac{2}{i} \left(\frac{\pi i}{\sqrt{3}} \right) = \frac{2\pi}{\sqrt{3}}$.

Example 46. *Evaluate* $\int_0^{2\pi} \frac{d\theta}{1 - 2a \sin\theta + a^2}$, *$0 < a < 1$.* (C.U. June 2010)

Sol. Put $z = e^{i\theta}$ so that $\sin\theta = \frac{1}{2i}\left(z - \frac{1}{z} \right)$ and $d\theta = \frac{dz}{iz}$.

Then, $\int_0^{2\pi} \frac{d\theta}{1 - 2a \sin\theta + a^2} = \oint_C \frac{1}{1 - 2a \cdot \frac{1}{2i}\left(z - \frac{1}{z} \right) + a^2} \frac{dz}{iz}$

$$= -\oint_C \frac{dz}{az^2 - i(a^2 + 1)z - a} = -\oint_C \frac{dz}{(az - i)(z - ia)}$$

where C is the circle $| z | = 1$.

The integrand has simple poles at $z = \frac{i}{a}$ and $z = ia$ of which only $z = ia$ lies inside the circle C. $[\because \ 0 < a < 1]$

Residue at $z = ia$ is $\underset{z \to ia}{\text{Lt}} (z - ia) \frac{1}{(az - i)(z - ia)} = \underset{z \to ia}{\text{Lt}} \frac{1}{az - i} = \frac{1}{i(a^2 - 1)}$

$\therefore$ By residue theorem,

$$\oint_C \frac{dz}{(az - i)(z - ia)} = 2\pi i \cdot \frac{1}{i(a^2 - 1)} = \frac{2\pi}{a^2 - 1}$$

Hence $\int_0^{2\pi} \frac{d\theta}{1 - 2a \sin\theta + a^2} = -\oint_C \frac{dz}{(az - i)(z - ia)} = \frac{2\pi}{1 - a^2}$.

Example 47. *Prove that* $\int_0^{2\pi} \frac{\sin^2\theta}{a + b\cos\theta} d\theta = \frac{2\pi}{b^2}\left(a - \sqrt{a^2 - b^2} \right)$, *where $0 < b < a$.*

Sol. Let $\mathrm{I} = \int_0^{2\pi} \frac{\sin^2\theta}{a + b\cos\theta} d\theta = \int_0^{2\pi} \frac{1 - \cos 2\theta}{2(a + b\cos\theta)} d\theta$

$$= \text{Real part of } \int_0^{2\pi} \frac{1 - e^{2i\theta}}{2a + 2b\cos\theta} d\theta$$

Put $z = e^{i\theta}$ so that $\cos\theta = \frac{1}{2}\left(z + \frac{1}{z} \right)$ and $d\theta = \frac{dz}{iz}$

Then $$\int_0^{2\pi} \frac{1-e^{2i\theta}}{2a+2b\cos\theta}\,d\theta = \oint_C \frac{1-z^2}{2a+b\left(z+\frac{1}{z}\right)}\frac{dz}{iz} = \oint_C \frac{1-z^2}{i(bz^2+2az+b)}\,dz$$

where C is the circle $|z| = 1$.

The poles of the integrand are the roots of $bz^2 + 2az + b = 0$, *viz.*

$$z = \frac{-2a \pm \sqrt{4a^2-4b^2}}{2b} = \frac{-a \pm \sqrt{a^2-b^2}}{b}$$

Let $$\alpha = \frac{-a+\sqrt{a^2-b^2}}{b} \quad \text{and} \quad \beta = \frac{-a-\sqrt{a^2-b^2}}{b}$$

Clearly $|\beta| > 1$ so that $z = \alpha$ is the only simple pole inside C.

Also $bz^2 + 2az + b = b(z-\alpha)(z-\beta)$

Residue at $z = \alpha$ is

$$\underset{z\to\alpha}{\text{Lt}}\ (z-\alpha)\cdot\frac{1-z^2}{ib(z-\alpha)(z-\beta)} = \underset{z\to\alpha}{\text{Lt}}\ \frac{1-z^2}{ib(z-\beta)} = \frac{1-\alpha^2}{ib(\alpha-\beta)}$$

$$= \frac{\alpha\left(\frac{1}{\alpha}-\alpha\right)}{ib(\alpha-\beta)} = \frac{\alpha(\beta-\alpha)}{ib(\alpha-\beta)} \qquad [\because \ \alpha\beta = 1]$$

$$= -\frac{\alpha}{ib} = \frac{a-\sqrt{a^2-b^2}}{ib^2}$$

$\therefore$ By residue theorem,

$$\oint_C \frac{1-z^2}{i(bz^2+2az+b)}\,dz = 2\pi i\cdot\frac{a-\sqrt{a^2-b^2}}{ib^2} = \frac{2\pi}{b^2}\left(a-\sqrt{a^2-b^2}\right)$$

Hence I = Real part of $\oint_C \frac{1-z^2}{i(bz^2+2az+b)}\,dz = \frac{2\pi}{b^2}\left(a-\sqrt{a^2-b^2}\right)$.

Example 48. *Evaluate* $\int_0^{\pi} \frac{d\theta}{a+b\cos\theta}$, *where* $a > |b|$. (C.U. June 2006; Dec. 2007)

Sol. Since $$\int_0^{2a} f(x)\,dx = 2\int_0^{a} f(x)\,dx, \text{ if } f(2a-x) = f(x)$$

$$\therefore \quad \int_0^{2\pi} \frac{d\theta}{a+b\cos\theta} = 2\int_0^{\pi} \frac{d\theta}{a+b\cos\theta} \qquad [\because \ \cos(2\pi-\theta) = \cos\theta]$$

or $$\int_0^{\pi} \frac{d\theta}{a+b\cos\theta} = \frac{1}{2}\int_0^{2\pi} \frac{d\theta}{a+b\cos\theta} \qquad ...(1)$$

Putting $z = e^{i\theta}$, so that $\cos\theta = \frac{1}{2}\left(z+\frac{1}{z}\right)$ and $d\theta = \frac{dz}{iz}$, we have

$$\int_0^{2\pi} \frac{d\theta}{a+b\cos\theta} = \oint_C \frac{1}{a+\frac{b}{2}\left(z+\frac{1}{z}\right)}\frac{dz}{iz} = \oint_C \frac{2dz}{i(bz^2+2az+b)}$$

where C is the circle $|z| = 1$.

Proceeding as in example 3, residue at $z = \alpha$ is

$$= \underset{z \to \alpha}{\text{Lt}} (z - \alpha) . \frac{2}{ib(z - \alpha)(z - \beta)} = \underset{z \to \alpha}{\text{Lt}} \frac{2}{ib(z - \beta)} = \frac{2}{ib(\alpha - \beta)}$$

$$= \frac{2}{ib} . \frac{b}{2\sqrt{a^2 - b^2}} = \frac{1}{i\sqrt{a^2 - b^2}}$$

$\therefore$ By residue theorem,

$$\oint_C \frac{2dz}{i(bz^2 + 2az + b)} = 2\pi i . \frac{1}{i\sqrt{a^2 - b^2}} = \frac{2\pi}{\sqrt{a^2 - b^2}}$$

Hence from (1), $\displaystyle\int_0^{\pi} \frac{d\theta}{a + b\cos\theta} = \frac{\pi}{\sqrt{a^2 - b^2}}$.

(2) **Integrals of the type $\displaystyle\int_{-\infty}^{\infty} \frac{f(x)}{F(x)} dx$, where f(x) and F(x) are polynomials in x such that $\dfrac{x f(x)}{F(x)} \to 0$ as $x \to \infty$ and F(x) has no zeros on the real axis.**

Consider the integral $\displaystyle\oint_C \frac{f(z)}{F(z)} dz$

over the closed contour C consisting of the real axis from – R to R and the semi-circle C_1 of radius R in the upper half plane.

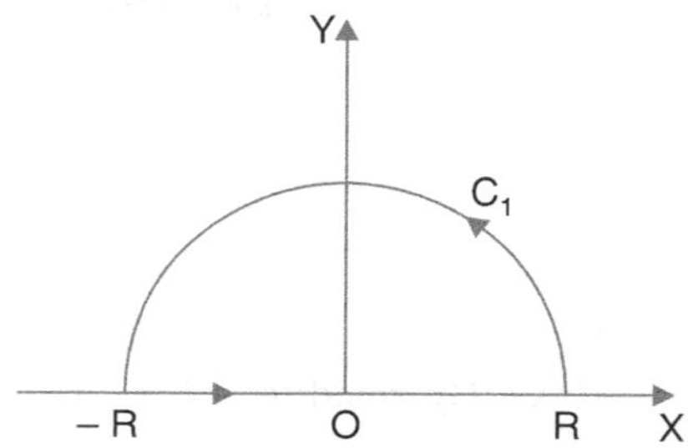

We take R large enough so that all the poles of $\dfrac{f(z)}{F(z)}$ in the upper half plane lie within C.

By residue theorem, we have

$$\oint_C \frac{f(z)}{F(z)} dz = 2\pi i \left[\text{sum of the residues of } \frac{f(z)}{F(z)} \text{ in the upper half plane}\right]$$

or $$\oint_{C_1} \frac{f(z)}{F(z)} dz + \int_{-R}^{R} \frac{f(x)}{F(x)} dx = 2\pi i \left[\text{sum of the residues of } \frac{f(z)}{F(z)} \text{ in the upper half plane}\right] \quad ...(1)$$

($\because$ on the real axis, $z = x$)

If we put $z = Re^{i\theta}$ in the first integral on the left side, then R is constant on C_1 and as z moves along C_1, θ varies from 0 to π.

$$\therefore \quad \int_{C_1} \frac{f(z)}{F(z)} dz = \int_0^{\pi} \frac{f(Re^{i\theta})}{F(Re^{i\theta})} Re^{i\theta}\, i\, d\theta$$

For large R, $\displaystyle\left|\int_0^{\pi} \frac{f(Re^{i\theta})}{F(Re^{i\theta})} Re^{i\theta}\, i d\theta\right| \to 0$ $\quad\Big|$ is of the order $\dfrac{Rf(R)}{F(R)}$

$$\therefore \quad \int_0^{\pi} \frac{f(Re^{i\theta})}{F(Re^{i\theta})} Re^{i\theta}\, i d\theta \to 0 \text{ when } R \to \infty$$

Hence from (1), we have $\displaystyle\int_{-\infty}^{\infty} \frac{f(x)}{F(x)} dx = 2\pi i$

$$\left[\text{Sum of the residues of } \frac{f(z)}{F(z)} \text{ in the upper half plane}\right].$$

ILLUSTRATIVE EXAMPLES

Example 49. *Evaluate* $\int_{-\infty}^{\infty} \frac{x^2}{(x^2+a^2)(x^2+b^2)}\, dx \ (a > 0,\ b > 0)$. (C.U. June 2006)

Sol. The poles of $\phi(z) = \frac{z^2}{(z^2+a^2)(z^2+b^2)}$ are $z = \pm ia, \pm ib$.

Of these, $z = ia$ and $z = ib$ lie in the upper half of the z-plane.

Residue of $\phi(z)$ at $z = ia$ is

$$\underset{z \to ia}{\text{Lt}} (z - ia) \cdot \frac{z^2}{(z^2+a^2)(z^2+b^2)} = \underset{z \to ia}{\text{Lt}} \frac{z^2}{(z+ia)(z^2+b^2)} = \frac{-a^2}{2ia(-a^2+b^2)} = \frac{a}{2i(a^2-b^2)}$$

Residue of $\phi(z)$ at $z = ib$ is

$$\underset{z \to ib}{\text{Lt}} (z - ib) \cdot \frac{z^2}{(z^2+a^2)(z^2+b^2)} = \underset{z \to ib}{\text{Lt}} \frac{z^2}{(z^2+a^2)(z+ib)} = \frac{-b^2}{(-b^2+a^2)(2ib)} = \frac{-b}{2i(a^2-b^2)}$$

$$\therefore \int_{-\infty}^{\infty} \frac{x^2\, dx}{(x^2+a^2)(x^2+b^2)} = 2\pi i \text{ [sum of residues of } \phi(z) \text{ in the upper half of } z\text{-plane]}$$

$$= 2\pi i \left[\frac{a}{2i(a^2-b^2)} - \frac{b}{2i(a^2-b^2)}\right] = \pi\left[\frac{a-b}{a^2-b^2}\right] = \frac{\pi}{a+b}.$$

Example 50. *Evaluate* $\int_0^{\infty} \frac{dx}{x^4+1}$.

Sol. The poles of $\phi(z) = \frac{1}{z^4+1}$ are obtained by solving $z^4 + 1 = 0$.

Now $z^4 + 1 = 0$.

$$\Rightarrow \quad z = (-1)^{1/4} = (\cos\pi + i\sin\pi)^{1/4} = [\cos(2n\pi + \pi) + i\sin(2n\pi + \pi)]^{1/4}$$

$$= \cos\frac{(2n+1)\pi}{4} + i\sin\frac{(2n+1)\pi}{4} \qquad \text{(By De Moivre's theorem)}$$

where $n = 0, 1, 2, 3$.

When $n = 0$, $z = \cos\frac{\pi}{4} + i\sin\frac{\pi}{4} = \frac{1}{\sqrt{2}} + i\frac{1}{\sqrt{2}}$

When $n = 1$, $z = \cos\frac{3\pi}{4} + i\sin\frac{3\pi}{4} = -\frac{1}{\sqrt{2}} + i\frac{1}{\sqrt{2}}$

When $n = 2$, $z = \cos\frac{5\pi}{4} + i\sin\frac{5\pi}{4} = -\frac{1}{\sqrt{2}} - i\frac{1}{\sqrt{2}}$

When $n = 3$, $z = \cos\frac{7\pi}{4} + i\sin\frac{7\pi}{4} = \frac{1}{\sqrt{2}} - i\frac{1}{\sqrt{2}}$

Of these, only the poles corresponding to $n = 0, 1$, *viz*, $z = e^{i\frac{\pi}{4}}$ and $z = e^{3i\frac{\pi}{4}}$ lie in the upper half of z-plane.

Residue of $\phi(z)$ at $z = e^{i\frac{\pi}{4}}$ is $\underset{z \to e^{i\frac{\pi}{4}}}{\text{Lt}} \dfrac{z - e^{i\frac{\pi}{4}}}{z^4 + 1}$ | Form $\frac{0}{0}$

$$= \underset{z \to e^{i\frac{\pi}{4}}}{\text{Lt}} \frac{1}{4z^3} \qquad \text{| By L' Hospital's rule}$$

$$= \frac{1}{4e^{3i\frac{\pi}{4}}} = \frac{1}{4} e^{-3i\frac{\pi}{4}}$$

Similarly, residue of $\phi(z)$ at $z = e^{3i\frac{\pi}{4}}$ is $\frac{1}{4} e^{-9i\frac{\pi}{4}}$

$$\therefore \quad \int_0^{\infty} \frac{dx}{x^4 + 1} = \frac{1}{2} \int_{-\infty}^{\infty} \frac{dx}{x^4 + 1}$$

$$= \frac{1}{2} \,.\, 2\pi i \text{ [sum of residues of } \phi(z) \text{ in the upper half of } z\text{-plane]}$$

$$= \pi i \left[\frac{1}{4} e^{-3i\frac{\pi}{4}} + \frac{1}{4} e^{-9i\frac{\pi}{4}}\right] = \frac{1}{4} \pi i \left[\left(\cos \frac{3\pi}{4} - i \sin \frac{3\pi}{4}\right) + \left(\cos \frac{9\pi}{4} - i \sin \frac{9\pi}{4}\right)\right]$$

$$= \frac{1}{4} \pi i \left[-\frac{1}{\sqrt{2}} - \frac{i}{\sqrt{2}} + \frac{1}{\sqrt{2}} - \frac{i}{\sqrt{2}}\right] = \frac{1}{4} \pi i(-i\sqrt{2}) = \frac{\pi\sqrt{2}}{4}.$$

Note. The above method can also be applied to some cases where $f(x)$ contains trigonometric functions also.

Example 51. *Evaluate* $\int_0^{\infty} \frac{\cos ax}{x^2 + 1} dx, a \geq 0.$ (C.U. Dec. 2009)

Sol. Since cos ax is the real part of e^{iax}, we consider the function $\phi(z) = \dfrac{e^{iaz}}{z^2 + 1}$

This has poles at $z = \pm i$, of which only $z = i$ lies in the upper half of z-plane.

Residue of $\phi(z)$ at $z = i$ is $\underset{z \to i}{\text{Lt}} \dfrac{(z - i)e^{iaz}}{z^2 + 1} = \underset{z \to i}{\text{Lt}} \dfrac{(z - i)e^{iaz}}{(z + i)(z - i)} = \underset{z \to i}{\text{Lt}} \dfrac{e^{iaz}}{z + i} = \dfrac{e^{-a}}{2i}$

$$\therefore \quad \oint_C \frac{e^{iaz}}{z^2 + i} dz = 2\pi i \,.\, \frac{e^{-a}}{2i} = \pi e^{-a} \qquad \text{...(1)}$$

where C is the contour of Art. 1.26 (2).

On the semi-circle C_1, $z = Re^{i\theta}$.

$$\therefore \quad z \,.\, \frac{e^{iaz}}{z^2 + 1} = Re^{i\theta} \,.\, \frac{e^{ia R (\cos \theta + i \sin \theta)}}{R^2 e^{2i\theta} + 1} = \frac{(e^{ia R \cos \theta} e^{i\theta})\, e^{-a R \sin \theta}\, R^{-1}}{e^{2i\theta} + R^{-2}}$$

which $\to 0$ as $R \to \infty$, since

$$| e^{iaR\cos\theta} . e^{i\theta} | = | \cos(\theta + aR\cos\theta) + i\sin(\theta + aR\cos\theta) | \le 1,$$
$$| e^{-aR\sin\theta} | \le 1, \ | e^{2i\theta} + R^{-2} | \ne 0 \quad \text{and} \quad R^{-1} \to 0$$

$\therefore$ The integral over C_1 vanishes and (1) gives $\displaystyle\int_{-\infty}^{\infty} \frac{e^{iax}}{x^2+1} dx = \pi e^{-a}$

Equating real parts, we get $\displaystyle\int_{-\infty}^{\infty} \frac{\cos ax}{x^2+1} dx = \pi e^{-a}$

Hence $\displaystyle\int_0^{\infty} \frac{\cos ax}{x^2+1} dx = \frac{1}{2}\int_{-\infty}^{\infty} \frac{\cos ax}{x^2+1} dx = \frac{\pi e^{-a}}{2}.$

(3) Integrals of the type $\displaystyle\int_{-\infty}^{\infty} \frac{f(x)}{F(x)} dx$, when F(x) has zeros on the real axis.

In such cases we proceed in a manner similar to above, except that the singularities on the real axis are enclosed in small semi-circles to avoid their inclusion in C, *i.e.*, the contour C is indented at these singularities.

Example 52. *Evaluate* $\displaystyle\int_0^{\infty} \frac{\sin mx}{x} dx, m > 0.$

Sol. Since $\sin mx$ is the imaginary part of e^{imx}, we consider the function

$$\phi(z) = \frac{e^{imz}}{z}.$$

This has a simple pole at $z = 0$, which lies on the real axis. Enclose this singularity by a small semi-circle $C_2 : | z | = r$. Evaluate the function $\phi(z)$ over the contour C shown in the figure consisting of parts of the real axis from $-R$ to $-r$ and r to R, the small semi-circle C_2 and the large semi-circle C_1. Since the function has no singularity within this contour, by Cauchy's theorem, we have

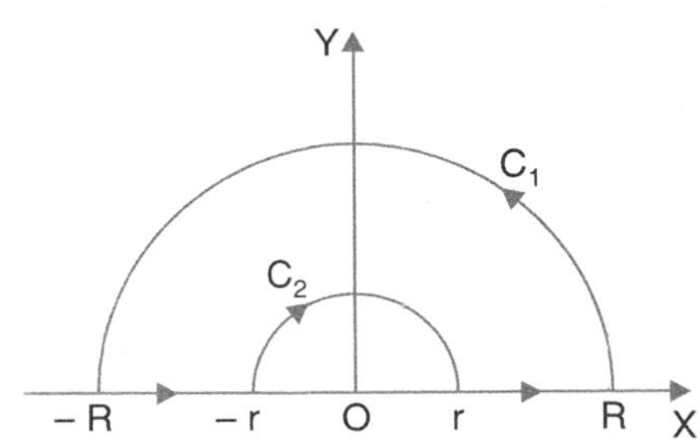

$$\oint_C \phi(z)\, dz = 0$$

$$\Rightarrow \quad \int_{-R}^{-r} \phi(x)\, dx + \int_{C_2} \phi(z)\, dz + \int_r^R \phi(x)\, dx + \int_{C_1} \phi(z)\, dz = 0$$

$$\Rightarrow \quad \int_{-R}^{-r} \frac{e^{imx}}{x} dx + \int_{C_2} \frac{e^{imz}}{z} dz + \int_r^R \frac{e^{imx}}{x} dx + \int_{C_1} \frac{e^{imz}}{z} dz = 0 \qquad ...(1)$$

Substituting $-x$ for x in the first integral and combining it with the third integral, we get

$$\int_r^R \frac{e^{imx} - e^{-imx}}{x} dx + \int_{C_2} \frac{e^{imz}}{z} dz + \int_{C_1} \frac{e^{imz}}{z} dz = 0$$

or
$$2i\int_r^R \frac{\sin mx}{x} dx + \int_{C_2} \frac{e^{imz}}{z} dz + \int_{C_1} \frac{e^{imz}}{z} dz = 0 \qquad ...(2)$$

Now $$\int_{C_2} \frac{e^{imz}}{z}\, dz = \int_{C_2} \frac{1}{z}\, dz + \int_{C_2} \frac{e^{imz}-1}{z}\, dz \qquad ...(3)$$

On C_2, $z = re^{i\theta}$

$$\therefore \quad \int_{C_2} \frac{1}{z}\, dz = \int_{\pi}^{0} \frac{re^{i\theta} i\, d\theta}{re^{i\theta}} = -\int_0^{\pi} i d\theta = -i\pi$$

Also $$\left| \int_{C_2} \frac{e^{imz}-1}{z}\, dz \right| \le M \int_{C_2} \frac{|dz|}{|z|} = \pi M$$

where M is the maximum value on C_2 of $| e^{imz} - 1 | = |e^{imr(\cos\theta + i \sin\theta)} - 1 |$

Clearly, $M \to 0$ as $r \to 0$

$$\therefore \quad \text{From (3), } \int_{C_2} \frac{e^{imz}}{z}\, dz = -i\pi \qquad ...(4)$$

Putting $z = Re^{i\theta}$ in the integral over C_1, we get

$$\int_{C_1} \frac{e^{imz}}{z}\, dz = \int_0^{\pi} \frac{e^{imR(\cos\theta + i\sin\theta)}}{Re^{i\theta}} Re^{i\theta}\, i\, d\theta = i\int_0^{\pi} e^{imR\cos\theta} \,.\, e^{-mR\sin\theta}\, d\theta$$

Since $| e^{imR\cos\theta} | \le 1$

$$\therefore \quad \left| \int_{C_1} \frac{e^{imz}}{z}\, dz \right| \le \int_0^{\pi} e^{-mR\sin\theta}\, d\theta = 2\int_0^{\pi/2} e^{-mR\sin\theta}\, d\theta$$

Also $\frac{\sin\theta}{\theta}$ continually decreases from 1 to $\frac{2}{\pi}$ as θ increases from 0 to $\frac{\pi}{2}$.

$\therefore$ For $0 \le \theta \le \frac{\pi}{2}$, $\frac{\sin\theta}{\theta} \ge \frac{2}{\pi}$ or $\sin\theta \ge \frac{2\theta}{\pi}$

$$\therefore \quad \left| \int \frac{e^{imz}}{z}\, dz \right| \le 2\int_0^{\pi/2} e^{-2mR\theta/\pi} d\theta = \left[-\frac{\pi}{mR} e^{-2mR\theta/\pi} \right]_0^{\pi/2} = \frac{\pi}{mR}(1 - e^{-mR})$$

As $R \to \infty$, $\frac{\pi}{mR}(1 - e^{-mR}) \to 0$

$$\therefore \quad \int_{C_1} \frac{e^{imz}}{z}\, dz = 0$$

Hence from (2), on taking the limit as $r \to 0$ and $R \to \infty$, we get

$$2i\int_0^{\infty} \frac{\sin mx}{x}\, dx - i\pi = 0 \quad \text{or} \quad \int_0^{\infty} \frac{\sin mx}{x}\, dx = \frac{\pi}{2}.$$

TEST YOUR KNOWLEDGE

Evaluate the following integrals by contour integration:

1. $\displaystyle\int_0^{2\pi} \frac{d\theta}{5 - 3\cos\theta}$ (*C.U. Dec. 2010*)

2. $\displaystyle\int_0^{2\pi} \frac{d\theta}{a + b\sin\theta}$, where $a > |b|$ (*C.U. June 2006*)

3. $\displaystyle\int_0^{\pi} \frac{\cos 3\theta}{5 - 4\cos\theta}\, d\theta$ (*C.U. Dec. 2008*)

4. $\displaystyle\int_0^{2\pi} \frac{\cos 2\theta}{5 + 4\cos\theta}\, d\theta$ (*C.U. June 2007*)

5. $\displaystyle\int_0^{2\pi} \frac{d\theta}{1 - 2p\cos\theta + p^2}$, $0 < p < 1$ (*C.U. June 2007, 10*)

6. $\displaystyle\int_0^{2\pi} \frac{\cos 2\theta\, d\theta}{1 - 2p\cos\theta + p^2}$, $0 < p < 1$

7. (*a*) $\displaystyle\int_0^{\pi} \frac{a\, d\theta}{a^2 + \sin^2\theta}$ (*b*) $\displaystyle\int_0^{\pi} \frac{d\theta}{17 - 8\cos\theta}$

8. $\displaystyle\int_0^{\infty} \frac{dx}{(x^2 + 1)^2}$

9. $\displaystyle\int_{-\infty}^{\infty} \frac{dx}{x^4 + 1}$

10. $\displaystyle\int_0^{\infty} \frac{dx}{x^6 + 1}$

11. $\displaystyle\int_{-\infty}^{\infty} \frac{dx}{(x^2 + a^2)(x^2 + b^2)}$

12. $\displaystyle\int_{-\infty}^{\infty} \frac{x^2 - x + 2}{x^4 + 10x^2 + 9}\, dx$

13. $\displaystyle\int_0^{\infty} \frac{x^2\, dx}{(x^2 + 9)(x^2 + 4)^2}$

14. $\displaystyle\int_0^{\infty} \frac{x\sin x}{x^2 + a^2}\, dx,\ a > 0$

15. $\displaystyle\int_{-\infty}^{\infty} \frac{\cos x}{(x^2 + a^2)(x^2 + b^2)}\, dx,\ a > b > 0$

16. $\displaystyle\int_0^{\infty} \frac{\sin mx}{x(x^2 + a^2)}\, dx,\ m > 0, a > 0$

17. $\displaystyle\int_0^{2\pi} \frac{d\theta}{(5 - 3\cos\theta)^2}$

18. $\displaystyle\int_{-\infty}^{\infty} \frac{x^2}{(x^2 + 1)(x^2 + 4)}\, dx$

19. $\displaystyle\int_0^{\infty} \frac{\cos x}{x}\, dx$

20. $\displaystyle\int_{-\infty}^{\infty} \frac{\sin x}{x^2 + 4x + 5}\, dx.$

Answers

1. $\dfrac{\pi}{2}$ **2.** $\dfrac{2\pi}{\sqrt{a^2 - b^2}}$ **3.** $\dfrac{\pi}{24}$ **4.** $\dfrac{\pi}{6}$

5. $\dfrac{2\pi}{1 - p^2}$ **6.** $\dfrac{2\pi p^2}{1 - p^2}$ **7.** (*a*) $\dfrac{\pi}{\sqrt{1 + a^2}}$ (*b*) $\dfrac{\pi}{15}$ **8.** $\dfrac{\pi}{4}$

9. $\dfrac{\pi}{\sqrt{2}}$ **10.** $\dfrac{\pi}{3}$ **11.** $\dfrac{\pi}{ab(a + b)}$ **12.** $\dfrac{5\pi}{12}$

13. $\dfrac{\pi}{200}$ **14.** $\dfrac{1}{2}\pi e^{-a}$ **15.** $\dfrac{\pi}{a^2 - b^2}\left(\dfrac{e^{-b}}{b} - \dfrac{e^{-a}}{a}\right)$ **16.** $\dfrac{\pi}{2a^2}(1 - e^{-ma})$

17. $\dfrac{5\pi}{32}$ **18.** $\dfrac{\pi}{3}$ **19.** 0 **20.** $\dfrac{-\pi\sin 2}{e}$.

UNIVERSITY QUESTIONS WITH SOLUTION

Q. 1. *If a function is analytic, prove that it is independent of* $\bar{z}$.

Sol. Let $w = f(z) = u + iv$ be the analytic function.

If $\dfrac{dw}{d\bar{z}} = 0$, it is independent of $\bar{z}$.

Since $z = x + iy$ and $\bar{z} = x - iy$, $x = \dfrac{1}{2}(z + \bar{z})$ and $y = \dfrac{z - \bar{z}}{2i}$.

We have
$$\frac{dw}{d\bar{z}} = \frac{du}{d\bar{z}} + i\frac{dv}{d\bar{z}}$$

Now,
$$\frac{du}{d\bar{z}} = \frac{\partial u}{\partial x}\cdot\frac{\partial x}{\partial \bar{z}} + \frac{\partial u}{\partial y}\cdot\frac{\partial y}{\partial \bar{z}} = \frac{\partial u}{\partial x}\left(\frac{1}{2}\right) + \frac{\partial u}{\partial y}\left(-\frac{1}{2i}\right)$$

$$\frac{dv}{d\bar{z}} = \frac{\partial v}{\partial x}\cdot\frac{\partial x}{\partial \bar{z}} + \frac{\partial v}{\partial y}\cdot\frac{\partial y}{\partial \bar{z}} = \frac{\partial v}{\partial x}\left(\frac{1}{2}\right) + \frac{\partial v}{\partial y}\left(-\frac{1}{2i}\right)$$

$\therefore$
$$\frac{dw}{d\bar{z}} = \frac{1}{2}\left(\frac{\partial u}{\partial x} - \frac{\partial v}{\partial y}\right) - \frac{1}{2i}\left(\frac{\partial u}{\partial y} + \frac{\partial v}{\partial x}\right)$$

$$= \frac{1}{2}\times 0 - \frac{1}{2i}\times 0 \qquad \text{(Using C-R eqns.)}$$

$$= 0.$$

Thus an analytic function is independent of $\bar{z}$.

Q. 2. *If* $f(z)$ *is an analytic function, show that* $\left[\dfrac{\partial}{\partial x}|f(z)|\right]^2 + \left[\dfrac{\partial}{\partial y}|f(z)|\right]^2 = |f'(z)|^2$.

Sol. Let
$$f(z) = u + iv$$
$$[f(z)]^2 = u^2 + v^2$$

Differentiating partially w.r.t. x,
$$2|f(z)|\frac{\partial}{\partial x}|f(z)| = 2u\,.\frac{\partial u}{\partial x} + 2v\frac{\partial v}{\partial x}$$

i.e.,
$$|f(z)|\frac{\partial}{\partial x}|f(z)| = u\frac{\partial u}{\partial x} + v\frac{\partial v}{\partial x} \qquad ...(1)$$

Differentiating partially w.r.t. y,
$$|f(z)|\frac{\partial}{\partial y}|f(z)| = u\frac{\partial u}{\partial y} + v\frac{\partial v}{\partial y} \qquad ...(2)$$

Squaring and adding eq. (1) and (2), we get
$$|f(z)|^2\left[\frac{\partial}{\partial x}|f(z)|\right]^2 + |f(z)|^2\left[\frac{\partial}{\partial y}|f(z)|\right]^2$$
$$= \left(u\frac{\partial u}{\partial x} + v\frac{\partial v}{\partial x}\right)^2 + \left(u\frac{\partial u}{\partial y} + v\frac{\partial v}{\partial y}\right)^2$$

$$= \left(u\frac{\partial u}{\partial x} + v\frac{\partial v}{\partial x}\right)^2 + \left[u\left(-\frac{\partial v}{\partial x}\right) + v\left(\frac{\partial u}{\partial x}\right)\right]^2, \text{ using C-R equations}$$

$$= u^2\left(\frac{\partial u}{\partial x}\right)^2 + v^2\left(\frac{\partial v}{\partial x}\right)^2 + 2uv\frac{\partial u}{\partial x}\frac{\partial v}{\partial x} + u^2\left(\frac{\partial v}{\partial x}\right)^2 + v^2\left(\frac{\partial v}{\partial x}\right)^2$$

$$- 2uv\,\frac{\partial u}{\partial x}\cdot\frac{\partial v}{\partial x}$$

$$= u^2\left[\left(\frac{\partial u}{\partial x}\right)^2 + \left(\frac{\partial v}{\partial x}\right)^2\right] + v^2\left[\left(\frac{\partial v}{\partial x}\right)^2 + \left(\frac{\partial u}{\partial x}\right)^2\right]$$

$$= u^2\,|f'(z)|^2 + v^2\,|f'(z)|^2, \qquad \left[\because\ f'(z) = \frac{\partial u}{\partial x} + i\frac{\partial v}{\partial x}\right]$$

i.e.,

$$|f(z)|^2\left\{\left[\frac{\partial}{\partial x}|f(z)|\right]^2 + \left[\frac{\partial}{\partial y}|f(z)|\right]^2\right\} = (u^2 + v^2)\ |f'(z)|^2 = |f(z)|^2\ |f'(z)|^2$$

$\therefore$

$$\left\{\left[\frac{\partial}{\partial x}|f(z)|\right]^2 + \left[\frac{\partial}{\partial y}|f(z)|\right]\right\}^2 = |f'(z)|^2.$$

Q. 3. *Show that an analytic function f(z) = u + iv with (i) constant real part (ii) constant imaginary part (iii) constant modulus is constant.* (C.U. June 2006, 2009, 2010)

Sol. (*i*) If the real part is constant, *i.e.,* u = a constant.

$$\therefore \qquad \frac{\partial u}{\partial x} = 0 \quad \text{and} \quad \frac{\partial u}{\partial y} = 0$$

Since $f(z)$ is analytic, by C-R equations,

$$\frac{\partial v}{\partial x} = -\frac{\partial u}{\partial y} = 0 \quad \text{and} \quad \frac{\partial v}{\partial y} = \frac{\partial u}{\partial x} = 0.$$

i.e. v is a constant.

Hence $u + iv = f(z)$ is constant.

(*ii*) As above.

(*iii*) If $|f(z)| = a$ constant.

i.e., $\sqrt{u^2 + v^2}$ = a constant. *i.e.,* $u^2 + v^2$ = a constant

Differentiating partially w.r.t. x and y,

$$2u\frac{\partial u}{\partial x} + 2v\frac{\partial v}{\partial x} = 0 \quad i.e. \quad u\frac{\partial u}{\partial x} + v\frac{\partial v}{\partial x} = 0$$

and

$$u\frac{\partial u}{\partial y} + v\frac{\partial v}{\partial y} = 0$$

i.e.,

$$u\frac{\partial u}{\partial x} - v\frac{\partial u}{\partial y} = 0$$

and

$$u\frac{\partial u}{\partial y} + v\frac{\partial u}{\partial x} = 0 \qquad \text{...(2)} \quad \text{(Using C-R equations)}$$

Multiply eq. (1) by u and eq. (2) by v, adding and get

$$\left(u^2\frac{\partial u}{\partial x} - uv\frac{\partial u}{\partial y}\right) + \left(uv\frac{\partial u}{\partial y} + v^2\frac{\partial u}{\partial x}\right) = 0$$

i.e., $$(u^2 + v^2)\frac{\partial u}{\partial x} = 0$$

i.e., $$\frac{\partial u}{\partial x} = 0, \qquad (\because \quad u^2 + v^2 \neq 0)$$

In a similar way, we can prove that $\frac{\partial u}{\partial y} = 0, \frac{\partial v}{\partial x} = 0$ and $\frac{\partial v}{\partial y} = 0$.

$\therefore$ u and v are constant and hence $f(z)$ is constant.

Q. 4. *Is there any analytic function $f(z) = u + iv$ for which $v = e^{y/x}$.* (C.U. June 2006)

Sol. If $f(z)$ is analytic then its real and imaginary parts are harmonic.

Here if $f(z)$ is analytic then $\frac{\partial^2 v}{\partial x^2} + \frac{\partial^2 v}{\partial y^2} = 0$

$$\frac{\partial v}{\partial x} = e^{y/x} \cdot \frac{-y}{x^2} = \frac{-y}{x^2}e^{y/x}$$

$$\frac{\partial v}{\partial y} = e^{y/x} \cdot \frac{1}{x} = \frac{1}{x}e^{y/x}$$

$$\frac{\partial^2 v}{\partial x^2} = -y\left[\frac{e^{y/x}}{x^2} \times \frac{-y}{x^2} + e^{y/x}\left(\frac{-2}{x^3}\right)\right] = \frac{y\,e^{y/x}}{x^4}[y + 2x]$$

$$\frac{\partial^2 v}{\partial y^2} = \frac{1}{x}e^{y/x} \cdot \frac{1}{x} = \frac{e^{y/x}}{x^2}$$

$$\therefore \qquad \frac{\partial^2 v}{\partial x^2} + \frac{\partial^2 v}{\partial y^2} \neq 0.$$

Since, v is not harmonic and hence there is no $f(z)$ with given v as imaginary part.

Q. 5. *If $w = u + iv$ is an analytic function and if $v = x^2 - y^2 + \frac{x}{x^2 + y^2}$, determine u.*

(C.U. Dec. 2008)

Sol. $$v = x^2 - y^2 + \frac{x}{x^2 + y^2}$$

$$\frac{\partial v}{\partial x} = 2x + \frac{(x^2 + y^2) - x \cdot 2x}{(x^2 + y^2)^2} = 2x + \frac{y^2 - x^2}{(x^2 + y^2)^2}$$

$$\frac{\partial v}{\partial y} = -2y + \frac{-x}{(x^2 + y^2)^2} \cdot 2y = -2y - \frac{2xy}{(x^2 + y^2)^2}$$

Since w is analytic, $\frac{\partial u}{\partial x} = \frac{\partial v}{\partial y}$ and $\frac{\partial u}{\partial y} = -\frac{\partial v}{\partial x}$

$$\frac{\partial u}{\partial x} = \frac{\partial v}{\partial y} = -2y - \frac{2xy}{(x^2+y^2)^2}$$

Integrating w.r.t. x,

$$u = \int \frac{\partial u}{\partial x}\, dx = -2xy - \frac{-y}{x^2+y^2} + \phi(y),$$

$\phi(y)$ is an arbitrary function of y.

$$u = \frac{y}{x^2+y^2} - 2xy + \phi(y)$$

$$\left[\begin{array}{l}\text{Put } x^2 + y^2 = u, \text{ then } 2xdx = du \\ \int \frac{2xy}{(x^2+y^2)^2}\, dx = y\int \frac{du}{u^2} = y\left(\frac{u^{-1}}{-1}\right) = \frac{-y}{x^2+y^2}\end{array}\right]$$

Now differentiating w.r.t. y,

$$\frac{\partial u}{\partial y} = -2x + \frac{(x^2+y^2) - y \cdot 2y}{(x^2+y^2)^2} + \phi'(y)$$

$$= -2x + \frac{x^2-y^2}{(x^2+y^2)^2} + \phi'(y)$$

But $$\frac{\partial u}{\partial y} = -\frac{\partial v}{\partial x} = -2x + \frac{x^2-y^2}{(x^2+y^2)^2}$$

$\therefore$ $\phi'(y) = 0$, *i.e.*, $\phi(y) = c$, a constant

$\therefore$ $$u = \frac{y}{x^2+y^2} - 2xy + c.$$

Q. 6. *Test whether sin y sin x – i cos x cos y is analytic, or not.* (C.U. Dec. 2008)

Sol. Let $f(z) = u + iv = \sin x \sin y - i \cos x \cos y$

If $f(z)$ is analytic then, $\frac{\partial^2 u}{\partial x^2} + \frac{\partial^2 u}{\partial y^2} = 0$ and $\frac{\partial^2 v}{\partial x^2} + \frac{\partial^2 v}{\partial y^2} = 0$

$u = \sin x \sin y$ and $v = -\cos x \cos y$

$$\frac{\partial u}{\partial x} = \cos x \sin y, \qquad \frac{\partial^2 u}{\partial x^2} = -\sin x \sin y$$

$$\frac{\partial u}{\partial y} = \sin x \cos y, \qquad \frac{\partial^2 u}{\partial y^2} = -\sin x \sin y$$

$\therefore$ $$\frac{\partial^2 u}{\partial x^2} + \frac{\partial^2 u}{\partial y^2} = -2 \sin x \sin y \neq 0.$$

$\therefore$ The given function is not analytic.

Q. 7. *Show that $v = e^{2x}$ [y cos 2y + x sin 2y] satisfies Laplace equation. Find f(z) = u + iv.* (C.U. Dec. 2008)

Sol. If $\frac{\partial^2 v}{\partial x^2} + \frac{\partial^2 v}{\partial y^2} = 0$, v satisfies the Laplace equation

$$\frac{\partial v}{\partial x} = 2e^{2x} [y \cos 2y + x \sin 2y] + e^{2x} [\sin 2y]$$

$$= e^{2x} [2y \cos 2y + 2x \sin 2y + \sin 2y]$$

$$\frac{\partial^2 v}{\partial x^2} = 2e^{2x} [2y \cos 2y + 2x \sin 2y + \sin 2y] + e^{2x} [2 \sin 2y]$$

$$= 2e^{2x} [2y \cos 2y + 2x \sin 2y + 2 \sin 2y]$$

$$\frac{\partial v}{\partial y} = e^{2x} [\cos 2y - 2y \sin 2y + 2x \cos 2y]$$

$$\frac{\partial^2 v}{\partial y^2} = e^{2x} [- 2 \sin 2y - 2 \sin 2y - 4y \cos 2y - 4x \sin 2y]$$

$$= - 2e^{2x} [2 \sin 2y + 2y \cos 2y + 2x \sin 2y]$$

$$= - \frac{\partial^2 v}{\partial x^2}$$

$\therefore \quad \frac{\partial^2 v}{\partial x^2} + \frac{\partial^2 v}{\partial y^2} = 0$. Hence v is harmonic.

To find $f(z) = u + iv$.

We have, if $f(z) = u + iv$ is analytic, $f'(z) = \frac{\partial u}{\partial x} + i \frac{\partial v}{\partial x}$

i.e., $f'(z) = \frac{\partial v}{\partial y} + i \frac{\partial v}{\partial x}$, using C-R equations

$$= \phi_1(x, y) + \phi_2(x, y)$$

Now $\phi_1(x, y) = \frac{\partial v}{\partial y} = e^{2x} [\cos 2y - 2y \sin 2y + 2x \cos 2y]$

and $\phi_2(x, y) = \frac{\partial v}{\partial x} = e^{2x} [2y \cos 2y + 2x \sin 2y + \sin 2y]$

Using Milne-Thomson method,

$$f'(z) = \phi_1(z, 0) + i \phi_2(z, 0)$$

$$= e^{2z} [1 + 2z]$$

$$\therefore \quad f(z) = \int f'(z)\, dz = \int e^{2z} [1 + 2z]\, dz$$

$$= (1 + 2z) \frac{e^{2z}}{2} - (2)\frac{e^{2z}}{4} + c$$

$$= \frac{e^{2z}}{2} [1 + 2z - 1] + c = ze^{2z} + c$$

$$\mathbf{f(z) = ze^{2z} + c.}$$

Q. 8. *Determine the analytic function whose real part is* $\dfrac{\sin 2x}{\cosh 2y - \cos 2x}$.

(C.U. June 2006, Dec. 2010)

Sol. Let $f(z) = u + iv$ be the required analytic function.

Given $$u = \frac{2\sin 2x}{e^{2y} + e^{-2y} - 2\cos 2x} \qquad \left[\because \cosh 2y = \frac{e^{2y}+e^{-2y}}{2}\right]$$

$$\frac{\partial u}{\partial x} = \frac{(e^{2y} + e^{-2y} - 2\cos 2x)\, 4\cos 2x - 2\sin 2x(4\sin 2x)}{(e^{2y} + e^{-2y} - 2\cos 2x)^2}$$

$$\frac{\partial u}{\partial y} = \frac{-4\sin 2x(e^{2y} - e^{-2y})}{(e^{2y} + e^{-2y} - 2\cos 2x)^2}$$

If $f(z) = u + iv$ is analytic, $f'(z) = \dfrac{\partial u}{\partial x} + i\dfrac{\partial v}{\partial x} = \dfrac{\partial u}{\partial x} - i\dfrac{\partial u}{\partial y}$, using C-R equations.

$$f'(z) = \phi_1(x, y) + i\phi_2(x, y)$$

By Milne-Thomson Method,

$$f'(z) = \phi_1(z, 0) + i\phi_2(z, 0)$$

$$= \frac{4(2 - 2\cos 2z)\cos 2z - 8\sin^2 2z}{(2 - 2\cos 2z)^2} - i \times 0$$

$$= \frac{8\cos 2z - 8}{4(1 - \cos 2z)^2} = \frac{-8(1 - \cos 2z)}{4(1 - \cos 2z)^2}$$

$$= \frac{-2}{1 - \cos 2z}$$

$\therefore$ $$f(z) = \int f'(z)\, dz = \int \frac{-2\, dz}{1 - \cos 2z}$$

$$= \int -\text{cosec}^2 z\, dz$$

$\therefore$ $$\mathbf{f(z) = \cot z + c.}$$

Q. 9. *Find the bilinear transformation that maps 1, i and – 1 of the z-plane onto 0, 1 and ∞ of the w-plane.* (C.U. June 2006)

Sol. Let $w = \dfrac{az + b}{cz + d}$, $ad - bc \neq 0$ be the required bilinear transformation.

Since the cross ratio is invariant under a bilinear transformation,

We have $$\frac{(z - z_1)(z_2 - z_3)}{(z - z_3)(z_2 - z_1)} = \frac{(w - w_1)(w_2 - w_3)}{(w - w_3)(w_2 - w_1)}$$

Let $z_1 = 1, z_2 = i, z_3 = -1, w_1 = 0, w_2 = 1, w_3 = \infty$.

Then $$\frac{(z - 1)(i + 1)}{(z + 1)(i - 1)} = \frac{(w - 0)(1 - \infty)}{(w - \infty)(1 - 0)}$$

i.e., $$\frac{(z-1)(i+1)}{(z+1)(i-1)} = \frac{w}{1} \cdot \underset{t\to\infty}{\text{Lt}} \left(\frac{1-t}{w-t}\right) = \frac{w}{1} \underset{t\to\infty}{\text{Lt}}\ 1 = w$$ [Using L' Hospital's rule]

i.e., $$\frac{(z-1)}{(z+1)} \cdot \frac{(1+i)(i+1)}{(i-1)(-i-1)} = w$$

i.e., $$w = \frac{(z-1)}{(z+1)} \frac{(1+2i-1)}{2} = \frac{i(z-1)}{(z+1)}$$

$$\therefore \quad w = \frac{i(z-1)}{(z+1)}.$$

Q. 10. *Prove that the cross ratio is invariant under a bilinear transformation.*

(C.U. Dec. 2006)

Sol. Let $w = \dfrac{az+b}{cz+d}$ be the bilinear transformation.

Let z_1, z_2, z_3 and z_4 be mapped into w_1, w_2, w_3, w_4 respectively.

Let $$w_1 = \frac{az_1+b}{cz_1+d}$$

$$w - w_1 = \frac{az+b}{cz+d} - \frac{az_1+b}{cz_1+d} = \frac{(az+b)(cz_1+d)-(az_1+b)(cz+d)}{(cz+d)(cz_1+d)}$$

$$= \frac{(ad-bc)(z-z_1)}{(cz+d)(cz_1+d)}$$

Similarly, $$w_1 - w_2 = \frac{(ad-bc)(z_1-z_2)}{(cz_1+d)(cz_2+d)}$$

$$w_3 - w_4 = \frac{(ad-bc)(z_3-z_4)}{(cz_3+d)(cz_4+d)}$$ and so on.

The cross ratio of four points w_1, w_2, w_3, w_4 is

$$\frac{(w_1-w_2)(w_3-w_4)}{(w_1-w_4)(w_3-w_2)} = \frac{\dfrac{(ad-bc)(z_1-z_2)}{(cz_1+d)(cz_2+d)} \times \dfrac{(ad-bc)(z_3-z_4)}{(cz_3+d)(cz_4+d)}}{\dfrac{(ad-bc)(z_1-z_4)}{(cz_1+d)(cz_4+d)} \times \dfrac{(ad-bc)(z_3-z_2)}{(cz_3+d)(cz_2+d)}}$$

$$= \frac{(z_1-z_2)(z_3-z_4)}{(z_1-z_4)(z_3-z_2)}$$

which is the cross ratio of the points z_1, z_2, z_3 and z_4.

Q. 11. *Discuss the transformation $w = \sinh z$.*

Sol. $$w = \sinh z = \frac{1}{i} \sin (iz)$$

i.e., $$iw = \sin (iz)$$

Let $Z = iz$, $W = iw$, then $W = \sin z$.

The transformation iz is a rotation of every point in the z-plane through an angle $\pi/2$ in the anti-clockwise direction. In a similar way iw is a rotation of every point in the w-plane through an angle $\pi/2$ in the anti-clockwise direction. We've already discussed the transformation $w = \sin z$.

Thus, $w = \sinh z$ is the transformation $w = \sin z$ with a rotation of the axes in the z-plane and w-plane through an angle $\pi/2$ in the anti-clockwise direction.

Q. 12. *Find the fixed points of* $w = \dfrac{3z - 5i}{iz - 1}$. (C.U. Dec. 2010)

Sol. Invariant points are obtained by $w = z$

$$\therefore \quad z = \frac{3z - 5i}{iz - 1}$$

i.e., $iz^2 - z - 3z + 5i = 0$

i.e., $iz^2 - 4z + 5i = 0$

$$\therefore \quad z = \frac{4 \pm \sqrt{16 - 20i^2}}{2i} = \frac{4 \pm 6}{2i}$$

$$z = -5i \text{ or } z = i.$$

Q. 13. *Obtain the expansion of* $\dfrac{z-1}{z^2}$ *in a Taylor series in powers of* $(z - 1)$.

(C.U. Dec. 2010)

Sol.
$$\frac{z-1}{z^2} = \frac{(z-1)}{(z-1+1)^2} = (z-1)[1 + z - 1]^{-2}$$
$$= (z-1)[1 - 2(z-1) + 3(z-1)^2 - 4(z-1)^3 + \ldots], \text{ if } |z - 1| < 1$$
$$= (z-1) - 2(z-1)^2 + 3(z-1)^3 - 4(z-1)^4 + \ldots \text{ is the required series.}$$

Q. 14. *Expand* $f(z) = \dfrac{7z-2}{z(z-2)(z+1)}$ *in Laurent's series valid in the annulus* $1 < |z + 1| < 3$.

(C.U. Dec. 2008)

Sol. Splitting $f(i)$ into partial fraction,

Let
$$f(z) = \frac{7z-2}{z(z-2)(z+1)} = \frac{A}{z} + \frac{B}{z-2} + \frac{C}{z+1}$$
$$7z - 2 = A(z-2)(z+1) + Bz(z+1) + Cz(z-2)$$

Put $z = 2$, $\quad 6B = 12 \quad \therefore \quad B = 2$

Put $z = -1$, $\quad 3C = -9 \quad \therefore \quad C = -3$

Put $z = 0$, $\quad -2A = -2 \quad \therefore \quad A = 1$

Thus $\dfrac{7z-2}{z(z-2)(z+1)} = \dfrac{1}{z} + \dfrac{2}{z-2} - \dfrac{3}{z+1}$

Given $1 < |z + 1| < 3$. *i.e.,* $|z + 1| > 1$ and $|z + 1| < 3$.

$$\therefore \quad \left|\frac{1}{z+1}\right| < 1 \quad \text{and} \quad \left|\frac{z+1}{3}\right| < 1.$$

Now,
$$f(z) = \frac{1}{z+1-1} + \frac{2}{z+1-3} - \frac{3}{z+1}$$
$$= \frac{1}{(z+1)\left[1 - \dfrac{1}{(z+1)}\right]} - \frac{2}{3\left[1 - \dfrac{z+1}{3}\right]} - \frac{3}{z+1}$$

$$= \frac{1}{(z+1)}\left[1 - \frac{1}{(z+1)}\right]^{-1} - \frac{2}{3}\left[1 - \frac{z+1}{3}\right]^{-1} - \frac{3}{z+1}$$

$$= \frac{1}{z+1}\left[1 + \frac{1}{z+1} + \frac{1}{(z+1)^2} + \ldots\right] - \frac{2}{3}\left[1 + \frac{z+1}{3} + \frac{(z+1)^2}{3^2} + \ldots\right] - \frac{3}{z+1}$$

$$= \left[\frac{1}{z+1} + \frac{1}{(z+1)^2} + \frac{1}{(z+1)^3} + \ldots\right] - \frac{2}{3}\left[1 + \frac{z+1}{3} + \frac{(z+1)^2}{3^2} + \ldots\right] - \frac{3}{z+1}$$

$$= \left[-\frac{2}{z+1} + \frac{1}{(z+1)^2} + \frac{1}{(z+1)^3} + \ldots\right] - \frac{2}{3}\left[1 + \frac{z+1}{3} + \frac{(z+1)^2}{3^2} + \ldots\right]$$

Thus $f(z) = \ldots \frac{1}{(z+1)^3} + \frac{1}{(z+1)^2} - \frac{2}{z+1} - \frac{2}{3} - \frac{2}{3}\left[\frac{(z+1)}{3} + \left(\frac{z+1}{3}\right)^2 + \ldots\right]$ is the required series.

Q. 15. *Find the Laurent's expansion of* $\frac{z-1}{z-2}$ *for* $|z-1| < 1$. (C.U. June 2010)

Sol. We have to express $\frac{z-1}{z-2}$ in terms of $(z-1)$.

$$\frac{z-1}{z-2} = \frac{z-1}{z-1-1}$$

$$= (z-1) \cdot \frac{1}{-[1-(z-1)]} = -(z-1)[1-(z-1)]^{-1}$$

$$= -(z-1)[1 + (z-1) + (z-1)^2 + \ldots], \text{ since } |z-1| < 1.$$

$$\therefore \quad \frac{z-1}{z-2} = -(z-1) - (z-1)^2 - (z-1)^3 - \ldots$$

Q. 16. *Find the Laurent's series for* $f(z) = \frac{z}{(z^2-1)(z^2+4)}$ *if* $1 < |z| < 2$.

(C.U. June 2009)

Sol. Let $\quad f(z) = \frac{A}{(z-1)} + \frac{B}{z+1} + \frac{C}{z+2i} + \frac{D}{z-2i} = \frac{z}{(z^2-1)(z^2+4)}$

i.e., $\quad z = A(z+1)(z^2+4) + B(z-1)(z^2+4) + C(z^2-1)(z-2i) + D(z^2-1)(z+2i)$

$z = 1 \Rightarrow \quad A = \frac{1}{10}$

$z = -1 \Rightarrow \quad B = \frac{1}{10}$

$z = 2i \Rightarrow \quad D = \frac{-1}{10}$

$z = -2i \Rightarrow \quad D = \frac{-1}{10}.$

$$\therefore \quad \frac{z}{(z^2-1)(z^2+4)} = \frac{1}{10(z-1)} + \frac{1}{10(z+1)} - \frac{1}{10(z+2i)} - \frac{1}{10(z-2i)}$$

Given $1 < |z| < 2$. $\therefore$ $\dfrac{1}{|z|} < 1$ and $|z| < 2$

$$\therefore \quad f(z) = \frac{1}{10z\left[1-\dfrac{1}{z}\right]} + \frac{1}{10z\left[1+\dfrac{1}{z}\right]} - \frac{1}{20i\left[1+\dfrac{z}{2i}\right]} + \frac{1}{20i\left[1-\dfrac{z}{2i}\right]}$$

$$f(z) = \frac{1}{10z}\left[1-\frac{1}{z}\right]^{-1} + \frac{1}{10z}\left[1+\frac{1}{z}\right]^{-1} - \frac{1}{20i}\left[1+\frac{z}{2i}\right]^{-1} + \frac{1}{20i}\left[1-\frac{z}{2i}\right]^{-1}$$

$$= \frac{1}{10z}\left[1+\frac{1}{z}+\frac{1}{z^2}+\ldots\right] + \frac{1}{10z}\left[1-\frac{1}{z}+\frac{1}{z^2}-\frac{1}{z^3}+\ldots\right]$$

$$- \frac{1}{20i}\left[1-\frac{z}{2i}+\left(\frac{z}{2i}\right)^2-\left(\frac{z}{2i}\right)^3+\ldots\right] + \frac{1}{20i}\left[1+\frac{z}{2i}+\left(\frac{z}{2i}\right)^2+\ldots\right]$$

$$\therefore \quad f(z) = \frac{1}{5}\left[\frac{1}{z}+\frac{1}{z^3}+\frac{1}{z^5}+\ldots\right] - \frac{1}{10}\left[\frac{z}{2}-\left(\frac{z}{2}\right)^3+\left(\frac{z}{2}\right)^5-\ldots\right]$$

Q. 17. *Evaluate* $\displaystyle\int_C \frac{z^2+1}{z^2-1}\,dz$ *if C is a circle of unit radius with centre z = – 1.*

Sol. Here singular points are $z = \pm 1$ and $z = -1$ is inside the circle C.

$$\int_C \frac{z^2+1}{z^2-1}\,dz = \int_C \frac{\left(\dfrac{z^2+1}{z-1}\right)}{z+1}\,dz$$

$$= \int_C \frac{f_1(z)\,dz}{z+1}, \quad \text{where } f_1(z) = \frac{z^2+1}{z-1} \text{ which is analytic within and on C.}$$

$= 2\pi i\, f_1(-1)$, using Cauchy's integral formula.

$= 2\pi i(-1)$

$= -2\pi i$.

Q. 18. *If the points z = a and z = b are both interior points of the domain D bounded by a simple closed curve C, show that* $\displaystyle\int_C \frac{dz}{(z-a)(z-b)} = 0.$

Sol. Let C_1 and C_2 be two non-intersecting closed curves containing the points a and b respectively.

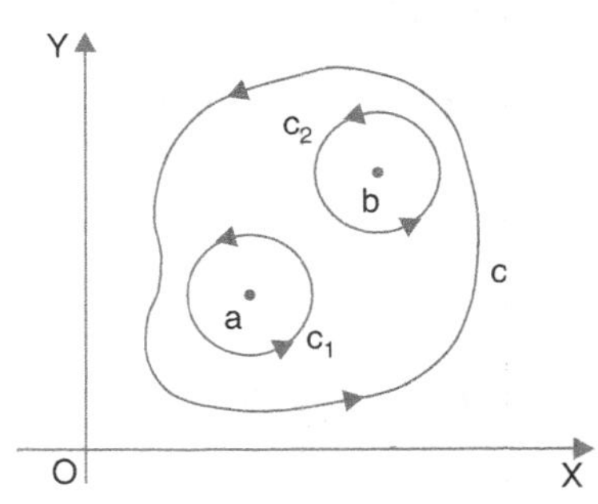

$$\int_C \frac{dz}{(z-a)(z-b)} = \int_{C_1} \frac{dz}{(z-a)(z-b)} + \int_{C_2} \frac{dz}{(z-a)(z-b)}$$

Now

$$\int_{C_1} \frac{dz}{(z-a)(z-b)} = \int_{C_1} \frac{\left(\dfrac{1}{z-b}\right)dz}{z-a} = \int_{C_1} \frac{f_1(z)\,dz}{z-a}$$

$$= 2\pi i\, f_1(a) \text{ by Cauchy's integral formula,}$$

where $f_1(z) = \dfrac{1}{z-b}$ is analytic within and on C_1

$$= 2\pi i\left(\frac{1}{a-b}\right) = \frac{2\pi i}{a-b}.$$

In a similar way.

$$\int_{C_2} \frac{dz}{(z-a)(z-b)} = \int_{C_2} \frac{\left(\dfrac{1}{z-a}\right) dz}{z-b}$$

$$= \int_{C_2} \frac{f_2(z)\, dz}{z-b}, \text{ where } f_2(z) = \frac{1}{z-a} \text{ is analytic within and on } C_2.$$

$$= 2\pi i\ f_2(b)$$

$$= \frac{2\pi i}{b-a}$$

$$\therefore \quad \int_C \frac{dz}{(z-a)(z-b)} = 2\pi i\left[\frac{1}{a-b} + \frac{1}{b-a}\right]$$

$$= 2\pi i\ [0]$$

$$\mathbf{= 0.}$$

Q. 19. *If C is a simple closed curve containing the origin, show that* $\dfrac{1}{2\pi i}\displaystyle\int_C \frac{e^{az}}{z^{n+1}}\, dz = \frac{a^n}{n!}$.

Sol. We know that $\displaystyle\int_C \frac{f(z)}{(z-z_0)^{n+1}}\, dz = \frac{2\pi i}{n!} f^n(z_0)$, where $f(z)$ is analytic in the region bounded by C, and z_0 is a point inside C.

Here $\quad f(z) = e^{az}$ and $z_0 = 0$.

$\therefore \quad f'(z) = ae^{az}, f''(z) = a^2e^{az}, ..., f^n(z) = a^n e^{az}$.

$\therefore \quad f^n(0) = a^n$

$$\therefore \quad \int_C \frac{f(z)}{z^{n+1}}\, dz = \frac{2\pi i}{n!} a^n$$

i.e.,

$$\mathbf{\frac{1}{2\pi i}\int_C \frac{e^{az}}{z^{n+1}}\, dz = \frac{a^n}{n!}.}$$

Q. 20. *Find the singularities of* (*i*) $\dfrac{1}{\sin(\pi/z)}$ (*ii*) $\dfrac{e^z}{z^2+\pi^2}$ (*iii*) $\dfrac{1-e^{2z}}{z^4}$.

Sol. (*i*) Singularities are the zeros of the denominator $\sin(\pi/z)$.

i.e.,
$$\frac{\pi}{z} = n\pi$$

$$\therefore \quad z = \frac{1}{n} \qquad \textit{i.e.,} \quad z = \pm 1, \pm\frac{1}{2}, \pm\frac{1}{3}, ...$$

(*ii*) Poles are obtained by, $z^2 + \pi^2 = 0$.

i.e.,
$$z = \pm i\pi$$

(iii) $$\frac{1-e^{2z}}{z^4} = \frac{1}{z^4}\left[1-\left(1+2z+\frac{4z^2}{2!}+\frac{8z^3}{3!}+\frac{16z^4}{4!}+\ldots\right)\right]$$

$$= -\left(\frac{2}{z^3}+\frac{2}{z^2}+\frac{4}{3z}+\frac{2}{3}+\ldots\ldots\right)$$

i.e., $z = 0$ is a pole of order 3.

Q. 21. *Evaluate using Cauchy's integral formula* $\int_C \frac{z+1}{z^2+2z+4}\,dz$ *where C is the circle* $|z+1+i| = 2.$ (C.U. June 2006)

Sol. Poles are $z = -1 \pm i\sqrt{3}$

C is a circle with centre $(-1, -1)$ and radius 2.

The point $z = -1 - i\sqrt{3}$ is inside C.

$\therefore$ By Cauchy's integral formula, $\int_C \frac{f(z)\,dz}{z-a} = 2\pi i\, f(a)$

$$\therefore \quad \int_C \frac{z+1\,dz}{z^2+2z+4} = 2\pi i\, f(-1-i\sqrt{3}), \quad f(z) = \frac{z+1}{z-(-1+i\sqrt{3})}$$

$$= 2\pi i\left(\frac{-1-i\sqrt{3}+1}{(-1-i\sqrt{3})-(-1+i\sqrt{3})}\right) = 2\pi i\left(\frac{-i\sqrt{3}}{-2i\sqrt{3}}\right)$$

$$= 2\pi i\left(\frac{1}{2}\right)$$

$$= \boldsymbol{\pi i}.$$

Q. 22. *Evaluate* $\int_C \frac{\sin \pi z^2 + \cos \pi z^2}{(z-1)(z-2)}\,dz$, *where C is the circle* $|z| = 3.$

(C.U. June 2009, Oct. 2011)

Sol. Let $f(z) = \frac{\sin \pi z^2 + \cos \pi z^2}{(z-1)(z-2)}$. Singular points are at $z = 1$ and 2 and both inside C.

Putting $\frac{1}{(z-1)(z-2)}$ into partial fraction, $\frac{1}{(z-1)(z-2)} = \frac{-1}{z-1} + \frac{1}{z-2}$

$$\therefore \quad f(z) = \frac{\sin \pi z^2 + \cos \pi z^2}{(z-1)(z-2)} = \frac{-(\cos \pi z^2 + \sin \pi z^2)}{z-1} + \frac{(\cos \pi z^2 + \sin \pi z^2)}{z-2}$$

$$\int_C f(z)\,dz = \int_C \frac{-f_1(z)\,dz}{z-1} + \int_C \frac{f_1(z)\,dz}{z-2}, \quad \text{where } f_1(z) = \cos \pi z^2 + \sin \pi z^2.$$

$= -2\pi i\, f_1(1) + 2\pi i\, f_1(2)$, by Cauchy's integral formula

$= -2\pi i\,[\cos \pi + \sin \pi] + 2\pi i\,[\cos 4\pi + \sin 4\pi]$

$= -2\pi i\,[-1] + 2\pi i\,[1]$

$= \boldsymbol{4\pi i}.$

Q. 23. *If* $f(\xi) = \int_C \frac{4z^2+z+5}{z-\xi}\,dz$ *where C is the ellipse* $\frac{x^2}{4}+\frac{y^2}{9} = 1$. *Find* $f(1), f(i), f'(-1)$ *and* $f''(-i)$. (C.U. Dec. 2007)

Sol. $f(1) = \int_C \frac{4z^2 + z + 5}{z - 1}\, dz$. The point $z = 1$ is inside C and $4z^2 + z + 5$ is analytic within and on C.

∴ By Cauchy's integral theorem

∴ $f(1) = 2\pi i\, \phi(1),$ where $\phi(z) = 4z^2 + z + 5$

$= 2\pi i \times 10 = \mathbf{20i\pi}.$

$$f(i) = \int_C \frac{4z^2 + z + 5}{z - i}\, dz.$$

The point $z = i$ is inside C and the function $4z^2 + z + 5$ is analytic within and on C.

∴ $f(i) = 2\pi i\, [4(i)^2 + i + 5]$, by Cauchy's integral theorem.

$= 2\pi i[1 + i] = \mathbf{2\pi[i - 1]}.$

$$f(\xi) = \int_C \frac{4z^2 + z + 5}{z - \xi}\, dz = 2\pi i\, [4\xi^2 + \xi + 5],$$

if ξ is a point inside C, by Cauchy's integral formula.

i.e. $f(\xi) = 2\pi i\, [4z^2 + z + 5]_{z = \xi} = 2\pi i\, [4\xi^2 + \xi + 5]$ ...(1)

Here the points $\xi = -1$ and $-i$ are all inside C.

Differentiating w.r.t. ξ, $f'(\xi) = 2\pi i\, [8\xi + 1]$

∴ $f'(-1) = 2\pi i\, [8(-1) + 1] = \mathbf{-14\pi i.}$

Again diff. (1) w.r.t. ξ,

$f''(\xi) = 2\pi i\, [8] = 16i\pi$

∴ $\mathbf{f''(-i) = 16\pi i.}$

Thus, $f(1) = 20\pi i,\ f(i) = 2\pi\, [i - 1],\ f'(-1) = -14\pi i$ and $f''(-i)\ 16i\pi$.

Q. 24. *Find the value of the integral* $\int_C \frac{dz}{z^2(z+4)}$, *where C:* $|z + 2| = 3$. (C.U. Oct. 2011)

Sol. C: $|z + 2| = 3$ is a circle having centre $(-2, 0)$ and radius 3 units.

Then $z = 0$ and $z = -4$ are inside C.

Putting $\frac{1}{z^2(z+4)}$ into partial fraction,

$$\frac{1}{z^2(z+4)} = \frac{Az + B}{z^2} + \frac{C}{z + 4}$$

i.e., $(Az + B)(Z + 4) + Cz^2 = 1$

when $z = 0$, $4B = 1$ ∴ $B = \frac{1}{4}$

when $z = -4$, $16C = 1$ ∴ $C = \frac{1}{16}$

Equating coefficients of z^2 on both sides.

$$A + C = 0. \quad \therefore \quad A = -C = \frac{-1}{16}$$

∴ $$f(z) = \frac{1}{z^2(z+4)} = \frac{-1}{16z} + \frac{1}{4z^2} + \frac{1}{16(z+4)}$$

∴ $$\int_C f(z)\, dz = \frac{-1}{16}\int_C \frac{dz}{z} + \frac{1}{4}\int_C \frac{dz}{z^2} + \frac{1}{16}\int_C \frac{dz}{z+4}$$

$$= \frac{-1}{16} \times 2\pi i\, f_1(0) + \frac{1}{4} \times 2\pi i \left[\frac{d}{dz} f_2(z)\right]_{z=0} + \frac{1}{16} \times 2\pi i\, f_3(-4),$$

by Cauchy's integral formula.

$$= \frac{-i\pi}{8} \times 1 + \frac{i\pi}{2} \times 0 + \frac{i\pi}{8} \times 1, \text{ where } f_1(z) = 1, f_2(z) = 1 = f_3(z).$$

$$= \mathbf{0}.$$

Q. 25. *If $w = f(z)$ is an analytic function of z, prove that* $\left(\frac{\partial^2}{\partial x^2} + \frac{\partial^2}{\partial y^2}\right) \log |f'(z)| = 0.$

(C.U. Dec. 2006, June 2007)

Sol. We know that

$$\frac{\partial^2 w}{\partial z\, \partial \bar{z}} = \frac{\partial^2 w}{\partial x^2} + \frac{\partial^2 w}{\partial y^2}$$

Let $w = \log |f'(z)| = \frac{1}{2} \log |f'(z)|^2$

$$= \frac{1}{2} \log f'(z)\overline{f'(z)} \qquad [\because\ z\bar{z} = |z|^2]$$

$$= \frac{1}{2} [\log f'(z) + \log \overline{f'(z)}]$$

$$\therefore \left(\frac{\partial^2}{\partial x^2} + \frac{\partial^2}{\partial y^2}\right) \log |f'(z)| = 4\frac{\partial^2}{\partial z \partial \bar{z}}\left[\frac{1}{2}\log f'(z) + \log \overline{f'(z)}\right]$$

$$= 4\frac{\partial^2}{\partial z \partial \bar{z}}\left[\frac{1}{2}\log f'(z) + \frac{1}{2}\log f'(\bar{z})\right] = 4\frac{\partial}{\partial z}\left[\frac{1}{2}\left(\frac{f''(\bar{z})}{f'(\bar{z})}\right)\right] = 0$$

Thus, $\left(\frac{\partial^2}{\partial \mathbf{x}^2} + \frac{\partial^2}{\partial \mathbf{y}^2}\right) \mathbf{\log |f'(z)| = 0}.$

Q. 26. *Show that the transformation $w = \cosh z$, maps the lines parallel to x-axis and lines parallel to y-axis into confocal central conics.*

Sol. $w = \cosh z = \cosh (x + iy) = \cos (ix - y)$ $\qquad [\because\ \cos (ix) = \cosh x]$

i.e., $u + iv = \cos (ix) \cos y + \sin (ix) \sin y$

$= \cosh x \cos y + i \sinh x \sin y$

$\therefore$ $u = \cosh x \cos y,\ v = \sinh x \sin y.$

Eliminating x from these expressions,

$$\frac{u^2}{\cos^2 y} - \frac{v^2}{\sin^2 y} = \cosh^2 x - \sinh^2 x = 1 \qquad ...(1)$$

Eliminating y,

$$\frac{u^2}{\cosh^2 x} + \frac{v^2}{\sinh^2 x} = \cos^2 y + \sin^2 y = 1 \qquad ...(2)$$

The lines parallel to y-axis in z-plane are $x = a$, a constant.

Then (2) $\frac{u^2}{\cosh^2 a} + \frac{v^2}{\sinh^2 a} = 1$ which is the equation of an ellipse with foci $(1, 0)$ and $(-1, 0)$.

Now the lines parallel to x-axis are $y = b$, a constant.

Then from (1), $\dfrac{u^2}{\cos^2 b} - \dfrac{v^2}{\sin^2 b} = 1$, which is the equation of a hyperbola, with foci $(-1, 0)$ and $(1, 0)$

When $a \le x \le b$ and $c \le y \le d$, the region in w-plane is shown below:

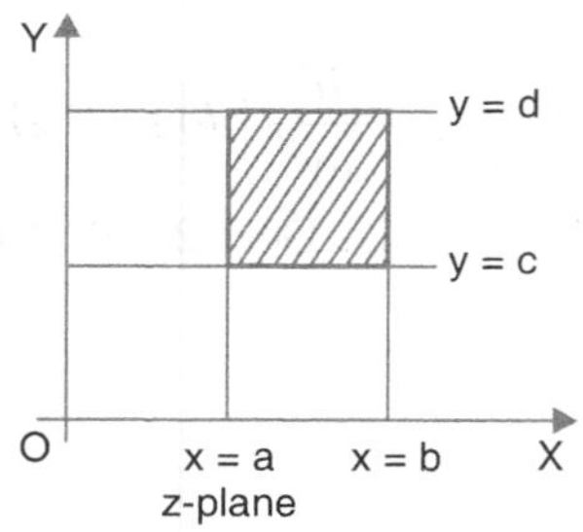

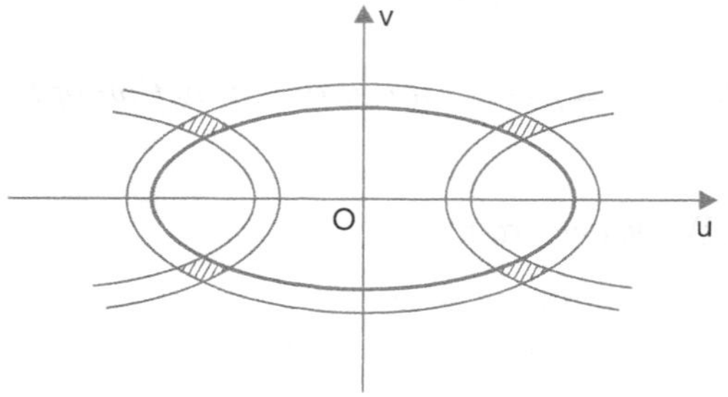

Q. 27. *If sin $(\theta + i\phi) = \cos\alpha + i\sin\alpha$, then prove that $\cos^2\theta = \pm\sin\alpha$.*

Sol. $\sin(\theta + i\phi) = \sin\theta\cosh\phi + i\cos\theta\sinh\phi = \cos\alpha + i\sin\alpha$, (given)

$\therefore$ $\sin\theta\cosh\phi = \cos\alpha$ and

$\cos\theta\sinh\phi = \sin\alpha$

$$\cosh^2\phi - \sinh^2\phi = 1 \Rightarrow \left(\frac{\cos\alpha}{\sin\theta}\right)^2 - \left(\frac{\sin\alpha}{\cos\theta}\right)^2 = 1$$

i.e., $$\cos^2\alpha\cos^2\theta - \sin^2\theta\sin^2\alpha = \sin^2\theta\cos^2\theta$$

i.e., $$\cos^2\theta(1 - \sin^2\alpha) - \sin^2\theta\sin^2\alpha = \sin^2\theta\cos^2\theta$$

i.e., $$\cos^2\theta - \sin^2\alpha(\cos^2\theta + \sin^2\theta) = \sin^2\theta\cos^2\theta$$

i.e., $$\cos^2\theta - \sin^2\theta\cos^2\theta = \sin^2\alpha$$

i.e., $$\cos^2\theta \,.\, \cos^2\theta = \sin^2\alpha.$$

$\therefore$ $$\mathbf{\cos^2\theta = \pm\sin\alpha.}$$

Q. 28. *If $w = u + iv$ is analytic, then prove that* $\dfrac{dw}{dz} = \dfrac{\partial w}{\partial x} = -\dfrac{i\partial w}{\partial y}$.

Sol. Let $w = f(z) = u + iv$ be analytic in a region R, then $f'(z) = \dfrac{dw}{dz}$ exists uniquely at every point of the region.

$$f'(z) = \underset{\Delta z \to 0}{\text{Lt}} \frac{f(z + \Delta z) - f(z)}{\Delta z} = \underset{\Delta z \to 0}{\text{Lt}} \frac{(u + \Delta u) + i(v + \Delta v) - (u + iv)}{\Delta z}$$

$$= \underset{\Delta z \to 0}{\text{Lt}} \frac{\Delta u + i\Delta v}{\Delta z} \quad ...(1)$$

Now let $\Delta z \to 0$ along lines parallel to x-axis. Then $\Delta y = 0$ and $\Delta z = \Delta x$.

$\therefore$ (1) becomes $f'(z) = \underset{\Delta x \to 0}{\text{Lt}} \dfrac{\Delta u + i\Delta v}{\Delta x} = \dfrac{\partial u}{\partial x} + \dfrac{i\partial v}{\partial x}$

i.e., $$\frac{dw}{dz} = \frac{\partial u}{\partial x} + \frac{i\partial v}{\partial x} = \frac{\partial}{\partial x}(u + iv) = \frac{\partial w}{\partial x}$$

Now let $\Delta z \to 0$ along a line parallel to y-axis. Then $\Delta x = 0$ and $\Delta z = i\Delta y$.

$\therefore$ (1) becomes $\dfrac{dw}{dz} = \underset{\Delta y \to 0}{\text{Lt}} \dfrac{\Delta u + i\Delta v}{i\Delta y} = \dfrac{1}{i}\dfrac{\partial u}{\partial y} + \dfrac{\partial v}{\partial y}$

$$= -i\left(\frac{\partial u}{\partial y} + \frac{i\partial v}{\partial y}\right) = -i\frac{\partial}{\partial y}(u + iv)$$

$$= -i\frac{\partial w}{\partial y}$$

Since $f'(z)$ is unique,

$$\mathbf{\frac{dw}{dz} = \frac{\partial w}{\partial x} = -i\frac{\partial w}{\partial y}}.$$

MORE UNIVERSITY QUESTIONS

1. If both $f(z)$ and its conjugate $\overline{f(z)}$ are analytic, prove that $f(z)$ is a constant. *(C.U. Dec. 2006)*
2. Show that $f(z) = \dfrac{(x+y)^2}{x^2+y^2}$ is discontinuous at the origin, given that $f(0) = 0$. *(C.U. June 2006)*
3. Show that $f(z) = z\bar{z}$ is differentiable but not analytic at $z = 0$.
   (C.U. June 2006, 2010, Dec. 2008, June 2009)
4. Write C-R equations in polar form. *(C.U. June 2006)*
5. Show that the function $V = e^x [x \sin y + y \cos y]$ is harmonic. *(C.U. June 2010)*
6. Find the fixed points of the transformation (*i*) $w = \dfrac{z-1}{z+2}$ (*ii*) $w = \dfrac{6z-9}{z}$.
7. Find the bilinear transformation which maps :
   (*i*) $z = 0, -1, \infty$ into the points $w = -1, -2-i, i$
   (*ii*) $z = 0, 1, -1$ into the points $w = i, \infty, 0$
   (*iii*) $z = 1, i, -1$ into the points $w = 0, 1, \infty$
   (*iv*) $z = -i, 0, i$ into the points $w = 0, -1, \infty$ *(C.U. June 2006)*
   (*v*) $z = 1, i, -1$ into the points $w = 2, i, -2$. *(C.U. June 2008)*
8. Find the bilinear transformation which has fixed points (*i*) $1, -1$ (*ii*) $i, -i$ and which transform $z = -i$ into $w = -i$.
9. Obtain the expansion of $\log(1 + z)$ when $|z| < 1$ using Taylor series. *(C.U. June 2006)*
10. Give two Laurent's series expansion in powers of z, of the function $f(z) = \dfrac{1}{z^2(1-z)}$ and specify the region in which those expansions are valid.
11. Evaluate $\displaystyle\int_C \frac{3z^2+7z+1}{z+1}\,dz$, where C : $|z + i| = 1$. *(C.U. Dec. 2010)*
12. Evaluate $\displaystyle\int_C \frac{e^z\,dz}{\cos \pi z}$ where C : $|z| = 1$. *(C.U. Dec. 2010)*
13. Evaluate $\displaystyle\int_0^{2\pi} \frac{d\theta}{5 - 3\cos\theta}$. *(C.U. Dec. 2010)*
14. Evaluate $\displaystyle\int_0^{2\pi} \frac{d\theta}{13 + 5\sin\theta}$. *(C.U. June 2006)*

15. Find the poles and residues of $f(z) = \dfrac{z^2}{(z-1)^2(z+2)}$ at each point. *(C.U. June 2006)*

16. Find the Laurent's series expansion of the function

$$f(z) = \frac{z^2 - 6z - 1}{(z-1)(z-3)(z+2)} \text{ valid in the region } 3 < |z+2| < 5.$$ *(C.U. Oct. 2011)*

17. Find the value of the integral $\int_C \dfrac{dz}{z^2(z+4)}$ taken counter clockwise around the circle (*i*) $|z| = 2$ (*ii*) $|z+2| = 3$.

Answers

6. (*i*) $\dfrac{-1 \pm i\sqrt{3}}{2}$ (*ii*) 3, 3

7. (*i*) $w = \dfrac{iz-2}{z+2}$ (*ii*) $w = \dfrac{i(z+1)}{1-z}$ (*iii*) $w = \dfrac{i(z-1)}{z+1}$

(*iv*) $w = \dfrac{z+i}{z-i}$ (*v*) $\dfrac{2i-6z}{iz-3}$

8. (*i*) $w = \dfrac{az+b}{a+bz}$ (*ii*) $w = \dfrac{az+b}{a-bz}$.

9. $z - \dfrac{z^2}{2} + \dfrac{z^3}{3} - \dfrac{z^4}{4} + \ldots$

10. $\dfrac{1}{z} + \dfrac{1}{z^2} + 1 + z + z^2 + \ldots$ in $|z| < 1$; $-\left(\dfrac{1}{z^3} + \dfrac{1}{z^4} + \ldots\right)$ in $|z| > 1$. **11.** 0

12. $-4i \sinh(1/2)$ [**Hint.** poles are $\pm\dfrac{1}{2}, \pm\dfrac{3}{2}, \pm\dfrac{5}{2}, \ldots$ but $z = \pm\dfrac{1}{2}$ lie inside $|z| = 1$]

13. $\pi/2$ **14.** $\pi/6$

15. Poles : 1 (double), – 2 (Simple) ; 5/9, 4/9

16. $\dfrac{1}{z+2} - \left[\dfrac{3}{z+2} + \left(\dfrac{3}{z+2}\right)^2 + \left(\dfrac{3}{z+2}\right)^3 + \ldots\right] + \dfrac{1}{5}\left[1 + \dfrac{z+2}{5} + \left(\dfrac{z+2}{5}\right)^2 + \ldots\right]$

17. (*i*) $\dfrac{i\pi}{8}$ (*ii*) 0.

UNIT 2
Integral Transforms—Fourier Transforms

2.1. INTEGRAL TRANSFORMS

The integral transform $\bar{f}(s)$ of a function $f(x)$ is defined by the equation

$$I\{f(x)\} = \bar{f}(s) = \int_a^b f(x)\, K(s, x)\, dx,$$

where $K(s, x)$ is a known function of s and x, called the **kernel** of the transform; s is called the **parameter** of the transform and $f(x)$ is called the **inverse transform** of $\bar{f}(s)$.

Some of the well-known transforms are given below:

(*i*) **Laplace Transform.** $K(s, x) = e^{-sx}$

$$L\{f(x)\} = \bar{f}(s) = \int_0^\infty f(x)\, e^{-sx}\, dx$$

(*ii*) **Complex Fourier Transform**

$$F\{f(x)\} = \bar{f}(s) = \int_{-\infty}^\infty f(x)\, e^{isx}\, dx$$

(*iii*) **Fourier Sine Transform**

$$F_s\{f(x)\} = \bar{f}(s) = \int_0^\infty f(x) \sin sx\, dx$$

(*iv*) **Fourier Cosine Transform**

$$F_c\{f(x)\} = \bar{f}(s) = \int_0^\infty f(x) \cos sx\, dx$$

(*v*) **Hankel Transform.** $K(s, x) = x\, J_n(sx)$

$$H_n\{f(x)\} = \bar{f}(s) = \int_0^\infty f(x)\, xJ_n\, (sx)\, dx$$

where $J_n(sx)$ is the Bessel function of the first kind and order n.

(*vi*) **Mellin Transform.** $K(s, x) = x^{s-1}$

$$M\{f(x)\} = \bar{f}(s) = \int_0^\infty f(x)\, x^{s-1}\, dx$$

We have already discussed Laplace transform and its application to the solution of ordinary differential equations. In the present chapter, we shall discuss fourier transforms and their application to the solution of partial differential equations.

The effect of applying an integral transform to a partial differential equation is to reduce the number of independent variables by one. The choice of a particular transform is decided by the nature of the boundary conditions and the facility with which the transform $\bar{f}(s)$ can be inverted to give $f(x)$.

2.2. FOURIER INTEGRAL THEOREM

Consider a function $f(x)$ satisfying Dirichlet's conditions in every interval $(-c, c)$, however large and $f(x)$ is absolutely integrable over $(-\infty, \infty)$.

$$f(x) = \frac{a_0}{2} + \sum_{n=1}^{\infty} \left(a_n \cos \frac{n\pi x}{c} + b_n \sin \frac{n\pi x}{c} \right) \quad ...(1)$$

where, $a_0 = \frac{1}{c}\int_{-c}^{c} f(t)\, dt$, $a_n = \frac{1}{c}\int_{-c}^{c} f(t) \cos \frac{n\pi t}{c}\, dt$ and $b_n = \frac{1}{c}\int_{-c}^{c} f(t) \sin \frac{n\pi t}{c}\, dt$

Substituting the values of a_0, a_n and b_n in (1), we get

$$f(x) = \frac{1}{2c}\int_{-c}^{c} f(t)\, dt + \frac{1}{c}\sum_{n=1}^{\infty}\int_{-c}^{c}\left[\cos\frac{n\pi x}{c}\cos\frac{n\pi t}{c} + \sin\frac{n\pi x}{c}\sin\frac{n\pi t}{c}\right] f(t)\, dt$$

$$= \frac{1}{2c}\int_{-c}^{c} f(t)\, dt + \frac{1}{c}\sum_{n=1}^{\infty}\int_{-c}^{c} \cos\frac{n\pi(t-x)}{c} \,.\, f(t)\, dt \quad ...(2)$$

Since $f(x)$ is absolutely integrable $\int_{-\infty}^{\infty} |f(x)|\, dx$ converges, then

$$\underset{c\to\infty}{\text{Lt}}\left[\frac{1}{2c}\int_{-c}^{c} f(t)\, dt\right] = 0$$

Putting $\frac{\pi}{c} = \Delta\lambda$, the second term in (2) becomes

$$\frac{1}{\pi}\sum_{n=1}^{\infty} \Delta\lambda \int_{-c}^{c} \cos\{n\Delta\lambda(t-x)\}\, f(t)\, dt$$

This is of the form $\sum_{n=1}^{\infty} F(n\Delta\lambda)\, \Delta\lambda$ whose limit as $\Delta\lambda \to 0$, is $\int_{0}^{\infty} F(\lambda)\, d\lambda$.

Hence as $c \to \infty$, (2) reduces to

$$f(x) = \frac{1}{\pi}\int_{0}^{\infty}\int_{-\infty}^{\infty} f(t) \cos \lambda(t-x)\, dt\, d\lambda \quad ...(3)$$

which is known as **Fourier integral** of $f(x)$.

Equation (3) is true at a point of continuity. At a point of discontinuity, the value of the integral on the right is

$$\frac{1}{2}\,[f(x+0) + f(x-0)].$$

2.3. FOURIER SINE AND COSINE INTEGRALS

We know that $\cos \lambda(t-x) = \cos \lambda t \cos \lambda x + \sin \lambda t \sin \lambda x$

$\therefore$ Fourier integral of $f(x)$ can be written as

$$f(x) = \frac{1}{\pi}\int_{0}^{\infty}\int_{-\infty}^{\infty} f(t)\{\cos \lambda t \cos \lambda x + \sin \lambda t \sin \lambda x\}\, dt\, d\lambda$$

$$= \frac{1}{\pi}\int_0^\infty \cos \lambda x \int_{-\infty}^\infty f(t) \cos \lambda t \, dt \, d\lambda + \frac{1}{\pi}\int_0^\infty \sin \lambda x \int_{-\infty}^\infty f(t) \sin \lambda t \, dt \, d\lambda \qquad ...(4)$$

When f(x) is an odd function, $f(t) \cos \lambda t$ is odd while $f(t) \sin \lambda t$ is even. Thus the first integral in (4) vanishes and we get

$$f(x) = \frac{2}{\pi}\int_0^\infty \sin \lambda x \int_0^\infty f(t) \sin \lambda t \, dt \, d\lambda \qquad ...(5)$$

This is called **Fourier sine integral.**

When f(x) is an even function, $f(t) \cos \lambda t$ is even while $f(t) \sin \lambda t$ is odd. Thus the second integral in (4) vanishes and we get

$$f(x) = \frac{2}{\pi}\int_0^\infty \cos \lambda x \int_0^\infty f(t) \cos \lambda t \, dt \, d\lambda \qquad ...(6)$$

This is called **Fourier cosine integral.**

2.4. COMPLEX FORM OF FOURIER INTEGRAL

Since $\cos \lambda(t - x)$ is an even function of λ, we have from (3),

$$f(x) = \frac{1}{2\pi}\int_{-\infty}^\infty \int_{-\infty}^\infty f(t) \cos \lambda(t - x) \, dt \, d\lambda \qquad ...(7)$$

$$\left[\because \; 2\int_0^a f(x)\, dx = \int_{-a}^a f(x)\, dx, \text{ if } f(x) \text{ is even}\right]$$

Also $\sin \lambda(t - x)$ is an odd function of λ, so that

$$0 = \frac{1}{2\pi}\int_{-\infty}^\infty \int_{-\infty}^\infty f(t) \sin \lambda(t - x) \, dt \, d\lambda \qquad ...(8)$$

$$\left[\because \; \int_{-a}^a f(x)\, dx = 0, \text{ if } f(x) \text{ is odd}\right]$$

Multiplying (8) by i and adding to (7), we get

$$f(x) = \frac{1}{2\pi}\int_{-\infty}^\infty \int_{-\infty}^\infty f(t) \{\cos \lambda(t - x) + i \sin \lambda(t - x)\} \, dt \, d\lambda$$

$$= \frac{1}{2\pi}\int_{-\infty}^\infty \int_{-\infty}^\infty f(t)\, e^{i\lambda(t-x)} \, dt \, d\lambda$$

$$= \frac{1}{2\pi}\int_{-\infty}^\infty e^{-i\lambda x} \int_{-\infty}^\infty f(t)\, e^{i\lambda t} \, dt \, d\lambda$$

which is known as the **complex form of Fourier integral.**

Example. *Express the function* $f(x) = \begin{cases} 1 & \text{for } |x| \le 1, \\ 0 & \text{for } |x| > 1, \end{cases}$

as a Fourier integral. Hence evaluate $\int_0^\infty \frac{\sin \lambda \cos \lambda x}{\lambda} d\lambda$. (C.U. June 2007, 2009)

Sol. The Fourier integral for $f(x)$ is

$$\frac{1}{\pi}\int_0^\infty \int_{-\infty}^\infty f(t)\cos\lambda(t-x)\,dt\,d\lambda$$

$$= \frac{1}{\pi}\int_0^\infty \int_{-1}^1 \cos\lambda(t-x)\,dt\,d\lambda$$

[$\because$ $f(t) = 0$ when $-\infty < t < -1$, $f(t) = 1$ when $-1 < t < 1$ and $f(t) = 0$ when $1 < t < \infty$]

$$= \frac{1}{\pi}\int_0^\infty \left[\frac{\sin\lambda(t-x)}{\lambda}\right]_{-1}^1 d\lambda = \frac{1}{\pi}\int_0^\infty \frac{\sin\lambda(1-x)-\sin\lambda(-1-x)}{\lambda}\,d\lambda$$

$$= \frac{1}{\pi}\int_0^\infty \frac{\sin\lambda(1+x)+\sin\lambda(1-x)}{\lambda}\,d\lambda = \frac{2}{\pi}\int_0^\infty \frac{\sin\lambda\cos\lambda x}{\lambda}\,d\lambda$$

$$\therefore \quad \int_0^\infty \frac{\sin\lambda\cos\lambda x}{\lambda}\,d\lambda = \frac{1}{2}\pi f(x) = \begin{cases}\frac{1}{2}\pi & \text{for } |x| < 1\\ 0 & \text{for } |x| > 1\end{cases}$$

At $|x| = 1$, *i.e.*, $x = \pm 1$, $f(x)$ is discontinuous and the integral has the value $\frac{1}{2}\left(\frac{\pi}{2}+0\right) = \frac{\pi}{4}$.

Note. Putting $x = 0$, we get $\int_0^\infty \frac{\sin\lambda}{\lambda}\,d\lambda = \frac{\pi}{2}$ or $\int_0^\infty \frac{\sin x}{x}\,dx = \frac{\pi}{2}$.

2.5. INVERSION FORMULAE FOR FOURIER TRANSFORMS

(1) *Fourier sine transform and its inversion formula*

Fourier sine integral is $f(x) = \frac{2}{\pi}\int_0^\infty \sin\lambda x \int_0^\infty f(t)\sin\lambda t\,dt\,d\lambda$

Replacing λ by s, we get $f(x) = \frac{2}{\pi}\int_0^\infty \sin sx \int_0^\infty f(t)\sin st\,dt\,ds$

Denoting the value of the inner integral by $F_s\{f(x)\}$, we have

$$f(x) = \frac{2}{\pi}\int_0^\infty F_s\{f(x)\}\sin sx\,ds \qquad ...(1)$$

where $$F_s\{f(x)\} = \bar{f}(s) = \int_0^\infty f(t)\sin st\,dt \qquad ...(2)$$

Equation (2) is defined as Fourier sine transform of the function $f(x)$. Equation (1) which determines the function $f(x)$ is known as the inversion formula for the Fourier sine transform.

Equations (1) and (2) together represent Fourier sine transform pair.

(2) *Fourier cosine transform and its inversion formula*

Fourier cosine integral is $f(x) = \frac{2}{\pi}\int_0^\infty \cos\lambda x \int_0^\infty f(t)\cos\lambda t\,dt\,d\lambda$

Replacing λ by s, we get $f(x) = \frac{2}{\pi}\int_0^\infty \cos sx \int_0^\infty f(t)\cos st\,dt\,ds$

Denoting the value of the inner integral by $F_c\{f(x)\}$, we have

$$f(x) = \frac{2}{\pi}\int_0^\infty F_c\{f(x)\}\cos sx\,ds \qquad ...(3)$$

where $$F_c\{f(x)\} = \bar{f}(s) = \int_0^\infty f(t) \cos st \, dt \qquad ...(4)$$

Equation (4) is defined as Fourier cosine transform of the function $f(x)$. Equation (3) which determines the function $f(x)$ is known as the inversion formula for the Fourier cosine transform. Equations (4) and (5) together represent Fourier cosine transform pair.

(3) *Complex Fourier transform and its inversion formula*

Complex form of Fourier integral is $f(x) = \frac{1}{2\pi}\int_{-\infty}^{\infty} e^{-i\lambda x} \int_{-\infty}^{\infty} f(t)\, e^{i\lambda t}\, dt\, d\lambda$

Replacing λ by s, we get $$f(x) = \frac{1}{2\pi}\int_{-\infty}^{\infty} e^{-isx} \int_{-\infty}^{\infty} f(t)\, e^{ist}\, dt\, ds$$

Denoting the value of the inner integral by $F\{f(x)\}$, we have

$$f(x) = \frac{1}{2\pi}\int_{-\infty}^{\infty} F\{f(x)\}\, e^{-isx}\, ds \qquad ...(5)$$

where $$F\{f(x)\} = \bar{f}(s) = \int_{-\infty}^{\infty} f(t)\, e^{ist}\, dt \qquad ...(6)$$

Equation (6) is defined as complex Fourier transform of the function $f(x)$. Equation (5) which determines the function $f(x)$ is known as the inversion formula for the complex Fourier transform. Equations (5) and (6) represent the complex Fourier transform pair.

ILLUSTRATIVE EXAMPLES

Example 1. *Using Fourier sine integral, show that*

$$\int_0^\infty \frac{1-\cos \pi\lambda}{\lambda} \sin x\lambda \, d\lambda = \begin{cases} \frac{1}{2}\pi, & \text{when } 0 < x < \pi \\ 0, & \text{when } x > \pi \end{cases}$$ (C.U. Dec. 2008)

Sol. Let $$f(x) = \begin{cases} \frac{1}{2}\pi, & \text{when } 0 < x < \pi \\ 0, & \text{when } x > \pi \end{cases}$$

Using Fourier sine integral, we have

$$f(x) = \frac{2}{\pi}\int_0^\infty \sin \lambda x \int_0^\infty f(t) \sin \lambda t \, dt\, d\lambda$$

$$= \frac{2}{\pi}\int_0^\infty \sin \lambda x \left[\int_0^\pi f(t) \sin \lambda t\, dt + \int_\pi^\infty f(t)\sin \lambda t\, dt\right] d\lambda$$

$$= \frac{2}{\pi}\int_0^\infty \sin \lambda x \int_0^\pi \frac{1}{2}\pi \sin \lambda t \, dt\, d\lambda \qquad \text{[On substituting for } f(t)]$$

$$= \int_0^\infty \sin \lambda x \left[-\frac{\cos \lambda t}{\lambda}\right]_0^\pi d\lambda = \int_0^\pi \frac{1-\cos \pi\lambda}{\lambda} \sin x\lambda\, d\lambda$$

$$\therefore \quad \int_0^\infty \frac{1-\cos \pi\lambda}{\lambda} . \sin x\lambda \, d\lambda = f(x) = \begin{cases} \frac{1}{2}\pi, & \text{when } 0 < x < \pi \\ 0, & \text{when } x > \pi \end{cases}$$

Example 2. *Find the Fourier sine transform of* $e^{-|x|}$. *Hence evaluate* $\int_0^\infty \frac{x \sin mx}{1+x^2}\,dx$.

(C.U. Dec. 2008)

Sol. In the interval $(0, \infty)$, x is positive so that $e^{-|x|} = e^{-x}$. Fourier sine transform of $f(x) = e^{-x}$ is given by

$$F_s\{f(x)\} = \int_0^\infty f(x) \sin sx\,dx = \int_0^\infty e^{-x} \sin sx\,dx$$

$$= \left[\frac{e^{-x}}{1+s^2}(-\sin sx - s\cos sx)\right]_0^\infty = \left(\frac{s}{1+s^2}\right)$$

Using inversion formula for Fourier sine transform, we get

$$f(x) = \frac{2}{\pi}\int_0^\infty F_s\{f(x)\} \sin sx\,ds \quad \text{or} \quad e^{-x} = \frac{2}{\pi}\int_0^\infty \frac{s}{1+s^2} \sin sx\,ds$$

Replacing x by m, we have $\quad e^{-m} = \frac{2}{\pi}\int_0^\infty \frac{s}{1+s^2} \sin ms\,ds = \frac{2}{\pi}\int_0^\infty \frac{x \sin mx}{1+m^2}\,dx$

Hence, $$\int_0^\infty \frac{x \sin mx}{1+m^2}\,dx = \frac{\pi}{2} e^{-m}.$$

Example 3. *Find the Fourier cosine transform of* e^{-x^2}. (C.U. Dec. 2008)

Sol. Fourier cosine transform of e^{-x^2} is given by

$$F_c\{e^{-x^2}\} = \int_0^\infty e^{-x^2} \cos sx\,dx = I \text{ (say)} \qquad \ldots(1)$$

Differentiating w.r.t. s, we have

$$\frac{dI}{ds} = -\int_0^\infty x e^{-x^2} \sin sx\,dx = \frac{1}{2}\int_0^\infty (\sin sx)(-2x\,e^{-x^2})\,dx$$

$$= \frac{1}{2}\left[\left\{\sin sx\, e^{-x^2}\right\}_0^\infty - s\int_0^\infty \cos sx\, e^{-x^2}\,dx\right] \qquad \text{(Integrating by parts)}$$

$$= -\frac{s}{2}\int_0^\infty e^{-x^2} \cos sx\,dx = -\frac{s}{2} I$$

or $$\frac{dI}{I} = -\frac{s}{2}\,ds$$

Integrating, we have

$$\log I = -\frac{s^2}{4} + \log A \quad \text{or} \quad I = A\,e^{-\frac{s^2}{4}} \qquad \ldots(2)$$

Now when $s = 0$, from (1), $\quad I = \int_0^\infty e^{-x^2}\,dx = \frac{\sqrt{\pi}}{2}$

$\therefore$ From (2), $\dfrac{\sqrt{\pi}}{2} = A$

Hence, $I = F_c\{e^{-x^2}\} = \dfrac{\sqrt{\pi}}{2}\, e^{-\frac{s^2}{4}}$.

Example 4. *Find the Fourier transform of,* $f(x) = \begin{cases} 1 - x^2, & \text{if } |x| < 1 \\ 0, & \text{if } |x| > 1. \end{cases}$

and use it to evaluate $\displaystyle\int_0^\infty \left(\frac{x \cos x - \sin x}{x^3}\right) \cos \frac{x}{2}\, dx.$ (C.U. Dec. 2006, 07, 09)

Sol. Fourier transform of $f(x)$ is given by

$$F\{f(x)\} = \int_{-\infty}^{\infty} f(x)\, e^{isx}\, dx = \int_{-1}^{1} (1 - x^2)\, e^{isx} dx$$

$$= \left[(1 - x^2) \cdot \frac{e^{isx}}{is} - (-2x) \frac{e^{isx}}{(is)^2} + (-2) \frac{e^{isx}}{(is)^3}\right]_{-1}^{1}$$

$$= \left[-\frac{2}{s^2}(e^{is} + e^{-is}) + \frac{2}{is^3}(e^{is} - e^{-is})\right]$$

$$= \left[-\frac{4}{s^2}\left(\frac{e^{is} + e^{-is}}{2}\right) + \frac{4}{s^3}\left(\frac{e^{is} - e^{-is}}{2i}\right)\right]$$

$$= 4\left[-\frac{\cos s}{s^2} + \frac{\sin s}{s^3}\right] = -4\left(\frac{s \cos s - \sin s}{s^3}\right)$$

By inversion formula for Fourier transform, we have

$$f(x) = \frac{1}{2\pi} \int_{-\infty}^{\infty} F\{f(x)\}\, e^{-isx}\, ds = -\frac{2}{\pi} \int_{-\infty}^{\infty} \left(\frac{s \cos s - \sin s}{s^3}\right) (\cos sx - i \sin sx)\, ds$$

$$= -\frac{2}{\pi} \int_{-\infty}^{\infty} \left(\frac{s \cos s - \sin s}{s^3}\right) \cos sx\, ds + \frac{2i}{\pi} \int_{-\infty}^{\infty} \left(\frac{s \cos s - \sin s}{s^3}\right) \sin sx\, ds$$

$$= -\frac{2}{\pi} \int_{-\infty}^{\infty} \left(\frac{s \cos s - \sin s}{s^3}\right) \cos sx\, ds$$

(Since the integrand in the second integral on R.H.S is odd)

$$= -\frac{4}{\pi} \int_{0}^{\infty} \left(\frac{s \cos s - \sin s}{s^3}\right) \cos sx\, ds$$

or $$\int_0^\infty \left(\frac{s \cos s - \sin s}{s^3}\right) \cos sx\, ds = -\frac{\pi}{4} f(x) = \begin{cases} -\dfrac{\pi}{4}(1 - x^2), & \text{if } |x| < 1 \\ 0, & \text{if } |x| > 1 \end{cases}$$

Taking $x = \dfrac{1}{2}$, we have $\displaystyle\int_0^\infty \left(\frac{s \cos s - \sin s}{s^3}\right) \cos \frac{s}{2}\, ds = -\frac{3\pi}{16}$

Hence, $$\int_0^{\infty}\left(\frac{x\cos x-\sin x}{x^3}\right)\cos\frac{x}{2}\,dx=-\frac{3\pi}{16}.$$

Example 5. *Solve the integral equation* $\int_0^{\infty} F(x)\cos px\,dx=\begin{cases}1-p, & 0\le p\le 1\\ 0, & p>1\end{cases}$, *hence deduce that* $\int_0^{\infty}\frac{\sin^2 t}{t^2}\,dt=\frac{\pi}{2}$.

Sol. Let $$\int_0^{\infty} F(x)\cos px\,dx=f(p),\text{ then } f(p)=\begin{cases}1-p, & 0\le p\le 1\\ 0, & p>1\end{cases}$$

$$\therefore\quad \frac{2}{\pi}\int_0^{\infty} F(x)\cos px\,dx=\frac{2}{\pi}f(p)=\bar{f}(p)$$

By inversion formula for Fourier cosine transform, we have

$$F(x)=\int_0^{\infty}\bar{f}(p)\cos px\,dp=\frac{2}{\pi}\int_0^{\infty}f(p)\cos px\,dp$$

$$=\frac{2}{\pi}\left[\int_0^1(1-p)\cos px\,dp+\int_1^{\infty}0\,.\cos px\,dp\right]$$

$$=\frac{2}{\pi}\left[(1-p)\,.\frac{\sin px}{x}-(-1)\,.\frac{-\cos px}{x^2}\right]_0^1=\frac{2}{\pi}\left[-\frac{\cos x}{x^2}+\frac{1}{x^2}\right]=\frac{2(1-\cos x)}{\pi x^2}.$$

Deduction. Since $\int_0^{\infty}F(x)\cos px\,dx=\begin{cases}1-p, & 0\le p\le 1\\ 0, & p>1\end{cases}$ where $F(x)=\frac{2(1-\cos x)}{\pi x^2}$

$$\therefore\quad \frac{2}{\pi}\int_0^{\infty}\frac{1-\cos x}{x^2}\,.\cos px\,dx=\begin{cases}1-p, & 0\le p\le 1\\ 0, & p>1\end{cases}$$

When $p=0$, we have $$\frac{2}{\pi}\int_0^{\infty}\frac{1-\cos x}{x^2}\,dx=1\quad\text{or}\quad\int_0^{\infty}\frac{2\sin^2\frac{x}{2}}{x^2}\,dx=\frac{\pi}{2}$$

Putting $x=2t$ so that $dx=2dt$, we get $\int_0^{\infty}\frac{\sin^2 t}{t^2}\,dt=\frac{\pi}{2}$.

TEST YOUR KNOWLEDGE

1. Find the Fourier integral representation of the function $f(x)=\begin{cases}0, & x<0\\ \frac{1}{2}, & x=0\\ e^{-x}, & x>0\end{cases}$

2. Using Fourier integrals, show that:

(*i*) $\int_0^{\infty}\frac{\sin\pi\lambda\sin x\lambda}{1-\lambda^2}\,d\lambda=\begin{cases}\frac{1}{2}\pi\sin x, & \text{when } 0\le x\le\pi\\ 0, & \text{when } x>\pi\end{cases}$

(*ii*) $\int_0^{\infty}\frac{\cos x\lambda}{1+\lambda^2}\,d\lambda=\frac{\pi}{2}e^{-x},\ x\ge 0$ (*iii*) $\int_0^{\infty}\frac{\lambda\sin\lambda x}{k^2+\lambda^2}\,d\lambda=\frac{\pi}{2}e^{-kx};\ x>0,\ k>0$.

(C.U. Dec. 2006, 07)

3. Find the Fourier sine transform of $\dfrac{e^{-ax}}{x}$. *(C.U. June 2007)*

4. Find the Fourier cosine transform of the function $f(x)$, if $f(x) = \begin{cases} \cos x, & 0 < x < a \\ 0, & x > a \end{cases}$.

5. Find the Fourier sine and cosine transforms of :

(i) $2e^{-5x} + 5e^{-2x}$ *(C.U. Dec. 2007)* (ii) $f(x) = \begin{cases} 1, & \text{for } 0 \le x < a \\ 0, & \text{for } x > a \end{cases}$

(C.U. June 2007, Dec. 2010)

(iii) $f(x) = \begin{cases} x, & \text{for } 0 < x < 1 \\ 2 - x, & \text{for } 1 < x < 2 \\ 0, & \text{for } x > 2 \end{cases}$.

6. Show that the Fourier transform of $f(x) = e^{-x^2/2}$ self reciprocal. *(C.U. Dec. 2006, 07, 08)*

7. Find the Fourier transform of :

(i) $f(x) = \begin{cases} 1, & |x| < a \\ 0, & |x| > a \end{cases}$ *(C.U. June 2009)* (ii) $f(x) = \begin{cases} x, & |x| < a \\ 0, & |x| > a \end{cases}$.

8. Solve the integral equation $\int_0^\infty f(x) \cos \lambda x \, dx = e^{-\lambda}$.

9. Solve for F(x) the integral equation $\int_0^\infty F(x) \sin tx \, dx = \begin{cases} 1, & 0 \le t < 1 \\ 2, & 1 \le t < 2 \\ 0, & t \ge 2 \end{cases}$.

Answers

1. $f(x) = \dfrac{1}{\pi} \int_0^\infty \dfrac{\lambda \sin \lambda x + \cos \lambda x}{1 + \lambda^2} \, d\lambda$

3. $\sqrt{\dfrac{2}{\pi}} \tan^{-1}\left(\dfrac{s}{a}\right)$

4. $\dfrac{1}{\sqrt{2\pi}} \left[\dfrac{\sin (1+s)a}{1+s} + \dfrac{\sin (1-p)a}{1-p}\right]$

5. (i) $s\sqrt{\dfrac{2}{\pi}}\left(\dfrac{2}{s^2+25} + \dfrac{5}{s^2+4}\right)$; $10\sqrt{\dfrac{2}{\pi}}\left(\dfrac{1}{s^2+25} + \dfrac{1}{s^2+4}\right)$

(ii) $\sqrt{\dfrac{2}{\pi}}\left(\dfrac{1-\cos as}{s}\right)$; $\sqrt{\dfrac{2}{\pi}} \cdot \dfrac{\sin as}{s}$

(iii) $\dfrac{2}{s^2}\sqrt{\dfrac{2}{\pi}} \sin s(1-\cos s)$; $\dfrac{2}{s^2}\sqrt{\dfrac{2}{\pi}} \cos s(1-\cos s)$

7. (i) $\sqrt{\dfrac{2}{\pi}} \cdot \dfrac{\sin as}{s}$

(ii) $i\sqrt{\dfrac{2}{\pi}}\left(\dfrac{as \cos as - \sin as}{s^2}\right)$

8. $f(x) = \dfrac{2}{\pi(1+x^2)}$

9. $F(x) = \dfrac{2}{\pi x} (1 + \cos x - 2 \cos 2x)$.

2.6. PROPERTIES OF FOURIER TRANSFORMS

Linearity. If F(s) and G(s) are the Fourier transform of the functions $f(x)$ and $g(x)$ respectively, then $F[af(x) + bg(x)] = aF(s) + bG(s)$ where a and b are constants.

Proof. By definition $F[af(x) + bg(x)] = \int_{-\infty}^{\infty} [af(x) + bg(x)] \, e^{isx} \, dx$

$$= \int_{-\infty}^{\infty} af(x)\, e^{isx}\, dx + \int_{-\infty}^{\infty} bg(x)\, e^{isx}\, dx$$

$$= a\mathrm{F}(s) + b\mathrm{G}(s).$$

Symmetry. If F(s) is the Fourier transform of $f(x)$, then $2\pi f(-s)$ is the transform of F(x).

Proof. We have, $\mathrm{F}(s) = \int_{-\infty}^{\infty} f(x)\, e^{isx}\, dx$ where $f(x) = \dfrac{1}{2\pi}\int_{-\infty}^{\infty} \mathrm{F}(s) e^{-isx}\, ds$

i.e.,
$$2\pi f(x) = \int_{-\infty}^{\infty} \mathrm{F}(s)\, e^{-isx}\, ds$$

Changing x to $-x$,

$$2\pi f(-x) = \int_{-\infty}^{\infty} \mathrm{F}(s)\,.\, e^{isx}\, ds$$

Now interchanging s and x,

$$2\pi f(-s) = \int_{-\infty}^{\infty} \mathrm{F}(x)\, e^{isx}\, dx$$ which is the Fourier transform of F(x).

Change of time scale. If F(s) is the Fourier transform of $f(x)$, then $\mathrm{F}[f(ax)] = \dfrac{1}{a}\mathrm{F}(s/a)$, where a is a positive real constant. (*C.U. Dec. 2009*)

Proof.
$$\mathrm{F}[f(ax)] = \int_{-\infty}^{\infty} f(ax)\, e^{isx}\, dx, \text{ by definition}$$

$$= \int_{-\infty}^{\infty} f(u)\, e^{is(u/a)} \frac{du}{a} \quad \text{Put } ax = 4, \text{ then } dx = \frac{du}{a}.$$

$$= \frac{1}{a}\int_{-\infty}^{\infty} f(u)\,.\, e^{iu(s/a)}\, du = \frac{1}{a}\mathrm{F}(s/a)$$

Hence,
$$\mathrm{F}[f(x)] = \frac{1}{a}\, \mathrm{F}[s/a].$$

Remark. If $a < 0$, $\mathrm{F}[f(ax)] = \left(\dfrac{1}{a}\right) \mathrm{F}(s/a)$.

In general, the scaling property is $\mathrm{F}\,[f(ax)] = \dfrac{1}{|a|}\, \mathrm{F}(s/a)$.

Time shifting. $\mathrm{F}[f(x-a)] = e^{isa}\, \mathrm{F}(s)$, where F($s$) is the Fourier transform of $f(x)$. (*C.U. June 2006*)

Proof. By definition,

$$\mathrm{F}[f(x-a)] = \int_{-\infty}^{\infty} f(x-a)\, e^{isx}\, dx$$

$$= \int_{-\infty}^{\infty} f(u)\, e^{is(u+a)}\, du \qquad \text{Put } x - a = u,\ du = dx,\ x = u + a.$$

$$= \int_{-\infty}^{\infty} f(u)\, e^{isu}\,.\, e^{isa}\, du = e^{isa}\int_{-\infty}^{\infty} f(u)\, e^{isu}\, du$$

$$= \mathbf{e^{isa}\, F(s)}$$

Using this property, we can recover the function from its transform.

Frequency shifting. If a is a real constant then, $F[e^{iax}f(x)] = F(s + a)$, where F(s) is the Fourier transform of $f(x)$. *(C.U. Dec. 2009)*

Proof. We have $F[e^{iax} f(x)] = \int_{-\infty}^{\infty} e^{iax} f(x) e^{isx} \, dx$

$$= \int_{-\infty}^{\infty} e^{i(s+a)x} f(x) \, dx$$

$= F(s + a)$, by definition.

Modulation theorem. If $F(s) = \int_{-\infty}^{\infty} e^{isx} f(x) \, dx$, then

$$F(f(x) \cos ax) = \frac{1}{2}[F(s+a) + F(s-a)]$$ *(C.U. June 2007)*

Proof. $F[f(x) \cos ax] = \int_{-\infty}^{\infty} f(x) \cos ax \, e^{isx} \, dx$, by definition

$$= \int_{-\infty}^{\infty} f(x) e^{isx} \frac{[e^{iax} + e^{-iax}]}{2} \, dx \qquad \left[\because \cos ax = \frac{e^{iax} + e^{-iax}}{2}\right]$$

$$= \frac{1}{2} \int_{-\infty}^{\infty} [e^{i(s+a)x} f(x) + e^{i(s-a)x} f(x)] \, dx$$

$$= \frac{1}{2} [F(s+a) + F(s-a)]$$

In a similar way, $F[\sin ax \, f(x)] = \frac{1}{2}[F(s+a) - F(s-a)]$.

Time differentiation. Let $F[f(x)] = F(s)$. If $f(x)$ is continuous and $f'(x)$ is at least piece-wise continuous on $(-\infty, \infty)$ and if $f(x)$ and $f'(x)$ are absolutely integrable, then $F[f'(x)] = -is\,F(s)$.

Proof. We have $F[f'(x)] = \int_{-\infty}^{\infty} f'(x) e^{isx} \, dx$

$$= \left[e^{isx} \cdot f(x)\right]_{-\infty}^{\infty} - \int_{-\infty}^{\infty} (is) e^{isx} f(x) \, dx \qquad \text{[on integration]}$$

$$= 0 - is \int_{-\infty}^{\infty} e^{isx} f(x) \, dx$$

$$\left\{\because f(t) \text{ is absolutely integrable } \left[e^{isx} \cdot f(x)\right]_{-\infty}^{\infty} = 0\right\}$$

$$F[f'(x)] = -is\,F(s)$$

Remark. In a similar way,

$$F[f''(x)] = (-is)\,F[f'(x)] = (-is)(-is)\,F(s) = (-is)^2 F(s)$$

$$F[f'''(x)] = (-is)^3 F(s)$$

$$\vdots$$

$$F[f^n(x)] = (-is)^n F(s).$$

Frequency differentiation. If F(s) = F[f(x)], then

(i) F′(s) = F[ixf(x)] (ii) F[xf(x)] = – i F′(s) and

(iii) $F[x^n f(x)] = (-i)^n F^n(s)$ where f(x) is absolutely integrable on (– ∞, ∞).

(C.U. June 2007, Dec. 2007)

Proof. (i) $$F'(s) = \frac{d}{ds}\left[\int_{-\infty}^{\infty} f(x)\,e^{isx}\,dx\right], \text{ by definition}$$

$$= \int_{-\infty}^{\infty} \frac{d}{ds}[f(x)\,e^{isx}]\,dx = \int_{-\infty}^{\infty} f(x)\,e^{isx}(ix)\,dx$$

$$= \int_{-\infty}^{\infty} [ixf(x)]\,e^{isx}\,dx$$

= F[ix f(x)], by definition of Fourier transform.

Equivalently, F[xf(x)] = – i F(s).

In general, if $x^n f(x)$ is absolutely integrable on (– ∞, ∞) and if $x^n f(x)$ has a Fourier transform, then (for all integer values of n),

$$F[x^n f(x)] = (-i)^n F^n(s)$$

Note. From the above two properties $F[x^m f^n(x)] = (-i)^{m+n} \frac{d^m}{ds^m}[s^n F(s)]$, m, n = 1, 2, 3, ...

2.7. CONVOLUTION OF TWO FUNCTIONS

Convolution of two functions f(x) and g(x) over the interval (a, x – a), denoted by f ∗ g is given by

$$(f * g)(x) = \int_a^{x-a} f(u)\,g(x-u)\,du$$

When a = 0, the convolution $\int_0^x f(u)\,g(x-u)\,du$ is called the unilateral convolution of f and g in (0, x).

i.e., $$(f * g)\,(x) = \int_0^x f(u)\,g(x-u)\,du$$

The convolution of f and g from – ∞ to ∞ is called the bilateral convolution, *i.e.*, (f ∗ g)(x) $= \int_{-\infty}^{\infty} f(u)\,g(x-u)\,du$. Both unilateral and bilateral convolution has an important role in Fourier transformation.

2.8. CONVOLUTION THEOREM FOR FOURIER TRANSFORM *F[f(x) ∗ g(x)] = F[f(x)] . F[g(x)]*

That is the Fourier transform of the convolution of f(x) and g(x) is the product of their transforms.

Proof. By definition, $$F[f(x) * g(x)] = F\left[\int_{-\infty}^{\infty} f(u)\,.\,g(x-u)\,du\right]$$

$$= \int_{-\infty}^{\infty} e^{isx}\left[\int_{-\infty}^{\infty} f(u)\, g(x-u)\, du\right] dx$$

$$= \int_{-\infty}^{\infty} f(u)\left[\int_{-\infty}^{\infty} e^{isx}\, g(x-u)\, dx\right] du, \quad \text{changing the order of integration.}$$

$$= \int_{-\infty}^{\infty} f(u) . \left[\int_{-\infty}^{\infty} e^{isx} * e^{-isu}\, g(x-u)\, d(x-u)\right] e^{isu}\, du$$

$$= \int_{-\infty}^{\infty} \left[\int_{-\infty}^{\infty} e^{+is(x-u)}\, g(x-u)\, d(x-u)\right] f(u)\, e^{isu}\, du$$

$$= \int_{-\infty}^{\infty} f(u)\, e^{isu}\left[\int_{-\infty}^{\infty} e^{+ist}\, g(t)\, dt\right] du, \quad [\text{By putting } x-u=t \quad \therefore \quad dx = dt]$$

$$= \int_{-\infty}^{\infty} f(u)\, e^{isu}\, du * F[g(x)]$$

$$= F[f(x)] . F[g(x)]$$

i.e., $F[f(x) * g(x)] = \mathbf{F[f(x)] . F[g(x)]}$

2.9. PARSEVAL'S IDENTITY FOR FOURIER TRANSFORMS

If F(s) and G(s) are the Fourier transforms of $f(x)$ and $g(x)$ respectively, then

(*a*) $\dfrac{1}{2\pi}\displaystyle\int_{-\infty}^{\infty} F(s)\overline{G(s)}\, ds = \int_{-\infty}^{\infty} f(x)\overline{g(x)}\, dx$

(*b*) $\dfrac{1}{2\pi}\displaystyle\int_{-\infty}^{\infty} |F(s)|^2\, ds = \int_{-\infty}^{\infty} |f(x)|^2\, dx$, where $\overline{G(s)}$, $\overline{g(x)}$ denote the complex conjugate.

Proof. We know the Fourier transform pair of $f(x)$ is $F(s) = \int_{-\infty}^{\infty} f(x)\, e^{isx}\, dx$ and

$$f(x) = \frac{1}{2\pi}\int_{-\infty}^{\infty} F(s)\, e^{-isx}\, dx.$$

(*a*) Now, $\displaystyle\int_{-\infty}^{\infty} f(x)\overline{g(x)}\, dx = \int_{-\infty}^{\infty} f(x)\left[\frac{1}{2\pi}\int_{-\infty}^{\infty} \overline{G}(s)\, e^{isx}\, ds\right] dx$

$$\left[\overline{g(x)} = \frac{1}{2\pi}\int_{-\infty}^{\infty} \overline{G}(s)\, e^{isx}\, ds\right]$$

$$= \frac{1}{2\pi}\int_{-\infty}^{\infty} \overline{G}(s)\left(\int_{-\infty}^{\infty} f(x)\, e^{isx}\, dx\right) ds, \text{ changing the order of integration}$$

i.e., $$\int_{-\infty}^{\infty} f(x)\overline{g(x)}\, dx = \frac{1}{2\pi}\int_{-\infty}^{\infty} \overline{G}(s)\, F(s)\, ds.$$

(*b*) If $g(x) = f(x)$, in (*a*),

$$\int_{-\infty}^{\infty} f(x)\,\overline{f(x)}\, dx = \frac{1}{2\pi}\int_{-\infty}^{\infty} \overline{F}(s)\, F(s)\, ds = \frac{1}{2\pi}\int_{-\infty}^{\infty} |\overline{F}(s)|^2\, ds$$

i.e., $$\int_{-\infty}^{\infty} |f(x)|^2\, dx = \frac{1}{2\pi}\int_{-\infty}^{\infty} |\overline{F}(s)|^2\, ds.$$

ILLUSTRATIVE EXAMPLES

Example 6. *Find the Fourier transform of* $f(x) = \begin{cases} a - |x|, & for\ |x| < a \\ 0, & for\ |x| > a \end{cases}$. *Hence find* $\int_0^\infty \frac{sin^4 t}{t^4} dt.$ (C.U. Nov. 2010)

Sol.

$$F(f(x)) = \int_{-\infty}^{\infty} f(x)\, e^{isx}\, dx$$

$$= \int_{-a}^{0} (a + x)\, e^{isx}\, dx + \int_{0}^{a} (a - x)\, e^{isx}\, dx$$

$$= \left[(a + x)\frac{e^{isx}}{is} - 1 \times \frac{e^{isx}}{(is)^2}\right]_{-a}^{0} + \left[(a - x)\frac{e^{isx}}{is} - \frac{(-1)e^{isx}}{(is)^2}\right]_{0}^{a}$$

$$= \left(\frac{a}{is} - \frac{1}{(is)^2}\right) - \left(0 - \frac{e^{-ias}}{(is)^2}\right) + \left(0 + \frac{e^{ias}}{(is)^2}\right) - \left(\frac{a}{is} + \frac{1}{(is)^2}\right)$$

$$= \frac{-2}{(is)^2} + \frac{e^{ias} + e^{-ias}}{(is)^2} = \frac{+2}{(is)^2}[-1 + \cos as] = \frac{2}{s^2}[1 - \cos as]$$

i.e.,

$$F(s) = \frac{2}{s^2}[1 - \cos as]$$

$$= \mathbf{\frac{4}{s^2} \sin^2 (as/2)}$$

By Parseval's inequality,

$$\frac{1}{2\pi}\int_{-\infty}^{\infty} |F(s)|^2\, ds = \int_{-\infty}^{\infty} |f(x)|^2\, dx$$

i.e.,

$$\frac{1}{2\pi}\int_{-\infty}^{\infty} \left(\frac{4 \sin^2 (as/2)}{s^2}\right)^2 ds = \int_{-a}^{a} |(a - |x|)|^2\, dx = 2\int_0^a (a - x)^2\, dx = \left[\frac{2}{-3}(a - x)^3\right]_0^a$$

i.e.

$$= \frac{2}{-3}[0 - a^3] = \frac{2a^3}{3}$$

$$\frac{16}{\pi}\int_{-\infty}^{\infty} \frac{\sin^4 s\,(as/2)}{s^4}\, ds = \frac{2a^3}{3}$$

Put

$$\frac{as}{2} = u,\ ds = \frac{2}{a}du$$

$\therefore$

$$\frac{16}{\pi}\int_{-\infty}^{\infty} \frac{\sin^4 u}{\left(\frac{2u}{a}\right)^4} \times \frac{2du}{a} = \frac{2}{3}a^3$$

i.e., $$\frac{2a^3}{\pi}\int_{-\infty}^{\infty}\frac{\sin^4 u}{u^4}\,du=\frac{2}{3}a^3$$

∴ $$\frac{1}{\pi}\int_{-\infty}^{\infty}\frac{\sin^4 t}{t^4}\,dt=\frac{1}{3}$$

∴ $$\int_{-\infty}^{\infty}\frac{\sin^4 t}{t^4}\,dt=\frac{\pi}{3}$$

2.10. PROPERTIES OF FOURIER COSINE AND SINE TRANSFORMS

Fourier cosine and sine transform of the function $f(x)$ is defined as $F_c(s) = \int_0^{\infty} f(x)\cos sx\,dx$ and $F_s(s) = \int_0^{\infty} f(x)\sin sx\,dx$ respectively. Then $f(x) = \frac{2}{\pi}\int_0^{\infty} F_c(s)\cos sx\,ds$ is the inverse Fourier cosine transform and $f(x) = \frac{2}{\pi}\int_0^{\infty} F_s(s)\sin sx\,ds$ is the inverse Fourier sine transform.

1. Linearity property is valid in the case of Fourier sine and cosine transform.
2. Change of scale property : $F_c\,[f(ax)] = \frac{1}{a}F_c(s/a)$ and $F_s[f(ax)] = \frac{1}{a}F_s(s/a)$
3. Modulation theorem:

(i) $F_s[f(x)\cos ax] = \frac{1}{2}[F_s(s+a)+F_s(s-a)]$

(ii) $F_c[f(x)\sin ax] = \frac{1}{2}[F_s(s+a)-F_s(s-a)]$

(iii) $F_s[f(x)\sin ax] = \frac{1}{2}[F_c(s-a)-F_c(s+a)]$

4. $F_s[x\,f(x)] = -\frac{d}{ds}[F_c(s)]$ and $F_c[x\,f(x)] = \frac{d}{ds}[F_s(s)]$.

Proof. $$F_s[x\,f(x)] = \int_0^{\infty} x f(x)\,e^{isx}\,dx$$

Now, $$\frac{d}{ds}[F_c(s)] = \frac{d}{ds}\int_0^{\infty} f(x)\cos sx\,dx = \int_0^{\infty} f(x)\frac{d}{ds}(\cos sx)\,dx$$
$$= \int_0^{\infty} f(x)\,-x\sin sx\,dx = -\int_0^{\infty} x f(x)\sin sx\,dx$$
$$= -F_s[x\,f(x)]$$

∴ $$\mathbf{F_s[x\,f(x)] = -\frac{d}{ds}F_c(s)}$$

$$= \frac{d}{ds}[F_s(s)] = \frac{d}{ds}\int_0^{\infty} f(x)\sin sx\,dx$$
$$= \int_0^{\infty} f(x)\,.\cos sx\,(x)\,dx = \int_0^{\infty} x f(x)\cos sx\,dx$$

$$= F_c\,[x\,f(x)]$$

$\therefore$ $$\mathbf{F_c[x\,f(x)] = \frac{d}{ds}\,[F_s(s)]}$$

5. $F_c[f'(x)] = s\,F_s(s) - f(0)$ and
$F_s[f'(x)] = -\,s\,F_c(s)$ if $f(x) \to 0$ as $x \to \infty$.

Proof. We have $F_c[f'(x)] = \int_0^\infty f'(x)\,\cos x\,dx$

$$= \left[\cos sx\,.\,f(x)\right]_0^\infty - \int_0^\infty -\,s\sin sx\,f(x)\,dx \qquad \text{(on integration)}$$

$$= -\,f(0) + s\int_0^\infty f(x)\,\sin sx\,dx$$

i.e., $F_c[f'(x)] = s\,F_s(s) - f(0)$

Now, $F_s[f'(x)] = \int_0^\infty f'(x)\,\sin sx\,dx$

$$= \left[\sin sx\,f(x)\right]_0^\infty - \int_0^\infty s\cos sx\,f(x)\,dx$$

$$= -\,s\,F_c(s)$$

i.e., $\mathbf{F_s[f'(x)] = -\,s\,F_c(s)}$

Note. $F_s[f''(x)] = -\,s^2\,F_s(s) - f'(0)$ and $F_c[f''(x)] = -\,s^2\,F_s(s) + sf(0)$.

Parseval's identity for *Fourier* sine and cosine transform

(*i*) $\int_0^\infty f(x)\,g(x)\,dx = \frac{2}{\pi}\int_0^\infty F_c(s)\,G_c(s)\,ds$

(*ii*) $\int_0^\infty f(x)\,g(x)\,dx = \frac{2}{\pi}\int_0^\infty F_s(s)\,G_s(s)\,ds$

(*iii*) $\int_0^\infty |f(x)|^2\,dx = \frac{2}{\pi}\int_0^\infty [F_c(s)]^2$ and

(*iv*) $\int_0^\infty |f(x)|^2\,dx = \frac{2}{\pi}\int_0^\infty [F_s(s)]^2$.

Example 7. *Find the Fourier integral representation of the function* $f(x) = \begin{cases} 0, & x < 0 \\ \frac{1}{2}, & x = 0 \\ e^{-x}, & x > 0 \end{cases}$.

Sol. We know that $\int_0^\infty \frac{\cos\lambda x}{1+\lambda^2}\,d\lambda = \frac{\pi}{2}e^{-x},\ x > 0$ and $\int_0^\infty \frac{\lambda\sin\lambda x}{1+\lambda^2}\,d\lambda = \frac{\pi}{2}\,e^{-x},\ x > 0.$

Adding these, $\int_0^{\infty} \frac{\cos \lambda x + \lambda \sin \lambda x}{1+\lambda^2} d\lambda = \pi e^{-x}, x > 0.$

At $x = 0$, $\int_0^{\infty} \frac{\cos \lambda x + \lambda \sin \lambda x}{1+\lambda^2} d\lambda = \int_0^{\infty} \frac{d\lambda}{1+\lambda^2} = \left[\tan^{-1} x\right]_0^{\infty} = \frac{\pi}{2}.$

When $x < 0$, $\int_0^{\infty} \frac{\cos \lambda x + \lambda \sin \lambda x}{1+\lambda^2} d\lambda = \int_0^{\infty} \frac{\cos \lambda x - \lambda \sin \lambda x}{1+\lambda^2} dx = \frac{\pi}{2} e^{-x} - e^{-x}\frac{\pi}{2} = 0.$

$$\therefore \quad \int_0^{\infty} \frac{\cos \lambda x + \lambda \sin \lambda x}{1+\lambda^2} d\lambda = \begin{cases} 0, & x < 0 \\ \pi/2, & x = 0 \\ \pi e^{-x}, & x > 0. \end{cases}$$

Example 8. *Using Fourier integrals, ST*

(*a*) $\int_0^{\infty} \frac{\sin \pi\lambda \sin x\lambda}{1-\lambda^2} d\lambda = \begin{cases} \frac{\pi}{2} \sin x, & 0 \le x \le \pi \\ 0, & x > \pi \end{cases}$ (*b*) $\int_0^{\infty} \frac{\cos x\lambda}{1+\lambda^2} d\lambda = \frac{\pi}{2} e^{-x}, x \ge 0$

(*c*) $\int_0^{\infty} \frac{\lambda \sin \lambda x}{k^2+\lambda^2} d\lambda = \frac{\pi}{2} e^{-kx}, x > 0, k > 0.$ (C.U. Nov. 2010)

Sol. (*a*) Fourier sine integral is

$$F(x) = \frac{2}{\pi}\int_0^{\infty} \sin \lambda x \int_0^{\pi} f(x) \sin \lambda t \; dt \, d\lambda$$

i.e.,

$$\sin x = \frac{2}{\pi}\int_0^{\infty} \sin \lambda x \int_0^{\pi} \sin t \sin \lambda t \; dt \, d\lambda \qquad \boxed{f(x) = \sin x}$$

$$= \frac{1}{\pi}\int_0^{\infty} \sin \lambda x \int_0^{\pi} [\cos (1-\lambda)t - \cos (1+\lambda)t] \; dt \, d\lambda$$

$$= \frac{1}{\pi}\int_0^{\infty} \sin \lambda x \left[\frac{\sin (1-\lambda)t}{1-\lambda} - \frac{\sin (1+\lambda)t}{1+\lambda}\right]_0^{\pi} d\lambda$$

$$= \frac{1}{\pi}\int_0^{\infty} \sin \lambda x \left[\frac{\sin \lambda\pi}{1-\lambda} + \frac{\sin \lambda\pi}{1+\lambda}\right] d\lambda = \frac{2}{\pi}\int_0^{\infty} \sin \lambda x \left[\frac{\sin \lambda\pi}{1-\lambda^2}\right] d\lambda$$

$$\Rightarrow \quad \int_0^{\infty} \frac{\sin \lambda x \, . \, \sin \lambda\pi}{1-\lambda^2} d\lambda = \begin{cases} \frac{\pi}{2} \sin x, & 0 \le x \le \pi \\ 0, & x > \pi \end{cases}$$

(*b*) Fourier cosine integral is

$$f(x) = \frac{2}{\pi}\int_0^{\infty} \cos \lambda x \int_0^{\infty} f(t) \cos \lambda t \; dt \, d\lambda$$

$$e^{-x} = \frac{2}{\pi}\int_0^{\infty} \cos \lambda x \int_0^{\infty} e^{-t} \cos \lambda t \; dt \, d\lambda \qquad \boxed{f(x) = e^{-x}}$$

$$= \frac{2}{\pi}\int_0^{\infty} \cos \lambda x \left(\frac{1}{1+\lambda^2}\right) d\lambda \qquad \text{after integration}$$

$$\Rightarrow \quad \int_0^{\infty} \frac{\cos \lambda x}{1+\lambda^2} d\lambda = \frac{\pi}{2} e^{-x}, x \ge 0.$$

(*c*) Fourier sine integral

$$f(x) = \frac{2}{\pi}\int_0^{\infty} \sin \lambda x \int_0^{\infty} f(t) \sin \lambda t \; dt \; d\lambda$$

$$e^{-kx} = \frac{2}{\pi}\int_0^{\infty} \sin \lambda x \int_0^{\infty} e^{-kt} \sin \lambda t \; dt \; d\lambda \qquad \boxed{f(x) = e^{-kx}}$$

$$= \frac{2}{\pi}\int_0^{\infty} \sin \lambda x \left(\frac{\lambda}{k^2+\lambda^2}\right) d\lambda \qquad \text{on integration}$$

$$\int_0^{\infty} \frac{\lambda \sin \lambda x}{k^2+\lambda^2} = \frac{\pi}{2} e^{-kx}, \; x > 0, \; k > 0.$$

Example 9. *Find the Fourier sine transform of* $\frac{e^{-ax}}{x}$. (C.U. Dec. 2008)

Sol. (*a*) $$F_s(s) = \int_0^{\infty} \frac{e^{-ax}}{x} \sin sx \, dx = I \text{ (say)} \qquad ...(1)$$

Diff. (1) w.r.t. s,

$$\frac{dI}{ds} = \frac{d}{ds}\left[\int_0^{\infty} \frac{e^{-ax}}{x} \sin sx\right] = \int_0^{\infty} \frac{e^{-ax}}{x} . x \cos sx \, dx = \int_0^{\infty} e^{-ax} \cos sx \, dx = \frac{a}{s^2+a^2}.$$

Integration w.r.t. s yields, $I = \tan^{-1}(s/a) + c$ ...(2)

When $s = 0$, $I = 0$ $\therefore$ $c = 0$

$\therefore$ From (2), $I = \tan^{-1}(s/a)$

Example 10. *Find the Fourier cosine transform of the function f(x), if*

$$f(x) = \begin{cases} \cos x, & 0 < x < a \\ 0, & x > a. \end{cases}$$

Sol. $$F_c(s) = \int_0^a f(x) \cos sx \, dx = \int_0^a \cos x \cos sx \, dx = \frac{1}{2}\int_0^a [\cos(1+s)x + \cos(1-s)x] \, dx$$

$$= \frac{1}{2}\left[\frac{\sin(1+s)x}{1+s} + \frac{\sin(1-s)x}{1-s}\right]_0^a = \frac{1}{2}\left[\frac{\sin(1+s)a}{1+s} + \frac{\sin(1-s)a}{1-s}\right].$$

Example 11. *Find the Fourier sine and cosine transform of*

(*i*) $2e^{-5x} + 5e^{-2x}$ (*ii*) $f(x) = \begin{cases} 1, & 0 \le x < a \\ 0, & x > a \end{cases}$ (*iii*) $f(x) = \begin{cases} x, & 0 < x < 1 \\ 2-x, & 1 < x < 2 \\ 0, & x > 2. \end{cases}$

(C.U. Oct. 2011)

Sol. (*i*) $$F_s(s) = \int_0^{\infty} f(x) \sin sx \, dx$$

$$= 2\int_0^{\infty} e^{-5x} \sin x \, dx + 5\int_0^{\infty} e^{-2x} \sin sx \, dx = \frac{2s}{s^2+25} + \frac{5s}{s^2+4}$$

$$F_c(s) = \int_0^\infty f(x)\cos sx\,dx = 2\int_0^\infty e^{-5x}\cos sx\,dx + 5\int_0^\infty e^{-2x}\cos sx\,dx$$

$$= \frac{10}{s^2+25} + \frac{10}{s^2+4}.$$

(*ii*) $$F_s(s) = \int_0^a \sin sx\,dx = \left(\frac{-\cos sx}{s}\right)_0^a = \frac{1-\cos as}{s}$$

$$F_c(s) = \int_0^a \cos sx\,dx = \frac{\sin as}{s}.$$

(*iii*) $$F_c(s) = \int_0^\infty f(x)\sin sx\,dx = \int_0^1 x\sin sx\,dx + \int_1^2 (2-x)\sin sx\,dx$$

$$= \left\{x\left(\frac{-\cos sx}{s}\right)\right\}_0^1 - \int_0^1\left(\frac{-\cos sx}{s}\right)dx + \left[(2-x)\left(\frac{-\cos sx}{s}\right)\right]_1^2 - \int_0^2(-1)\left(\frac{-\cos sx}{s}\right)dx\Bigg\}$$

$$= \frac{-\cos s}{s} + \left(\frac{\sin sx}{s^2}\right)_0^1 + \frac{\cos s}{s} - \left(\frac{\sin sx}{s^2}\right)_1^2$$

$$= \frac{2\sin s}{s^2} - \frac{\sin 2s}{s^2} = \frac{2\sin s(1-\cos s)}{s^2}$$

$$F_c(s) = \int_0^\infty f(x)\cos sx\,dx = \int_0^1 x\cos sx\,dx + \int_1^2 (2-x)\cos sx\,dx$$

$$= \left(\frac{x\sin sx}{s}\right)_0^1 - \int_0^1 \frac{\sin sx}{s}dx + \left[(2-x)\frac{\sin sx}{s}\right]_1^2 - \int_1^2(-1)\frac{\sin sx}{s}dx$$

$$= \frac{\sin s}{s} + \left(\frac{\cos sx}{s^2}\right)_0^1 - \frac{\sin s}{s} - \left(\frac{\cos sx}{s^2}\right)_1^2 = \frac{\cos s}{s^2} - \frac{1}{s^2} - \frac{\cos 2s}{s^2} + \frac{\cos s}{s^2}$$

$$= \frac{2\cos s}{s^2} - \frac{1+\cos 2s}{s^2} = \frac{2\cos s}{s^2} - \frac{2\cos^2 s}{s^2} = \frac{2\cos s}{s^2}[1-\cos s].$$

Example 12. *Find the Fourier transform of*

(*i*) $f(x) = \begin{cases} 1, & |x| < a \\ 0, & |x| > a \end{cases}$ (*ii*) $f(x) = \begin{cases} x, & |x| < a \\ 0, & |x| > a. \end{cases}$ (C.U. June 2009)

Sol. (*i*) $$F(s) = \int_{-a}^{a} e^{+isx}\,dx$$

$$= \left(\frac{e^{isx}}{is}\right)_{-a}^{a} = \frac{1}{is}[e^{ias} - e^{-ias}] = \frac{2}{s}\ \textbf{sin as}.$$

(*ii*) $$F(s) = \int_{-a}^{a} xe^{isx}\,dx = \int_{-a}^{a} x(\cos sx + i\sin sx)\,dx$$

$$= \int_{-a}^{a} x\cos ax\,dx + i\int_{-a}^{a} x\sin sx\,dx = 0 + 2i\int_0^a x\sin sx\,dx$$

$$= 2i \left\{ \left(x \cdot \frac{-\cos sx}{s} - (1) \cdot \frac{-\sin sx}{s^2} \right)_0^a \right\} = 2i \left[\frac{-a \cos as}{s} - 0 + \frac{\sin as}{s^2} - 0 \right]$$

$$= 2i \left[\frac{\sin as - as \cos as}{s^2} \right]$$

$$= \frac{\mathbf{2i}}{\mathbf{s^2}} [\mathbf{\sin as - as \cos as}].$$

Example 13. *Show that the Fourier transform of* $e^{-x^2/2}$ *is self reciprocal.*

(C.U. Nov. 2010; Oct. 2011)

Sol. By definition, $F(e^{-x^2/2}) = \int_{-\infty}^{\infty} e^{-x^2/2} . e^{isx} \, dx = \int_{-\infty}^{\infty} e^{isx - x^2/2} \, dx$

$$= \int_{-\infty}^{\infty} e^{\frac{2isx - x^2}{2}} \, dx = \int_{-\infty}^{\infty} e^{-\frac{1}{2}(x^2 - 2isx + (is)^2 - (is)^2)} \, dx$$

$$= \int_{-\infty}^{\infty} e^{-\frac{1}{2}(x - is)^2} . e^{-\frac{s^2}{2}} \, dx$$

$$= e^{-s^2/2} \int_{-\infty}^{\infty} e^{-t^2} . \sqrt{2} \, dt \qquad \left(\text{Put } \frac{x - is}{\sqrt{2}} = t, \text{ then } \quad dx = \sqrt{2} \, dt \right)$$

$$= \sqrt{2} . e^{-s^2/2} . \int_{-\infty}^{\infty} e^{-t^2} \, dt$$

$$= \sqrt{2} . e^{-s^2/2} \int_{-\infty}^{\infty} e^{-u} . \frac{du}{2\sqrt{u}} \qquad \left[\text{Put } t^2 = u, \, 2t \, dt = du, \, \therefore \quad dt = \frac{du}{2\sqrt{u}} \right)$$

$$= \frac{e^{-s^2/2}}{\sqrt{2}} \int_{-\infty}^{\infty} u^{-1/2} e^{-u} \, du = \frac{e^{-s^2/2}}{\sqrt{2}} \int_{-\infty}^{\infty} e^{-u} u^{\frac{1}{2} - 1} \, du$$

$$= \frac{e^{-s^2/2}}{\sqrt{2}} . \Gamma 1/2 \qquad \text{(By the definition of gamma function)}$$

$$= \sqrt{\frac{\pi}{2}} \, e^{-s^2/2}, \quad \because \quad \Gamma 1/2 = \sqrt{\pi} .$$

i.e., **$F(e^{-x^2/2})$ is a constant multiple of $e^{-s^2/2}$. Hence self reciprocal.**

Example 14. *Find the Fourier sine transform of* $f(x) = \begin{cases} 1, & 0 \le x < a \\ 0, & x \ge a \end{cases}$.

(C.U. Nov. 2010)

Sol. By definition, $F_s[f(x)] = \int_{-\infty}^{\infty} f(x) \sin sx \, dx$

$$= \int_0^a \sin sx \, dx + 0 = \left[\frac{-\cos sx}{s} \right]_0^a = \frac{-\cos as + 1}{s}$$

$$= \frac{\mathbf{1 - \cos as}}{\mathbf{s}}.$$

Example 15. *Find the Fourier transform of the function* $f(t) = e^{-a|t|}$, $-\infty < t < \infty$, $a > 0$.

(C.U. Nov. 2010)

Sol. Here $f(t)$ is an even function.

$$\therefore \quad F[f(t)] = 2\int_0^\infty f(t)\cos st\,dt = 2\int_0^\infty e^{-at}\cos st\,dt$$

$$= 2\left[\frac{e^{-at}}{a^2+s^2}[-a\cos st + s\sin st]\right]_0^\infty = 2\left[0 - \frac{-a}{a^2+s^2}\right]$$

$$= -\frac{\mathbf{2a}}{\mathbf{a^2+s^2}}.$$

Example 16. *Find the Fourier cosine transform of* $\dfrac{e^{-ax}}{x}$.

(C.U. Nov. 2010; Dec. 2006, 2008)

Sol. By definition, $\quad F_c(s) = \int_0^\infty f(x)\cos sx\,dx$

$$= \int_0^\infty \frac{e^{-ax}}{x}\cos sx\,dx = \text{I (say)} \qquad ...(1)$$

Differentiating (1) w.r.t. s,

$$\frac{dI}{ds} = \frac{d}{ds}\left[\int_0^\infty \frac{e^{-ax}}{x}\cos sx\,dx\right]$$

$$= \int_0^\infty \frac{d}{ds}\left(\frac{e^{-ax}}{x}\cos sx\right)dx = \int_0^\infty \frac{e^{-ax}}{x}[-x\sin sx]\,dx$$

$$= -\int_0^\infty e^{-ax}\sin sx\,dx = \text{Img.}\left(-\int_0^\infty e^{-ax}e^{isx}\,dx\right)$$

$$= -\text{Img.}\int_0^\infty e^{-x(a-is)}\,dx = -\text{Img.}\left[\frac{e^{-x(a-is)}}{is-a}\right]_0^\infty$$

$$= \text{Img.}\left[\frac{1}{is-a}\right] = \text{Img.}\frac{-(is+a)}{s^2+a^2} = \frac{-s}{s^2+a^2}.$$

Now integrating both sides w.r.t. s, we get $I = F_c(s) = \dfrac{-1}{2}\log(s^2+a^2)$.

Example 17. *Find the Fourier transform of* $f(x) = \begin{cases} 1-|x|, & \text{if } |x| < 1 \\ 0, & \text{for } |x| > 1 \end{cases}$

(C.U. June 2009)

Sol. Fourier transform,

$$F(s) = \int_{-\infty}^\infty f(x)e^{isx}\,dx$$

$$= \int_{-1}^0 (1+x)e^{isx}\,dx + \int_0^1 (1-x)e^{isx}\,dx$$

$$= \left[(1+x)\frac{e^{isx}}{is} - \frac{e^{isx}}{(is)^2}\right]_{-1}^{0} + \left[(1-x)\frac{e^{isx}}{is} - (-1)\frac{e^{isx}}{(is)^2}\right]_{0}^{1}$$

$$= \left[\frac{1}{is} - \frac{1}{(is)^2} - \left(0 - \frac{e^{-is}}{(is)^2}\right)\right] + \left[0 + \frac{e^{is}}{(is)^2} - \left(\frac{1}{is} + \frac{1}{(is)^2}\right)\right]$$

$$= \frac{1}{is} - \frac{1}{(is)^2} + \frac{e^{-is}}{(is)^2} + \frac{e^{is}}{(is)^2} - \frac{1}{is} + \frac{1}{(is)^2} = \frac{-2}{(is)^2} + \frac{e^{is}+e^{-is}}{(is)^2}$$

$$= \frac{2}{s^2} - \frac{2\cos s}{s^2} = \frac{2}{s^2}\,[1-\cos s], \text{ if } s \neq 0$$

Example 18. *Find the Fourier sine transform of* $e^{-x} + e^{-2x}$. (C.U. Dec. 2008)

Sol. Fourier sine transform,

$$F_s(s) = \int_0^\infty f(x)\sin sx\,dx$$

$$F_s(s) = \int_0^\infty (e^{-x} + e^{-2x})\sin sx\,dx$$

$$= \int_0^\infty e^{-x}\sin sx\,dx + \int_0^\infty e^{-2x}\sin sx\,dx$$

$$= \text{Img.}\int_0^\infty e^{-x}.e^{isx}\,dx + \text{Img.}\int_0^\infty e^{-2x}.e^{isx}\,dx$$

$$= \text{Img.}\left[\int_0^\infty e^{-x(1-is)}\,dx + \int_0^\infty e^{-x(2-is)}\,dx\right]$$

$$= \text{Img.}\left[\frac{e^{-x(1-is)}}{-(1-is)} + \frac{e^{-x(2-is)}}{-(2-is)}\right]_0^\infty = \text{Img.}\left[\frac{1}{1-is} + \frac{1}{2-is}\right]$$

i.e.,

$$F_s(s) = \text{Img.}\left(\frac{1}{1-is}\right) + \text{Img.}\left(\frac{1}{2-is}\right) = \text{Img.}\left[\frac{1+is}{1+s^2} + \frac{2+is}{4+s^2}\right]$$

$$= \frac{s}{1+s^2} + \frac{s}{4+s^2} = \frac{4s+s^3+s+s^3}{(1+s^2)(4+s^2)}$$

$$= \frac{\mathbf{5s+2s^3}}{\mathbf{(1+s^2)(4+s^2)}}.$$

Example 19. *Find the Fourier sine and cosine transform of* e^{-ax}, $x > 0$.

(C.U. June 2007; Dec. 2006)

Sol. Fourier sine transform,

$$F_s(s) = \int_0^\infty f(x)\sin sx\,dx$$

$$= \int_0^\infty e^{-ax}\sin sx\,dx$$

$$= \text{Img.} \int_0^\infty e^{-ax} \,.\, e^{isx}\, dx = \text{Img.} \int_0^\infty e^{-x(a-is)}\, dx$$

$$= \text{Img.} \left[\frac{e^{-x(1-is)}}{(is-a)} \right]_0^\infty = \text{Img.} \frac{1}{a-is} = \text{Img.} \frac{a+is}{a^2+s^2} = \frac{s}{s^2+a^2}$$

$$\mathbf{F_s(e^{-ax}) = \frac{s}{s^2+a^2}}$$

Fourier cosine transform,

$$\text{F}_c(s) = \int_0^\infty f(x) \cos sx\, dx = \int_0^\infty e^{-ax} \cos sx\, dx$$

$$= \text{Real} \int_0^\infty e^{-ax}\, e^{isx}\, dx = \text{Real} \int_0^\infty e^{-x(a-is)}\, dx$$

$$= \text{Real} \left(\frac{e^{-x(a-is)}}{is-a} \right)_0^\infty = \text{Real} \left(\frac{1}{a-is} \right) = \text{Real} \frac{a+is}{a^2+s^2}$$

$$= \mathbf{\frac{a}{a^2+s^2}}.$$

Example 20. *Find the Fourier cosine transform of* $\frac{1}{1+x^2}$ *and hence find the Fourier sine transform of* $\frac{x}{1+x^2}$.

Sol. $$\text{F}_c(s) = \int_0^\infty f(x) \cos sx\, dx = \int_0^\infty \frac{\cos sx}{1+x^2}\, dx = \text{I (say)} \qquad ...(1)$$

$$\therefore \quad \frac{d\text{I}}{ds} = \frac{d}{ds} \int_0^\infty \frac{\cos sx}{1+x^2}\, dx$$

$$= \int_0^\infty \frac{1}{1+x^2} \,.\, -\sin sx \,.\, x\, dx = -\int_0^\infty \frac{x \sin sx}{1+x^2}\, dx$$

$$= -\int_0^\infty \frac{x^2 \sin sx}{x(1+x^2)}\, dx = -\int_0^\infty \frac{(1+x^2-1)\sin sx}{x(1+x^2)}\, dx$$

$$= -\int_0^\infty \frac{\sin sx}{x}\, dx + \int_0^\infty \frac{\sin sx}{x(1+x^2)}\, dx$$

$$= -\frac{\pi}{2} + \int_0^\infty \frac{\sin sx}{x(1+x^2)}\, dx \qquad ...(2)$$

Now, $$\frac{d^2\text{I}}{ds^2} = \int_0^\infty \frac{x \cos sx}{x(1+x^2)}\, dx = \text{I}$$

$$\therefore \quad \frac{d^2\text{I}}{ds^2} - \text{I} = 0$$

i.e., $(D^2 - 1)\,I = 0$ where $D \equiv \dfrac{d}{ds}$.

Auxiliary eqn. is $m^2 - 1 = 0$. *i.e.,* $m = \pm 1$

$\therefore \quad I = Ae^{s} + Be^{-s}$ ...(3)

When $s = 0$, (1) $\Rightarrow$ $I = \displaystyle\int_0^\infty \frac{dx}{1+x^2} = \left[\tan^{-1} x\right]_0^\infty = \pi/2.$

From (2), $\dfrac{dI}{ds} = -\pi/2$

$\therefore$ From (3), $I = Ae^{s} + Be^{-s}$

i.e., $\dfrac{dI}{ds} = Ae^{s} - Be^{-s}$

At $s = 0$, $\dfrac{dI}{ds} = A - B$ $\left[\text{But } \dfrac{dI}{ds} = -\pi/2 \text{ at } s = 0.\right]$

$\therefore \quad A - B = \pi/2$

From (3), $A + B = \pi/2$ $[\because \; I = \pi/2 \text{ at } s = 0]$

Solving these, $2A = 0$ *i.e.,* $A = 0$

and $B = \pi/2.$

Thus, $I = \pi/2\, e^{-s}$

$\therefore \quad \displaystyle\int_0^\infty \frac{\cos sx}{1+x^2}\,dx = \frac{\pi}{2} e^{-s}$ *i.e.,* $F_c(s) = \dfrac{\pi}{2}\, e^{-s}$

Now, $F_s\left(\dfrac{x}{1+x^2}\right) = \displaystyle\int_0^\infty \frac{x}{1+x^2} \cdot \sin sx\, dx$

$= -\dfrac{dI}{ds}$

$= \dfrac{-\pi}{2} e^{-s}$ $\left[\text{Since } I = \dfrac{\pi}{2} e^{-s} \text{ and so } \dfrac{dI}{ds} = -\dfrac{\pi}{2} e^{-s}\right]$

Example 21. *Find the Fourier sine transform of* $\dfrac{1}{x}$.

Sol. $F_s(s) = \displaystyle\int_0^\infty f(x) \sin sx\, dx$

$= \displaystyle\int_0^\infty \frac{\sin sx}{x}\, dx,$ put $sx = u$

$= \displaystyle\int_0^\infty \frac{\sin u}{(u/s)} \frac{du}{s} = \int_0^\infty \frac{\sin u}{u}\, du$

$= \boldsymbol{\pi/2}.$

Example 22. *Verify the Parseval's theorem for the function,*

$$f(x) = \begin{cases} e^{-x}, & x > 0 \\ 0, & x < 0 \end{cases}$$ (C.U. Dec. 2006)

Sol. We have the identity,

$$\int_{-\infty}^{\infty} |f(x)|^2 \, dx = \frac{1}{2\pi} \int_{-\infty}^{\infty} |F(s)|^2 \, ds$$

Here, $\int_{-\infty}^{\infty} f^2(x)\, dx = \int_0^{\infty} e^{-2x}\, dx = \left[\frac{-1}{2} e^{-2x}\right]_0^{\infty} = \frac{1}{2}$ ...(1)

$$F(s) = \int_{-\infty}^{\infty} f(x)\, e^{isx}\, dx = \int_0^{\infty} e^{-x} . e^{isx}\, dx = \int_0^{\infty} e^{-x[1-is]}\, dx$$

$$= \frac{1}{1 - is}$$

$$\therefore \quad |F(s)|^2 = \left|\frac{1}{1-is}\right|^2 = \frac{1}{1+s^2}$$

$$\therefore \quad \int_{-\infty}^{\infty} |F(s)|^2\, ds = \int_{-\infty}^{\infty} \frac{ds}{1+s^2}\, dx = \left[\tan^{-1} s\right]_{-\infty}^{\infty} = \frac{\pi}{2} - (-\pi/2) = \pi$$

$\frac{1}{2\pi}\int_{-\infty}^{\infty} |F(s)|^2\, ds = \frac{1}{2\pi} \times \pi = \frac{1}{2}$ ...(2)

From (1) and (2), $\int_{-\infty}^{\infty} f^2(x)\, dx = \frac{1}{2\pi}\int_{-\infty}^{\infty} |F(s)|^2\, ds$

Hence the verification.

TEST YOUR KNOWLEDGE

1. Find the complex Fourier integral representation of the function

$$f(x) = \begin{cases} 0, & x < 0 \\ e^{-ax}, & x > 0 \end{cases} \text{ where } a > 0.$$

2. Find the Fourier transform of $f(x) = \begin{cases} \sin x, & 0 \le x \le \pi \\ 0, & \text{elsewhere.} \end{cases}$ *(C.U. Dec. 2007)*

3. Find the inverse Fourier transform of $e^{-|x|}$. *(C.U. Dec. 2008)*

4. Find the Fourier cosine transform of e^{-x^2}, $x > 0$. *(C.U. Dec. 2008)*

5. Find the Fourier transform of $f(x) = \begin{cases} e^{-ax}, & 0 < x < \infty \\ 0, & x < 0. \end{cases}$

6. Find the Fourier transform of $f(x) = \begin{cases} xe^{-x}, & x > 0 \\ 0, & x < 0. \end{cases}$

7. Find the Fourier transform of $f(x) = \begin{cases} 1 + x/a, & a < x < 0 \\ 1 - x/a, & 0 < x < a \\ 0, & \text{elsewhere.} \end{cases}$

8. Find the Fourier cosine transform of $f(x) = \begin{cases} \cos x, & 0 < x < a \\ 0, & x > a. \end{cases}$

Answers

1. $\dfrac{1}{2\pi}\displaystyle\int_{-\infty}^{\infty}\dfrac{e^{-isx}}{a-is}\,ds$	2. $\dfrac{1+e^{-is\pi}}{1-s^2}$	3. $\dfrac{2}{1+s^2}$
4. $\dfrac{\sqrt{\pi}}{2}e^{-s^2/4}$	5. $\dfrac{1}{a-is}$	6. $\dfrac{1}{(1-is)^2}$
7. $\dfrac{4}{as^2}\sin^2\left(\dfrac{as}{2}\right)$	8. $\dfrac{1}{2}\left[\dfrac{\sin a(s+1)}{s+1}+\dfrac{\sin a(s-1)}{s-1}\right]$.	

2.11. FOURIER TRANSFORMS OF THE DERIVATIVES OF A FUNCTION

Let $\overline{u}(s, t)$ be the Fourier transform of the function $u(x, t)$.

Then,
$$\overline{u}(s, t) = \frac{1}{\sqrt{2\pi}}\int_{-\infty}^{\infty} u(x, t)\, e^{isx}\, dx$$

Suppose u and $\dfrac{\partial u}{\partial x}$ both vanish as $x \to \pm\infty$. Then the Fourier transform of $\dfrac{\partial^2 u}{\partial x^2}$ is given by

$$F\left\{\frac{\partial^2 u}{\partial x^2}\right\} = \frac{1}{\sqrt{2\pi}}\int_{-\infty}^{\infty}\frac{\partial^2 u}{\partial x^2}e^{isx}\,dx$$

$$= \frac{1}{\sqrt{2\pi}}\left[\left\{e^{isx}\frac{\partial u}{\partial x} - ise^{isx}\,.\,u\right\}_{-\infty}^{\infty} + \int_{-\infty}^{\infty}(is)^2 e^{isx}\,.\,u\,dx\right]$$

$$= -\frac{s^2}{\sqrt{2\pi}}\int_{-\infty}^{\infty} ue^{isx}\,dx = -s^2\,\overline{u}$$

If $\overline{u}_s(s, t)$ and $\overline{u}_c(s, t)$ be the Fourier sine and cosine transforms of $u(x, t)$, then

$$\overline{u}_s(s, t) = \sqrt{\frac{2}{\pi}}\int_0^{\infty} u \sin sx\,dx \quad \text{and} \quad \overline{u}(s, t) = \sqrt{\frac{2}{\pi}}\int_0^{\infty} u\cos sx\,dx$$

The Fourier sine transform of $\dfrac{\partial^2 u}{\partial x^2}$ is given by

$$F_s\left\{\frac{\partial^2 u}{\partial x^2}\right\} = \sqrt{\frac{2}{\pi}}\int_0^{\infty}\frac{\partial^2 u}{\partial x^2}\sin sx\,dx$$

$$= \sqrt{\frac{2}{\pi}}\left[\left\{\sin sx\frac{\partial u}{\partial x} - s\cos sx\,.\,u\right\}_0^{\infty} - \int_0^{\infty} s^2 \sin sx\,.\,u\,dx\right]$$

$$= \sqrt{\frac{2}{\pi}}\left[s\{u\}_{x=0} - s^2\int_0^{\infty} u\sin sx\,dx\right] = \sqrt{\frac{2}{\pi}}\,[s\{u\}_{x=0} - s^2\,\overline{u}_s]$$

Similarly, we have

$$F_c\left\{\frac{\partial^2 u}{\partial x^2}\right\} = \sqrt{\frac{2}{\pi}}\left[-\left\{\frac{\partial u}{\partial x}\right\}_{x=0} - s^2\,\overline{u}_c\right].$$

2.12. APPLICATION OF FOURIER TRANSFORMS TO BOUNDARY VALUE PROBLEMS

This is illustrated through the following examples.

ILLUSTRATIVE EXAMPLES

Example 23. *Solve the equation* $\dfrac{\partial u}{\partial t} = \dfrac{\partial^2 u}{\partial x^2}$, $x > 0, t > 0$, *subject to the conditions*

(*i*) $u = 0$, *when* $x = 0, t > 0$ (*ii*) $u = \begin{cases} 1, & 0 < x < 1 \\ 0, & x \geq 1 \end{cases}$ *when* $t = 0$

and (*iii*) $u(x, t)$ *is bounded.*

Sol. Since $(u)_{x=0}$ is given, taking Fourier sine transform of both sides of the given equation, we have

$$\int_0^\infty \frac{\partial u}{\partial t} \sin sx \, dx = \int_0^\infty \frac{\partial^2 u}{\partial x^2} \sin sx \, dx$$

or $$\frac{\partial}{\partial t} \int_0^\infty u \sin sx \, dx = [s(u)_{x=0} - s^2 \overline{u}_s]$$

or $$\frac{d\overline{u}_s}{dt} + s^2 \overline{u}_s = s(u)_{x=0}$$

or $$\frac{d\overline{u}_s}{dt} + s^2 \overline{u}_s = 0 \quad \text{since } u = 0, t > 0 \text{ when } x = 0, t > 0, \text{ using } (i)$$

Its solution is $\overline{u}_s = Ae^{-s^2 t}$, where A is a constant ...(1)

Now, using (*ii*) when $t = 0$, Fourier sine transform of $u(x, t)$

i.e., $$\overline{u}_s(s, 0) = \int_0^\infty u(x, 0) \sin sx \, dx = \int_0^1 1 \,.\, \sin sx \, dx + \int_1^\infty 0 \,.\, \sin sx \, dx$$

$$= \left[-\frac{\cos sx}{s}\right]_0^1 = \left(\frac{1 - \cos s}{s}\right)$$

$\therefore$ From (1), $A = \overline{u}_s(s, 0) = \left(\dfrac{1 - \cos s}{s}\right)$ so that $\overline{u}_s = \left(\dfrac{1 - \cos s}{s}\right) e^{-s^2 t}$

Applying the inverse Fourier sine transform, we have

$$u(x, t) = \frac{2}{\pi} \int_0^\infty \frac{1 - \cos s}{s} e^{-s^2 t} \sin sx \, ds \quad \text{which is the required solution.}$$

Example 24. *If the initial temperature of an infinite bar is given by*

$$\theta(x) = \begin{cases} \theta_0 & \text{for } |x| < a \\ 0 & \text{for } |x| > a, \end{cases}$$

determine the temperature at any instant x and at any instant t.

Sol. To determine the temperature $\theta(x, t)$, we have to solve the heat-flow equation

$$\frac{\partial \theta}{\partial t} = c^2 \frac{\partial^2 \theta}{\partial t^2}, \qquad t > 0 \qquad ...(1)$$

subject to the initial condition $\theta(x, 0) = \begin{cases} \theta_0 & \text{for } |x| < a \\ 0 & \text{for } |x| > a \end{cases}$ ...(2)

Taking Fourier transform of (1), we get

$$\int_{-\infty}^{\infty} \frac{\partial \theta}{\partial t} e^{isx}\, dx = c^2 \int_{-\infty}^{\infty} \frac{\partial^2 \theta}{\partial t^2} e^{isx}\, dx$$

or $$\frac{d}{dt}\int_{-\infty}^{\infty} \theta\, e^{isx}\, dx = -\, c^2 s^2 \overline{\theta}$$

or $$\frac{d\overline{\theta}}{dt} = -\, c^2 s^2 \overline{\theta} \qquad ...(3)$$

Now taking the Fourier transform of (2), we get

$$\overline{\theta}(s, 0) = \int_{-\infty}^{\infty} \theta(x, 0)\, e^{isx}\, dx = \int_{-a}^{a} \theta_0\, e^{isx}\, dx = \theta_0 \left[\frac{e^{isx}}{is}\right]_{-a}^{a}$$

$$= \theta_0 \left[\frac{e^{isa} - e^{-isa}}{is}\right] = \frac{2\theta_0}{s}\left[\frac{e^{isa} - e^{-isa}}{2i}\right]$$

$$= \frac{2\theta_0 \sin sa}{s}$$

From (3), $$\frac{d\overline{\theta}}{\overline{\theta}} = -\, c^2 s^2\, dt \qquad ...(4)$$

Integrating $\log \overline{\theta} = -\, c^2 s^2 t + \log A$ or $\overline{\theta} = Ae^{-c^2 s^2 t}$

Since $\overline{\theta} = \dfrac{2\theta_0 \sin sa}{s}$ when $t = 0$, from (4), we get $A = \dfrac{2\theta_0 \sin sa}{s}$

$$\therefore \quad \overline{\theta} = \frac{2\theta_0 \sin sa}{s} e^{-c^2 s^2 t}$$

Taking its inverse Fourier transform, we get

$$\theta(x, t) = \frac{1}{2\pi}\int_{-\infty}^{\infty} \frac{2\theta_0 \sin as}{s} . e^{-c^2 s^2 t} . e^{-sx}\, ds$$

$$= \frac{\theta_0}{\pi}\int_{-\infty}^{\infty} \frac{\sin as}{s} . e^{-c^2 s^2 t} (\cos xs - i \sin xs)\, ds$$

$$= \frac{\theta_0}{\pi}\left[\int_{-\infty}^{\infty} \frac{\sin as}{s} . e^{-c^2 s^2 t} \cos xs\, ds - i\int_{-\infty}^{\infty} \frac{\sin as}{s} . e^{-c^2 s^2 t} \sin xs\, ds\right]$$

$$= \frac{\theta_0}{\pi}\int_{-\infty}^{\infty} \frac{\sin as}{s} . e^{-c^2 s^2 t} \cos xs\, ds$$

(The second integral vanishes since its integrand is an odd function)

$$= \frac{2\theta_0}{\pi}\int_{0}^{\infty} \frac{\sin as}{s} . e^{-c^2 s^2 t} \cos xs\, ds = \frac{\theta_0}{\pi}\int_{0}^{\infty} \frac{e^{-c^2 s^2 t}}{s} . 2 \sin as \cos xs\, ds$$

$$= \frac{\theta_0}{\pi}\int_{0}^{\infty} e^{-c^2 s^2 t} \left(\frac{\sin (a + x)\, s + \sin (a - x)}{s}\, s\right) ds$$

$$= \frac{\theta_0}{\pi}\int_{0}^{\infty} e^{-v^2} \left\{\sin \frac{(a + x)v}{c\sqrt{t}} + \sin \frac{(1 - x)v}{c\sqrt{t}}\right\} \frac{dv}{v} \quad \text{where } v^2 = c^2 s^2 t$$

$$= \frac{\theta_0}{2}\left\{erf\left(\frac{a + x}{2c\sqrt{t}}\right) + erf\left(\frac{a - x}{2c\sqrt{t}}\right)\right\}.$$

UNIT 3
Linear Algebra

3.1. VECTOR SPACES (LINEAR SPACES)

Definition. A non-empty set V with two operations called addition and scalar multiplication denoted by '+' and '.' respectively is a vector space over a field F, if it satisfies the following axioms. The elements of V are referred as vectors and that of F as scalars.

(*i*) for any $x, y \in V$, $x + y \in V$. (closure property under addition)

(*ii*) for any vectors $x, y, z \in V$, $(x + y) + z = x + (y + z)$.

[Associative property under addition]

(*iii*) there is a vector $0 \in V$, called zero vector such that for any $x \in V$, $0 + x = x = x + 0$.

(Existance of additive identity)

(*iv*) for every $x \in V$, there is a vector $-x \in V$ such that $x + (-x) = 0 = (-x) + x$.

(Existance of additive inverse)

(*v*) for any $x, y \in V$, $x + y = y + x$. [Commutative property under addition]

(*vi*) for any $x \in V$ and $a \in F$, $a \, . \, x \in V$. [Closure property under scalar multiplication]

(*vii*) for any $x, y \in V$ and $a \in F$, $a \, . \, (x + y) = a \, . \, x + a \, . \, y$. [Distributive property]

(*viii*) for any $x \in V$ and $a, b \in F$, $(ab) \, . \, x = a(b \, . \, x)$.

(*ix*) for any $x \in V$ and $a, b \in F$, $(a + b) \, . \, x = a \, . \, x + b \, . \, x$.

(*x*) for any $x \in V$, and $1 \in F$, $1 \, . \, x = x$.

Usually we denote $a.x$ as ax. In this unit we consider real vector space, unless otherwise stated. If F = Set of all real numbers R, V is called real vector space.

For example 1. Let R be any field. The set of elements $(x_1, x_2, ..., x_n)$ with vector addition and scalar multiplication defined by

$x + y = (x_1 + y_1, x_2 + y_2, ..., x_n + y_n)$ and $ax = (ax_1, ax_2, ..., ax_n)$ where

$x = (x_1, x_2, ..., x_n)$ and $y = (y_1, y_2, ..., y_n)$; x_i, y_i and $a \in R$. Here R^n is the vector space.

Verification

Let $x = (x_1, x_2, ..., x_n), y = (y_1, y_2, ..., y_n), z = (z_1, z_2, ..., z_n)$ are vectors of R^n and $a, b \in R$ are scalars.

(*i*) Here, $x + y = (x_1 + y_1, x_2 + y_2, ..., x_n + y_n)$ and since $x_i, y_i \in R$, $x_i + y_i \in R$.

$\therefore \quad x + y \in R^n$ (Closure property under addition)

(*ii*)
$$\begin{aligned}(x + y) + z &= (x_1 + y_1, x_2 + y_2, ..., x_n + y_n) + (z_1, z_2, ..., z_n)\\ &= (x_1 + y_1 + z_1, x_2 + y_2 + z_2, ..., x_n + y_n + z_n)\\ &= (x_1 + (y_1 + z_1), x_2 + (y_2 + z_2), ..., x_n + (y_n + z_n))\\ &= (x_1, x_2, ..., x_n) + (y_1 + z_1, y_2 + z_2, ..., y_n + z_n)\\ &= x + (y + z)\end{aligned}$$
[Associative property]

(*iii*) Since $0 \in R$, the n-tuple $(0, 0, ..., 0) = 0 \in R^n$.

Now $\quad x + 0 = (x_1 + 0, x_2 + 0, ..., x_n + 0) = (x_1, x_2, ..., x_n) = x$

(0, 0, ..., 0) is the zero vector in R^n

(*iv*) Now $\quad -x = -1(x_1, x_2, ..., x_n) = (-x_1, -x_2, ..., -x_n)$

$$x + (-x) = (x_1, x_2, ..., x_n) + (-x_1, -x_2, ..., -x_n) = (x_1 - x_1, x_2 - x_2, ..., x_n - x_n)$$
$$= (0, 0, ..., 0) = 0$$

$-x$ is the additive inverse of x in R^n.

(*v*)
$$x + y = (x_1 + y_1, x_2 + y_2, ..., x_n + y_n) = (y_1 + x_1, y_2 + x_2, ..., y_n + x_n)$$
$$= (y_1, y_2, ..., y_n) + (x_1, x_2, ..., x_n) = y + x.$$

(Commutativity under addition)

(*vi*) $\quad ax = (ax_1, ax_2, ..., ax_n) \in R^n$, since $ax_1, ax_2, ..., ax_n \in R$

Closure property under scalar multiplication.

(*vii*)
$$a(x + y) = a(x_1 + y_1, x_2 + y_2, ..., x_n + y_n) = (a(x_1 + y_1), a(x_2 + y_2), ..., a(x_n + y_n))$$
$$= (ax_1 + ay_1, ax_2 + ay_2, ..., ax_n + ay_n)$$
$$= (ax_1, ax_2, ..., ax_n) + (ay_1, ay_2, ..., ay_n)$$
$$= ax + by. \qquad \text{[Distributive property]}$$

(*viii*) Let $a, b \in R$,
$$(ab)x = (abx_1, abx_2, ..., abx_n) = (a(bx_1), a(bx_2), ..., a(bx_n))$$
$$= a(bx_1, bx_2, ..., bx_n) = a(bx)$$

(*ix*)
$$(a + b)x = ((a + b)x_1, (a + b)x_2, ..., (a + b)x_n)$$
$$= (ax_1 + bx_1, ax_2 + bx_2, ..., ax_n + bx_n)$$
$$= (ax_1, ax_2, .., ax_n) + (bx_1, bx_2, ..., bx_n)$$
$$= ax + bx$$

(*x*)
$$1.\, x = 1\,(x_1, x_2, ..., x_n) = (1x_1, 1x_2, ..., 1x_n)$$
$$= (x_1, x_2, ..., x_n) = x.$$

2. Let F be any field and S, any non-empty set. Then the set V of all functions from S into F is a vector space; the addition and scalar multiplication in V defined by $(f + g)(x) = f(x) + g(x)$ and $(af)(x) = a\,f(x)$, $f_1\, g \in V$ and $a \in F$.

   In this case, the zero vector in V is the zero function which maps any $x \in S$ into $0 \in F$. *i.e.* $0(x) = 0$, for all $x \in S$.

   Also Additive inverse of $f \in V$ is $-f$ such that $(-f)(x) = -f(x)$, for all $x \in S$.
3. Let V be the set of all $m \times n$ matrices with entries from a field F. Under usual matrix addition and scalar multiplication, V is a vector space.
4. The set V of all polynomials $a_0 + a_1x + a_2x^2 + ... + a_nx^n$ with coefficients from a field F. Then under usual addition of polynomials and multiplication of a polynomial with a scalar, V is a vector space.
5. Let $V = \{(x, y) : x, y \in R\}$. Define addition and scalar multiplication as $(x_1, y_1) + (x_2, y_2) = (x_1 + x_2, y_1 + y_2)$ and $a(x, y) = (ax, y)$. Then V is a vector space over R.

Remark: Let V be a vector space over a field F.

(*i*) $a0 = 0$, for any $a \in F$ and $0 \in V$.

(*ii*) $0x = 0$, for any $x \in V$ and $0 \in F$.

(*iii*) If $kx = 0$, then $k = 0$ or $x = 0$, for any $k \in F$ and $x \in V$.

(*iv*) $(-k)x = k(-x) = -kx$ for any scalar $k \in F$ and $x \in V$.

(*v*) $k(x - y) = kx - ky$, for any $k \in F$ and x and $y \in V$.

3.2. SUBSPACE

Let V be a vector space over a field F. A non-empty subset u of v is a subspace of V if u itself is a vector space under the same operations in V.

Let V be a vector space over a field F. Then V is a subset of itself and hence a subspace, called **trivial** or **improper subspace**. Also {0} consisting of the zero vector alone, is a subspace called **zero** subspace of V.

Theorem. *A non-empty subset U of a vector space V over a field F is a subspace of V if and only if*

(i) for every $x, y \in U$, $x + y \in U$ and (ii) for every $x \in V$ and $a \in F$, $ax \in U$.

Proof. Suppose u is a subspace of V. Then u itself is a vector space. Then clearly u is non-empty and conditions (*i*) and (*ii*) are satisfied.

Conversely assume that U is a non-empty set satisfying conditions (*i*) and (*ii*). To prove u is a vector space.

Since U is non-empty, $x \in U$. Then by (*ii*) $0x = 0 \in U$ *i.e.*, zero element is in U.

Now by (*i*), $\quad 0 + x = x \in U$.

Also $x \in U$ and $-1 \in F$ implies $(-1)x = -x \in U$, using (*ii*)

i.e., additive inverse of x is in U.

The elements of U are all elements of V and V is a vector space, associativity, commutativity, distributive property are all true in U. Thus U is a vector space under the same operations in v. Hence U is a subspace of V.

Note: Let $x, y \in U$ and $a, b \in F$. Then by the above theorem, $ax \in U$ and $by \in U$ (using (*ii*)). Then using (*i*) $ax + by \in U$.

Thus a non-empty subset U of a vector space. V is a subspace if and only if $ax + by \in U$ for any $x, y \in U$ and $a, b \in F$.

i.e. To prove U as a subspace of V, it is enough to prove this condition alone. *i.e.*, $ax + by \in U$, for any $x, y \in U$ and $a, b \in F$.

ILLUSTRATIVE EXAMPLES

Example 1. *The set $U = \{(x, y, 0); x, y \in R\}$. Prove that u is subspace of R^3.*

Sol. Clearly, $(0, 0, 0) \in U$. Hence U is non-empty.

We have to prove $\quad ax + by \in U$, for any $x, y \in U \quad$ and $\quad a, b \in R$.

Let $\quad x = (x_1, y_1, 0) \quad$ and $\quad y = (x_2, y_2, 0) \in U \quad$ and $\quad a, b \in R$

Now
$$ax + by = a(x_1, y_1, 0) + b(x_2, y_2, 0)$$
$$= (ax_1 + bx_2, ay_1 + by_2, 0) \in U$$

Thus U is a subspace of R^3.

Example 2. *Consider the set $\{(x, y, z) \in R^3 : 2x + 5y - 7z) = 0\}$.* (C.U. Dec. 2010)

Sol. Let U be the given set. Then U is non-empty as $(0, 0, 0) \in R^3$

$$[2 \times 0 + 5 \times 0 - 7 \times 0 = 0].$$

Let $x = (x_1, y_1, z_1)$ and $y = (x_2, y_2, z_2)$ be two elements in U and $a, b \in$ R.

$$ax + by = a(x_1, y_1, z_1) + b(x_2, y_2, z_2)$$
$$= (ax_1 + bx_2, ay_1 + by_2, az_1 + bz_2)$$

Now $2(ax_1 + bx_2) + 5(ay_1 + by_2) - 7(az_1 + bz_2)$

$$= a(2x_1 + 5y_1 - 7z_1) + b(2x_2 + 5y_2 - 7z_2)$$
$$= a \times 0 + b \times 0, \quad \because \quad x, y \in \text{U}.$$
$$= 0.$$

Thus $ax + by \in$ U, for any $x, y \in$ U and $a, b \in$ R. Hence a subspace.

Example 3. *Let V be the space of all $n \times n$ matrices, with usual matrix addition and scalar multiplication. U is the set consisting of all symmetric matrices.*

Sol. Clearly 0 matrix (with all entries zero) is in U. So U is non-empty.

Let A, B $\in$ U and A $= (a_{ij})$, B $= (b_{ij}) \in$ U.

Then $a_{ji} = a_{ij}$ and $b_{ji} = b_{ij}$

Now $a\text{A} + b\text{B} = a(a_{ij}) + b(b_{ij}) \quad a, b \in \text{R}$

$$= (aa_{ij} + bb_{ij}),$$

Since A and B are symmetric, $aa_{ji} + bb_{ji} = aa_{ij} + bb_{ij}$.

$\therefore$ aA + bB is symmetric and hence belongs to U. Thus for any A, B $\in$ U and $a, b \in$ R, aA + bB $\in$ U. So U is a subspace.

Example 4. *Show that $U = \{(x, y, z); x, y, z \in Q\}$, Q : set of rational numbers, is not a subspace of R^3.*

Sol. If atleast one condition (i) or (ii) doesn't hold, U is not a subspace.

Let $x = (x, y, z) \in$ U and choose $a = \sqrt{2} \in$ R.

$ax = \sqrt{2}(x, y, z) = (\sqrt{2x}, \sqrt{2y}, \sqrt{2z})$ which is not in U, as the components are not rational.

Hence U is not a subspace of R^3.

Example 5. *Show that U consisting of all singular matrices is not a subspace of V, which is the vector space of all 2×2 matrices over the field R.*

$$u = \left\{\begin{pmatrix} a & b \\ c & d \end{pmatrix}; ad - bc = 0\right\}. \begin{pmatrix} 0 & 0 \\ 0 & 0 \end{pmatrix} \in u, \textit{ hence non-empty.}$$

Sol. Let $\text{A} = \begin{pmatrix} 1 & 0 \\ 0 & 0 \end{pmatrix}$ and $\text{B} = \begin{pmatrix} 0 & 0 \\ 0 & 1 \end{pmatrix} \in \text{U}$

Then $|\text{A}| = 0$ and $|\text{B}| = 0$

$1 \in$ R,

$$\text{A} + \text{B} = \begin{pmatrix} 1 & 0 \\ 0 & 0 \end{pmatrix} + \begin{pmatrix} 0 & 0 \\ 0 & 1 \end{pmatrix} = \begin{pmatrix} 1 & 0 \\ 0 & 1 \end{pmatrix}$$

But $|\text{A} + \text{B}| = 1 \neq 0 \quad \therefore \quad \text{A} + \text{B} \notin \text{U}.$

So U is not a subspace.

3.3. LINEAR COMBINATIONS

Let v be a vector space over a field F and let $x_1, x_2, ..., x_n$ be vectors in V. Then any vector $x \in$ V is a linear combination of $x_1, x_2, ..., x_n$ if there exist scalars $a_1, a_2, ..., a_n$ such that

$$x = a_1x_1 + a_2x_2 + ... + a_nx_n.$$

Example 6. *Any vector in R^2 can be represented as a linear combination of (1, 0) and (0, 1).*

Sol. Let $(x, y) \in R^2$ be any vector in R^2

Then $(x, y) = x(1, 0) + y(0, 1)$

In general $(x_1, x_2, ..., x_n) = x_1(1, 0, ..., 0) + x_2(0, 1, ..., 0) + ... + x_n(0, 0, ..., 1)$ for any $(x_1, x_2, ..., x_n)$ in R^n.

Example 7. *Show that the vector (3, 9, – 4, 2) is a linear combination of the vectors (1, – 2, 0, 3), (2, 3, 0, – 1) and (2, – 1, 2, 1).* (C.U. June 2007, Dec. 2006)

Sol. Let $(3, 9, -4, -2) = a(1, -2, 0, 3) + b(2, 3, 0, -1) + c(2, -1, 2, 1)$

i.e., $a + 2b + 2c = 3, \quad -2a + 3b - c = 9, \quad 2c = -4, \quad 3a - b + c = -2$

$$c = -2 \quad \therefore \quad a + 2b = 7,$$
$$-2a + 3b = 7$$
$$3a - b = 0.$$

$\therefore \quad b = 3a; 7a = 7 \quad \Rightarrow \quad a = 1$

Thus $a = 1, b = 3$ and $c = -2$

$\therefore$ (3, 9, – 4, – 2) is a linear combination of the given vectors.

Example 8. *Express (3, – 1, 3) as a linear combination of (1, – 3, 1), (1, 1, – 1) and (2, 0, 3).* (C.U. Dec. 2006)

Sol. Let $(3, -1, 3) = a(1, -3, 1) + b(1, 1, -1) + c(2, 0, 3)$

i.e., $a + b + 2c = 3, \quad -3a + b = -1, \quad a - b + 3c = 3$

Changing the augmented matrix into echelon form,

$$\begin{bmatrix} 1 & 1 & 2 & 3 \\ -3 & 1 & 0 & -1 \\ 1 & -1 & 3 & 3 \end{bmatrix} \sim \begin{bmatrix} 1 & 1 & 2 & 3 \\ 0 & 4 & 6 & 8 \\ 0 & -2 & 1 & 0 \end{bmatrix} \sim \begin{bmatrix} 1 & 1 & 2 & 3 \\ 0 & 4 & 6 & 8 \\ 0 & 0 & 8 & 8 \end{bmatrix}$$

rank of Augmented matrix and coefficient matrix are equal. Hence a unique solution for the system of equations.

$$\therefore \quad c = 1, b = \frac{1}{2} \text{ and } a = \frac{1}{2}.$$

$$\therefore \quad (3, -1, 3) = \frac{1}{2}(1, -3, 1) + \frac{1}{2}(1, 1, -1) + (2, 0, 3).$$

Example 9. *For what value of k, the vector (1, – 2, k) is a linear combination of (3, 0, – 2) and (2, – 1, – 5).*

Sol. Let $(1, -2, k) = a(3, 0, -2) + b(2, -1, -5)$

i.e., $3a + 2b = 1, -b = -2, -2a - 5b = k$

From this, $b = 2, \quad \therefore \quad 3a = -3 \quad \therefore \quad a = -1$

Then $2 - 10 = k$ *i.e.,* $k = -8$.

Example 10. *Express* $\begin{pmatrix} 3 & -1 \\ 1 & -2 \end{pmatrix}$ *as a linear combination of* $\begin{pmatrix} 1 & 1 \\ 0 & -1 \end{pmatrix}, \begin{pmatrix} 1 & 1 \\ -1 & 0 \end{pmatrix}$ *and* $\begin{pmatrix} 1 & -1 \\ 0 & 0 \end{pmatrix}$.

Sol. Let
$$\begin{pmatrix} 3 & -1 \\ 1 & -2 \end{pmatrix} = a\begin{pmatrix} 1 & 1 \\ 0 & -1 \end{pmatrix} + b\begin{pmatrix} 1 & 1 \\ -1 & 0 \end{pmatrix} + c\begin{pmatrix} 1 & -1 \\ 0 & 0 \end{pmatrix}$$
$$= \begin{pmatrix} a+b+c & a+b-c \\ -b & -a \end{pmatrix}$$

Comparing,

$\therefore$ $\quad -b = 1, -a = -2, a + b + c = 3$ and $a + b - c = -1$

Solving $\quad a = 2, b = -1$ and $c = 2.$

Thus
$$\begin{pmatrix} 3 & -1 \\ 1 & -2 \end{pmatrix} = 2\begin{pmatrix} 1 & 1 \\ 0 & -1 \end{pmatrix} - \begin{pmatrix} 1 & 1 \\ -1 & 0 \end{pmatrix} + 2\begin{pmatrix} 1 & -1 \\ 0 & 0 \end{pmatrix}.$$

Example 11. *Also write* $\begin{pmatrix} 2 & 1 \\ -1 & -2 \end{pmatrix}$ *in terms of the above vectors.*

Sol. Let
$$\begin{pmatrix} 2 & 1 \\ -1 & -2 \end{pmatrix} = a\begin{pmatrix} 1 & 1 \\ 0 & -1 \end{pmatrix} + b\begin{pmatrix} 1 & 1 \\ -1 & 0 \end{pmatrix} + c\begin{pmatrix} 1 & -1 \\ 0 & 0 \end{pmatrix} \quad ...(1)$$
$$= \begin{pmatrix} a+b+c & a+b-c \\ -b & -a \end{pmatrix}$$

Equating, $\quad a = 2, b = 1, a + b + c = 2$ and $a + b - c = 1$

$\quad a + b + c = 2 \Rightarrow c = -1.$

But last equation is not satisfied.

So we can't find a, b, c such that (1) is satisfied.

Example 12. *Represent* $3t^2 + 8t - 5$ *as a linear combination of* $2t^2 + 3t - 4$ *and* $t^2 - 2t - 3$.

Sol. Let $\quad 3t^2 + 8t - 5 = a(2t^2 + 3t - 4) + b(t^2 - 2t - 3)$

$\quad = (2a + b)t^2 + (3a - 2b)t - (4a + 3b)$

Equating, $\quad 2a + b = 3, \quad 3a - 2b = 8, \quad 4a + 3b = 5$

Solving, $\quad b = -1, a = 2$

$\therefore$ $\quad 3t^2 + 8t - 5 = 2(2t^2 + 3t - 4) - (t^2 - 2t - 3).$

3.4. LINEAR SPAN

If S is a non-empty subset of a vector space V over a field F. The subspace of V formed by the linear combinations of vectors in S is called linear span of S or subspace generated by S, denoted by L(S).

Theorem. *If* $S = \{x_1, x_2, ..., x_n\}$ *be a set of vectors in V. Then span S is a subspace of V.*

Proof. Let U be the set of all linear combinations of vectors in S. U is non-empty. To prove U is a subspace of V.

Let $x, y \in$ U *i.e.*, x and y are linear combinations of vectors in S

Let $x = a_1x_1 + a_2x_2 + ... + a_nx_n$ and $y = b_1x_1 + b_2x_2 + ... + b_nx_n$ where $a_1, a_2, ... a_n, b_1, b_2, ... b_n$ are scalar.

Now $\quad ax + by = a(a_1x_1 + a_2x_2 + ... + a_nx_n) + b(b_1x_1 + b_2x_2 + ... + b_nx_n), a, b \in$ R.

$$= (aa_1 + bb_1)x_1 + (aa_2 + bb_2)x_2 + ... + (aa_n + bb_n)x_n,$$

which is a linear combination of $x_1, x_2, ..., x_n$ and $\in$ U.

Thus for any $x, y \in$ U and $a, b \in$ R, $ax + by \in$ U. Hence U is a subspace of V. *i.e.,* span S is a subspace of V.

Definition. (Linear Span)

The vectors $x_1, x_2, .., x_n$ in a vector space V are said to span V if every vector in V is a linear combination of $x_1, x_2, ..., x_n$. Also if S = $\{x_1, x_2, ..., x_n\}$, we can say that S spans V or span S = V. *(C.U. Oct. 2011)*

If any arbitrary vector in V can be represented as a linear combination of the vectors $x_1, x_2, ..., x_n$ in V, we can say that $\{x_1, x_2, ..., x_n\}$ spans V.

Example 13. *Show that (1, 1, 1), (0, 1, 1) and (0, 1, – 1) generate R^3.*

Sol. Let (x, y, z) be any element in R^3. If we can represent (x, y, z) as a linear combination of the given vectors, then they span R^3.

Let $$(x, y, z) = a(1, 1, 1) + b(0, 1, 1) + c(0, 1, -1)$$
$$= (a, a + b + c, a + b - c)$$

Comparing both sides,

$$x = a, y = a + b + c, z = a + b - c$$

$$\therefore \quad \begin{aligned} a + b + c &= y \\ a + b - c &= z \\ a &= x \end{aligned} \qquad \begin{bmatrix} 1 & 1 & 1 \\ 1 & 1 & -1 \\ 1 & 0 & 0 \end{bmatrix} \begin{bmatrix} a \\ b \\ c \end{bmatrix} = \begin{bmatrix} y \\ z \\ x \end{bmatrix}$$

Changing the augmented matrix into echelon form,

$$\begin{bmatrix} 1 & 1 & 1 & y \\ 1 & 1 & -1 & z \\ 1 & 0 & 0 & x \end{bmatrix} \sim \begin{bmatrix} 1 & 1 & 1 & y \\ 0 & 0 & -2 & z-y \\ 0 & -1 & -1 & x-y \end{bmatrix} \sim \begin{bmatrix} 1 & 1 & 1 & y \\ 0 & -1 & -1 & x-y \\ 0 & 0 & -2 & z-y \end{bmatrix}$$

which is in the echelon form.

$$\therefore \quad z - y = -2c \quad \therefore \quad c = \frac{z-y}{2}$$

$$b = y - x - c = \frac{3y - 2x - z}{2} \quad \text{and} \quad a = x$$

$$\therefore \text{ Any} \quad (x, y, z) = x(1, 1, 1) + \left(\frac{3y - 2x - z}{2}\right)(0, 1, 1) + \left(\frac{z-y}{2}\right)(0, 1, -1).$$

3.5. LINEAR DEPENDENCE AND INDEPENDENCE OF VECTORS

The vectors $x_1, x_2, ..., x_n$ of a vector space V over F is said to be **linear dependent** if there exist constants $a_1, a_2, ..., a_n$ not all zero such that $a_1x_1 + a_2x_2 + ... + a_nx_n = 0$.

If $a_1x_1 + a_2x_2 + ... + a_nx_n = 0$ implies $a_1 = a_2 = ... = a_n = 0$, the vectors are said to be **linearly independent.**

Example 14. *Check whether or not the vectors are linearly dependent.*

(i) (2, 0, 1), (1, 1, 1), (1, – 2, 0).

(ii) (2, 3, – 1), (3, 2, 2), (4, 4, – 1)

(iii) (1, 3, 2, – 2), (4, 1, – 1, 3), (1, 1, 2, 0), (0, 0, 0, 1)

Sol. (*i*) Let a, b, c be scalars and let $a(2, 0, 1) + b(1, 1, 1) + c(1, -2, 0) = (0, 0, 0)$. ...(1)

i.e., $(2a + b + c, b - 2c, a + b) = (0, 0, 0)$.

Comparing,
$$2a + b + c = 0$$
$$b - 2c = 0$$
$$a + b = 0$$

Solving these, $a = -b \quad \therefore \quad -b + c = 0$

$b - 2c = 0 \quad$ *i.e.,* $\quad b = 0$ and $c = 0$

So $a = 0$. Thus all the scalars are zero,

i.e., (1) $\Rightarrow$ $a = b = c = 0$. Hence by definition the given vectors are not linearly dependent *i.e.,* they are dependent.

(*ii*) Consider $a(2, 3, -1) + b(3, 2, 2) + c(4, 4, -1) = (0, 0, 0)$, where a, b, c are scalars. ...(1)

$$(2a + 3b + 4c, 3a + 2b + 4c, -a + 2b - c) = (0, 0, 0)$$

i.e.,
$$2a + 3b + 4c = 0$$
$$3a + 2b + 4c = 0$$
$$-a + 2b - c = 0$$

i.e.,
$$\begin{bmatrix} 2 & 3 & 4 \\ 3 & 2 & 4 \\ -1 & 2 & -1 \end{bmatrix} \begin{bmatrix} a \\ b \\ c \end{bmatrix} = \begin{bmatrix} 0 \\ 0 \\ 0 \end{bmatrix} \quad ...(2)$$

Changing the co-efficient matrix into echelon form,

$$A = \begin{bmatrix} 2 & 3 & 4 \\ 3 & 2 & 4 \\ -1 & 2 & -1 \end{bmatrix} \sim \begin{bmatrix} 1 & -2 & 1 \\ 2 & 3 & 4 \\ 3 & 2 & 4 \end{bmatrix} \sim \begin{bmatrix} 1 & -2 & 1 \\ 0 & 7 & 2 \\ 0 & 8 & 1 \end{bmatrix} \sim \begin{bmatrix} 1 & -2 & 1 \\ 0 & 1 & 2/7 \\ 0 & 0 & -9/7 \end{bmatrix}$$

Rank (A) = 3. So the homogeneous system (2) has only the trivial solution *i.e.,* $a = b = c = 0$

Thus (1) implies all the scalars zero. So the given vectors are linearly independent.

Note. To find whether or not the given vectors, linearly independent, it is enough to check whether the corresponding homogeneous system has trivial solution or not *i.e.,* whether rank (A) = number of unknowns.

Another Method

Form the matrix A with the given vectors as rows and find its determinant. If $|A| = 0$, then rank (A) < number of unknowns and hence there is a non-trivial solution. Hence the given vectors are dependent. If $|A| \neq 0$, rank (A) = number of unknowns and hence only the trivial solution. So the vectors are independent.

If the determinant of the matrix, formed with the given vectors is zero, the vectors are linearly dependent and otherwise linearly independent.

(*iii*) Let A be the matrix with these vectors as rows.

$$|A| = \begin{vmatrix} 1 & 3 & 2 & -2 \\ 4 & 1 & -1 & 3 \\ 1 & 1 & 2 & 0 \\ 0 & 0 & 0 & 1 \end{vmatrix} = 1 \begin{vmatrix} 1 & 3 & 2 \\ 4 & 1 & -1 \\ 1 & 1 & 2 \end{vmatrix} \neq 0.$$

Hence the given vectors are linearly independent.

Example 15. *Every non-zero vector x in a vector space is itself independent.*

Sol. Let $x \neq 0 \in V$. Then $ax = 0$ implies $a = 0$, $\therefore$ $x \neq 0$.

Hence independent.

Example 16. *If two of the vectors $x_1, x_2, ..., x_n$ are equal, the vectors are linearly dependent.*

Sol. Let $x_2 = x_3$

Then $0x_1 + x_2 - x_3 + 0x_4 + ... + 0x_n = 0$ with the coefficient of x_2 and x_3 non-zero. Hence by definition, $x_1, x_2, ..., x_n$ are linearly dependent.

3.6. LINEARLY INDEPENDENT OR DEPENDENT SET

Let $S = \{x_1, x_2, ..., x_n\}$ be a set of vectors. Then S is a linearly independent (or dependent) set if the vectors $x_1, x_2, ..., x_n$ in it are linearly independent (or dependent).

Example 17. *A set of vectors containing the zero vector is linearly dependent.*

Sol. Let $\{x_1, x_2, x_3\}$ be a set of vectors in which $x_2 = 0$.

Then the linear combination $a_1x_1 + a_2x_2 + a_3x_3 = 0$ with $a_2 \neq 0$

Hence by definition, the given set is linearly dependent.

Example 18. *Every subset of a linearly independent set is linearly independent.*

Sol. Let $S = \{x_1, x_2, ..., x_n\} = \{x_i\}_{i=1}^{n}$ be a linearly independent set.

Let $S_1 = \{x_1, x_2, ..., x_r\}, x_n$ be a subset of S.

To prove S_1 is linearly independent.

Consider $a_1x_1 + a_2x_2 + ... + a_rx_r = 0$ ...(1)

i.e., $a_1x_1 + a_2x_2 + ... + a_rx_r + 0x_{r+1} + ... + 0x_n = 0$. Since S is independent, $a_1 = a_2 = ... = a_r = 0$

Thus (1) implies $a_1 = a_2 = ... = a_r = 0$. Hence S_1 is independent.

Example 19. *Every superset of a linearly dependent set is dependent.*

Sol. Let $S = \{x_1, x_2, ..., x_r\}$ be linearly dependent.

Let $S_1 = \{x_1, x_2, ..., x_n\}$, $r < n$. To prove S_1 is linearly dependent.

Since S is dependent, there exist scalars $a_1, a_2, ..., a_r$ not all zero such that

$$a_1x_1 + a_2x_2 + ... + a_rx_r = 0. \text{ Let } a_i \neq 0$$

Now, $a_1x_1 + a_2x_2 + ... + a_ix_i + ... + a_rx_r + 0x_{r+1} + ... + 0x_n = 0$, with $a_i \neq 0$

So S_1 is dependent.

Example 20. *The non-zero vectors $x_1, x_2, ..., x_n$ in a vector space V are linearly dependent if and only if one of the vectors x_j, $j \geq 2$ is a linear combination of the preceding vectors $x_1, x_2, ..., x_{j-1}$.*

Sol. Let x_j be a linear combination of the preceding vectors.

To prove $x_1, x_2, ..., x_n$ are dependent.

Let $x_j = a_1x_1 + a_2x_2 + ... + a_{j-1}x_{j-1}$. [*i.e.,* a linear combination of $x_1, ..., x_{j-1}$]

Now $a_1x_1 + ... + a_{j-1}x_{j-1} + (-1)x_j + 0x_{j+1} + ... + 0x_n = x_j - x_j + 0 = 0$ with $a_j = -1 \neq 0$. Thus $x_1, x_2, ..., x_n$ are linearly dependent.

Conversely assume that the non-zero vectors $x_1, x_2, ..., x_n$ are linearly dependent. To prove x_j is a linear combination of $x_1, x_2, ..., x_{j-1}$.

Since $x_1, x_2, ..., x_n$ are dependent, $a_1x_1 + ... + a_nx_n = 0$ with some $a_i \neq 0$.

Let r be the highest integer for which $a_r \neq 0$;

Then if $r > 1$,

$$a_1x_1 + a_2x_2 + ... + a_rx_r + 0x_{r+1} + ... + 0x_n = 0$$

i.e., $$a_rx_r = -a_1x_1 - a_2x_2 - ... - a_{r-1}x_{r-1}$$

$\therefore$ $$x_r = \frac{-a_1}{a_r}x_1 - \frac{a_2}{a_r}x_2 - ... - \frac{a_{r-1}}{a_r}x_{r-1}$$ which is a linear combination of $x_1, x_2, ..., x_{r-1}$.

If $r = 1$,

$$a_1 \neq 0 \quad \text{and} \quad a_1v_1 = 0$$

i.e., $v_1 = 0$ which is a contradiction.

(Since the vectors are non-zero).

Hence $r > 1$

Thus if the non-zero vectors $x_1, x_2, ..., x_n$ are linearly dependent, any x_j is a linear combination of the preceding vectors $x_1, ..., x_{j-1}$.

Example 21. $S = \{x_i\}_{i=1}^{n}$ *is linearly dependent if and only if some vectors in S is a linear combination of the other vectors in S.*

Sol. Suppose that S is linearly dependent. To prove $x_j = b_1x_1 + ... + b_{j-1}x_{j-1} + b_{j+1}x_j + ... + b_nx_n$ for any x_j. Since S is linearly dependent, $a_1x_1 + ... + a_jx_j + ... + a_nx_n = 0$ with $a_j \neq 0$.

Then $$x_j = \frac{-a_1}{a_j}x_1 - \frac{a_2}{a_j}x_2 ... - \frac{a_n}{a_j}x_n$$

$= b_1x_1 + b_2x_2 + ... + b_nx_n$ which is a linear combination of the remaining vectors.

Conversely assume that any x_j is a linear combination of the remaining vectors. To prove $\{x_i\}_1^n$ is dependent $x_j = a_1x_1 + ... + a_{j-1}x_{j-1} + a_{j+1}x_{j+1} + ... + a_nx_n$

$\therefore$ $a_1x_1 + ... + a_{j-1}x_{j-1} + (-x_j) + a_{j+1}x_j + ... + a_nx_n = 0$ (by adding $-x_j$ on both sides) where $a_j = -1 \neq 0$

Thus $a_1x_1 + ... + a_nx_n = 0$ with some non-zero scalar, $(a_j = -1)$

$\therefore$ The vectors $x_1, x_2, ..., x_n$ are linearly dependent.

Remark (1). If $\{x_1, x_2, ..., x_n\}$ is linearly independent vectors in a vector space, then they must be distinct and none can be the zero vector.

Remark (2). The vectors x_1 and x_2 are linearly dependent if and only if one is a scalar multiple of other.

(In example 8, put $n = 2$).

Example 22. *If x_1, x_2, x_3 are linearly independent vectors in a vector space V, show that the vectors $x_1 + x_2, x_2 + x_3, x_3 + x_1$ are linearly independent.*

Sol. Let a, b, c be scalars such that $a(x_1 + x_2) + b(x_2 + x_3) + c(x_3 + x_1) = 0$

To prove that $a = b = c = 0$.

$(a + c)x_1 + (a + b)x_2 + (b + c)x_3 = 0$. Since x_1, x_2, x_3 are independent, $a + c = 0, a + b = 0, b + c = 0$

i.e. $$\begin{bmatrix} 1 & 0 & 1 \\ 1 & 1 & 0 \\ 0 & 1 & 1 \end{bmatrix}\begin{bmatrix} a \\ b \\ c \end{bmatrix} = \begin{bmatrix} 0 \\ 0 \\ 0 \end{bmatrix} \quad i.e., \quad AX = 0$$

Now $|A| \neq 0 \quad \therefore \quad a = b = c = 0.$

Hence $x_1 + x_2, x_2 + x_3, x_3 + x_1$, are independent.

Note 1. Any rearrangement of linearly independent vectors is also independent.

2. Null set is linearly independent.

3.7. BASIS AND DIMENSION

A set of vectors $\{x_1, x_2, ..., x_n\}$ is a basis of a vector space V over a field F if (*i*) $\{x_i\}_{i=1}^{n}$ spans V (*ii*) $\{x_i\}_1^n$ is linearly independent. Thus a set of linearly independent vectors which span the vector space is called basis. The number of elements in the basis is called the dimension of the vector space.

Example 23. *The set S = {(1, 0, 0), (0, 1, 0), (0, 0, 1)} is a basis of* R^3, *called the natural basis.*

i.e., *S spans* R^3 *and S is linearly independent.*

Consider the matrix with these vectors as rows

i.e., $$\begin{bmatrix} 1 & 0 & 0 \\ 0 & 1 & 0 \\ 0 & 0 & 1 \end{bmatrix}$$ *which is in echelon form and hence independent.*

Sol. Let (x, y, z) be any element in R^3.

Then $(x, y, z) = x(1, 0, 0) + y(0, 1, 0) + z(0, 0, 1).$

i.e., any element of R^3 can be represented as the linear combination of these vectors.

Thus S is a basis of R^3

In general the *n*-tuples $e_1 = (1, 0, 0, ..., 0), e_2 = (0, 1, 0, ..., 0), ... e_n = (0, 0, ..., 1)$ is a basis of R^n (natural basis).

Example 24. *The vectors (1, 2, – 3), (2, –1, 3) and (3, 1, 2) form a basis of* R^3.

(C.U. June 2007)

The determinent of the matrix A, formed with these vector as rows

$$|A| = \begin{bmatrix} 1 & 2 & -3 \\ 2 & -1 & 3 \\ 3 & 1 & 2 \end{bmatrix} \neq 0.$$ *Hence these vectors are independent.*

Sol. Let (x, y, z) be any vector in R^3. If (x, y, z) is a linear combination of the given vectors, they span R^3.

Let $$(x, y, z) = a(1, 2, -3,) + b(2, -1, 3) + c(3, 1, 2)$$
$$= (a + 2b + 3c, 2a - b + c, -3a + 3b + 2c)$$

i.e., $$\begin{bmatrix} 1 & 2 & 3 \\ 2 & -1 & 1 \\ -3 & 3 & 2 \end{bmatrix}\begin{bmatrix} a \\ b \\ c \end{bmatrix} = \begin{bmatrix} x \\ y \\ z \end{bmatrix} \quad AX = B \text{ (say)}$$

$$\text{Augmented matrix, (A : B)} = \begin{bmatrix} 1 & 2 & 3 & x \\ 2 & -1 & 1 & y \\ -3 & 3 & 2 & z \end{bmatrix} \sim \begin{bmatrix} 1 & 2 & 3 & x \\ 0 & -5 & -5 & y-2x \\ 0 & 9 & 11 & z-11x \end{bmatrix}$$

$$\sim \begin{bmatrix} 1 & 2 & 3 & x \\ 0 & 1 & 1 & \dfrac{2x-y}{5} \\ 0 & 9 & 11 & z-11x \end{bmatrix}$$

$$\sim \begin{bmatrix} 1 & 2 & 3 & x \\ 0 & 1 & 1 & \dfrac{2x-y}{5} \\ 0 & 0 & 2 & \dfrac{9y-73x+5z}{5} \end{bmatrix}$$

rank (A : B) = rank (A). Hence a unique solution for this system of equations

$$c = \frac{9y-73x+5z}{10}, \; b = \frac{77x - 11y - 5z}{10}, \; a = x - 2b - 3c.$$

Thus the given vectors are linearly independent and span R^3. Hence a basis of R^3.

Note. The vector space R^3 have more than one basis, and contains 3 vectors. *i.e.,* Every vector space may have many bases, but with same number of vectors in it.

3.8. FINITE DIMENSIONAL AND INFINITE DIMENSIONAL VECTOR SPACES

A vector space V is called finite dimensional if there are only a finite number of elements in the basis of V. If the number of basis elements is not finite, the vector space is of infinite dimensional. The vector space {0} is defined to have dimension 0. Dimension of V is denoted as dim V.

Example 25. *The set of* 2×3 *matrices* $\begin{pmatrix} 1 & 0 & 0 \\ 0 & 0 & 0 \end{pmatrix}, \begin{pmatrix} 0 & 1 & 0 \\ 0 & 0 & 0 \end{pmatrix}, \begin{pmatrix} 0 & 0 & 1 \\ 0 & 0 & 0 \end{pmatrix}, \begin{pmatrix} 0 & 0 & 0 \\ 1 & 0 & 0 \end{pmatrix},$ $\begin{pmatrix} 0 & 0 & 0 \\ 0 & 1 & 0 \end{pmatrix}, \begin{pmatrix} 0 & 0 & 0 \\ 0 & 0 & 1 \end{pmatrix}$ *is a basis of the vector space V of all* 2×3 *matrices.*

Then dim V = 6.

Note 4. In this chapter, unless otherwise stated, we consider finite dimensional vector spaces.

Theorem. *If* $\{x_i\}_1^n$ *is a basis of a vector space V, then every vector in V has a unique representation, as a linear combination of basis elements.*

Proof. Let $x \in$ V. Then x is a linear combination of basis elements (since those elements span V). To prove this representation of x is unique.

Let $\quad x = a_1x_1 + a_2x_2 + ... + a_nx_n$ and

$\quad x = b_1x_1 + b_2x_2 + ... + b_nx_n$ be two different representation of x.

$\therefore \quad x - x = 0 = (a_1 - b_1)x_1 + (a_2 - b_2)x_2 + ... + (a_n - b_n)x_n.$

But $\{x_i\}_1^n$ is linearly independent, being a basis,

$$a_1 - b_1 = a_2 - b_2 = ... = a_n - b_n = 0.$$

i.e., $\quad a_1 = b_1, a_2 = b_2, ..., a_n = b_n$

i.e., Both the representation of x are same.

i.e., the representation of x as a linear combination of the basis elements is unique.

Theorem. *If $S = \{x_i\}_{i=1}^{n}$ be a set of non-zero vectors in a vector space V and let U = span S. Then some subset of S is a basis of U.*

Proof. If S is linearly independent, it is a basis of U [$\because$ S spans U].

If S in linearly dependent

then $a_1x_1 + ... + a_nx_n = 0$ with some $a_i \neq 0$.

Now by a theorem, some x_j is a linear combination of the preceding vectors. Now we delete x_j from S. Let S_1 be the resulting subset of S. Then $S_1 = \{x_1, ..., x_{j-1}, x_{j+1}, ..., x_n\}$ also spans U.

Again if S_1 is linearly independent, it is a basis. If S_1 is dependent, delete a vector of S_1 which is a linear combination of the preceding vectors of S_1 and let S_2 be the new set, which spans U. Continuing like this, as S is finite, we can find a subset S_m of S which is linearly independent and spans U *i.e.,* S_m is a subset of S which is linearly independent and spans U. So it is a basis.

Theorem. *Suppose $\{x_1, x_2, ..., x_n\}$ generates a vector space V. If $\{y_1, y_2, ..., y_m\}$ is linearly independent, then $m \leq n$ and V is generated by a set of the form $\{y_1, y_2, ..., y_m, x_{i1}, x_{i2}, ..., x_{i(n-m)}\}$.*

Proof. Let $y_1 \in$ V. Since $\{x_1, x_2, ..., x_n\}$ generates V, y_1 is a linear combination of $x_1, x_2, ..., x_n$. So $S_1 = \{y_1, x_1, ..., x_n\}$ is linearly dependent and generates V. We've the theorem, $\{x_1, x_2, ..., x_n\}$ is linearly dependent if and only if one of them is a linear combination of the preceding vectors.

Thus one of the vector is $\{y_1, x_1, ..., x_n\}$ is a linear combination of the preceding vectors. This vector cannot be y_1, so it must be one of the x_i's say x_j. Now delete x_j from the set S_1 and obtain the generating set $S_2 = \{y_1, x_1, ..., x_{j-1}, x_{j+1}, ..., x_n\}$. Repeat this with $y_2 \in$ V. Since S_2 generates V, the set $S_3 = \{y_1, y_2, x_1, ..., x_{j-1}, x_{j+1}, ..., x_n\}$ generates V.

Again applying the above theorem, one of the vectors in S_3 is a linear combination of the preceding vectors. This vector cannot be y_1 or y_2 and hence it must be some x_i*'s* say x_k. Delete this x_k and $S_4 = \{y_1, y_2, x_1, ..., x_{j-1}, x_{j+1}, ..., x_{k-1}, x_{k+1}, ..., x_n\}$ generates V and Repeating these steps for m times, if $m \leq n$, $\{y_1, y_2, ..., y_m, x_{i1}, x_{i2}, ..., x_{i(n-m)}\}$ is a generating set of V [At each step we add one y_i's and delete one of the x_i's in the generating set].

If $m > n$, aften n steps, $\{y_1, y_2, ..., y_n\}$ generates V and y_{n+1} is a linear combination of $y_1, y_2, ..., y_n$ which contradicts the fact that $\{y_i\}$ is independent

$\therefore$ $m > n$ is not possible. Thus $m \leq n$.

Remark. If dim V = n, then any linearly independent set is part of a basis.

Theorem. *Every basis of a finite dimensional vector space has same number of vectors.*

Proof. Let V be a finite dimensional vector space.

Let $\{x_i\}_1^n$ and $\{y_i\}_1^m$ be two bases of V.

Since $\{x_i\}_1^n$ generates V and $\{y_i\}_1^m$ is linearly independent, by the above theorem,

$$m \leq n \quad ...(1)$$

Similarly $\{y_i\}_1^m$ generates V and $\{x_i\}_1^n$ is linearly independent, $n \leq m$. ...(2)

From (1) and (2), $m = n$ *i.e.,* the two bases have same number of elements.

Theorem. *If V is a finite dimensional vector space with dimension n. Then any set of (n + 1) or more vectors is linearly dependent.*

Proof. Given dim (V) = n. Let $\{x_i\}_1^n$ be a basis. Let $\{y_1, y_2, ..., y_m\}$ be a set of vectors in V, where $m > n$. Since $\{x_i\}_1^n$ is a basis, it generates V.

$$\therefore \quad y_1 = a_{11} x_1 + ... + a_{1n} x_n$$
$$y_2 = a_{21} x_1 + ... + a_{2n} x_n$$
$$\vdots$$
$$y_m = a_{m1} x_1 + ... + a_{mn} x_n,$$

To prove $\{y_1, ..., y_m\}$ is linearly dependent.

Let $\quad a_1 y_1 + a_2 y_2 + ... + a_m y_m = 0$

i.e., $\quad a_1(a_{11} x_1 + ... + a_{1n} x_n) + a_2(a_{21} x_1 + ... + a_{2n} x_n) + ... + a_m(a_{m1} x_1 + ... + a_{mn} x_n) = 0$

i.e., $\quad (a_1 a_{11} + a_2 a_{21} + ... + a_m a_{m1}) x_1 + ... + (a_1 a_{1n} + a_2 a_{2n} + ... + a_m a_{mn}) x_n = 0.$

Since $\{x_i\}_1^n$ is linearly independent, being a basis,

$$a_1 a_{11} + a_2 a_{21} + ... + a_m a_{n1} = 0,$$
$$\vdots$$
$$a_1 a_{1n} + a_2 a_{2n} + ... + a_m a_{mn} = 0 \quad (n \text{ equations in } m \text{ unknowns})$$

Since $m > n$, this system must have non-trivial solution.

$\therefore$ Some a_1 or a_2 or ... or a_m is non-zero.

Thus $a_1 y_1 + ... + a_m y_m = 0$ with some $a_i \neq 0$. Hence $\{y_i\}_1^m$ is linearly dependent.

Theorem. *If V is an n dimensional vector space and W a subspace of V. Then dim W* $\leq n$. *If dim W = n, then W = V.*

Proof. Since dim V = n, any set of more than n vectors is linearly dependent.

Since W is a subspace of V, a basis of W contains not more than n elements.

$$\therefore \quad \dim W \leq n.$$

If $\{x_1, x_2, ..., x_n\}$ is a basis of W, this set is linearly independent.

Since dim V = n, this set is also a basis of V.

Hence W = V.

Example 26. *Find a basis and dimension of the subspace U in R^4 generated by (1, – 1, 2, 4), (2, 1, 3, 0) and (1, 2, – 1, 0).* (C.U. Dec. 2007)

Sol. Form the matrix A with the given vectors as rows.

$$A = \begin{bmatrix} 1 & -1 & 2 & 4 \\ 2 & 1 & 3 & 0 \\ 1 & 2 & -1 & 0 \end{bmatrix} \sim \begin{bmatrix} 1 & -1 & 2 & 4 \\ 0 & 3 & -1 & -8 \\ 0 & 3 & -3 & -4 \end{bmatrix} \sim \begin{bmatrix} 1 & -1 & 2 & 4 \\ 0 & 3 & -1 & -8 \\ 0 & 0 & -2 & -4 \end{bmatrix},$$

which is in the echelon form.

The non-zero rows of the echelon matrix form the basis of U.

$\therefore$ dim U = 3; {(1, – 1, 2, 4), (0, 3, – 1, – 8), (0, 0, – 2, 4) is a basis of U.

Example 27. *Find a basis and dimension of the vector subspace V spanned by the vectors (4, – 1, 7), (3, 3, 4), (2, 1, 3) and (1, – 1, 2).* (C.U. June 2007)

Sol. Let A be the matrix formed with the given vectors as rows.

$$A = \begin{bmatrix} 4 & -1 & 7 \\ 3 & 3 & 4 \\ 2 & 1 & 3 \\ 1 & -1 & 2 \end{bmatrix} \sim \begin{bmatrix} 1 & -1 & 2 \\ 4 & -1 & 7 \\ 3 & 3 & 4 \\ 2 & 1 & 3 \end{bmatrix} \sim \begin{bmatrix} 1 & -1 & 2 \\ 0 & 3 & -1 \\ 0 & 6 & -2 \\ 0 & 3 & -1 \end{bmatrix} \sim \begin{bmatrix} 1 & -1 & 2 \\ 0 & 3 & -1 \\ 0 & 0 & 0 \\ 0 & 0 & 0 \end{bmatrix}$$ which is in echelon form.

The non-zero rows (1, – 1, 2), (0, 3, – 1) are independent and hence form a basis of V. dim V = 2.

Example 28. *Find the dimension and a basis of the solution space W of the system of linear equations*

$$x + 2y - 4z + 3r - S = 0$$
$$x + 2y - 2z + 2r + S = 0$$
$$2x + 4y - 2z + 3r + 4S = 0$$

Sol. The given system be AX = 0

$$A = \begin{bmatrix} 1 & 2 & -4 & 3 & -1 \\ 1 & 2 & -2 & 2 & 1 \\ 2 & 4 & -2 & 3 & 4 \end{bmatrix} \sim \begin{bmatrix} 1 & 2 & -4 & 3 & -1 \\ 0 & 0 & 2 & -1 & 2 \\ 0 & 0 & 6 & -3 & 6 \end{bmatrix} \sim \begin{bmatrix} 1 & 2 & -4 & 3 & -1 \\ 0 & 0 & 2 & -1 & 2 \\ 0 & 0 & 0 & 0 & 0 \end{bmatrix}$$

Now AX = 0 become $x + 2y - 4z + 3r - s = 0$

$2z - r + 2s = 0$ Two equations in 5 variables.

Hence dimension of the solution space W is 5 – 2 = 3.

dim W = 3.

To find the basis. Let y, r and s be the arbitrary variables. To obtain the independent vectors, set (*a*) $y = 1, r = s = 0$, (*b*) $r = 1, y = s = 0$, (*c*) $y = r = 0, s = 1$.

Solutions are (*a*) (– 2, 1, 0, 0, 0), (*b*) (– 1, 0, 0.5, 1, 0) and (*c*) (5, 0, 1, 0, 1)

The required basis is {(– 2, 1, 0, 0, 0), (– 1, 0, 0.5, 1, 0), (5, 0, 1, 0, 1)}.

Example 29. *Prove that the vectors* $\{x_i\}_1^n$ *is a basis of a vector space if and only if each vector of V is uniquely expressed as a linear combination of* $x_1, x_2, ..., x_n$. (C.U. Dec. 2006)

Sol. Suppose $\{x_i\}_1^n$ be a basis of V. To prove any $x \in$ V can be uniquely expressed as a linear combination of x_i's.

Let $x \in$ V and let $x = a_1x_1 + a_2x_2 + ... + a_nx_n$ ...(1)

and $x = b_1x_1 + b_2x_2 + ... + b_nx_n$ ...(2)

be two different expressions of x in terms of x_i's.

From (1) and (2), $a_1x_1 + a_2x_2 + ... + a_nx_n = b_1x_1 + b_2x_2 + ... + b_nx_n$.

i.e., $(a_1 - b_1)x_1 + (a_2 - b_2)x_2 + ... + (a_n - b_n)x_n = 0$

Since $\{x_i\}_1^n$ is linearly independent, $a_1 - b_1 = a_2 - b_2 = ... = a_n - b_n = 0$

i.e., $a_1 = b_1, a_2 = b_2, ..., a_n = b_n$

i.e., (1) and (2) are same. Hence the uniqueness.

Conversely suppose that any $x \in$ V can be uniquely expressed as a linear combination of x_i's. To prove that $\{x_i\}_1^n$ is a basis. *i.e.*, to prove $\{x_i\}$ generates V and is linearly independent.

Since any $x \in V$ is a linear combination of x_i's, $\{x_i\}_1^n$ spans V.

Now to prove $\{x_i\}$ is linearly independent.

Consider $\quad a_1x_1 + a_2x_2 + \ldots + a_nx_n = 0$

We have $\quad 0x_1 + 0x_2 + \ldots + 0x_n = 0, 0 \in V$

By our assumption, this is possible only if,

$$a_1 = 0, a_2 = 0, \ldots, a_n = 0.$$

Thus $\quad a_1x_1 + a_2x_2 + \ldots + a_nx_n = 0$ implies $a_1 = a_2 = \ldots = a_n = 0.$

i.e., $\quad \{x_i\}_1^n$ is linearly independent.

Hence $\{x_i\}_1^n$ is a basis of V.

3.9. ORDERED BASIS – COORDINATE VECTORS AND TRANSITION MATRIX

Let V be a finite dimensional vector space with dim V = n. Then every basis of V has n vectors. Let $\{x_1, x_2, \ldots, x_n\}$ be a basis of V arranged in certain order. Then $\{x_2, x_1, \ldots, x_n\}$ is another ordered basis of V.

If $S = \{x_i\}_1^n$ is an ordered basis of a finite dimensional vector space with dim V = n. Then any $x \in V$ has a unique representation as a linear combination of x_i's.

i.e., $\quad x = a_1x_1 + a_2x_2 + \ldots + a_nx_n$, *i.e.,* we can find n scalars $a_1, a_2, \ldots, a_n$ determined by the vector x and basis S. These scalars $a_1, a_2, .., a_n$ are called the *co-ordinates of* x in S and denoted by $[x]_S$ or simply $[x]$.

i.e., $\quad [x]_S = \begin{bmatrix} a_1 \\ a_2 \\ \vdots \\ a_n \end{bmatrix}$ is the co-ordinate vector of x w.r.t. the ordered basis S. Here the co-ordinate vector $[x]_S$ depends on the order in which the vectors in S are arranged. *i.e.,* any change in this arrangement may change the co-ordinates of x w.r.t. S.

If $S = \{x_i\}_1^n$ and $T = \{y_i\}_1^n$ be two different bases of a vector space V, and let $x \in V$.

Then there exist $a_1, a_2, \ldots, a_n$ corresponding to S such that

$[x]_S = \begin{bmatrix} a_1 \\ a_2 \\ \vdots \\ a_n \end{bmatrix}$. Also there are scalars $b_1, b_2, \ldots, b_n$ w.r.t. T such that

$$[x]_T = \begin{bmatrix} b_1 \\ \vdots \\ b_n \end{bmatrix}$$

Example 30. *Consider the basis {(2, 1), (1, – 1)} of R^2. Find the co-ordinate vector of (2, 3) in R^2 relative to this basis. Also find the co-ordinate vector relative to the natural basis T = {(1, 0), (0, 1)} of R^2.*

Sol. Let $(2, 3) = x$ and Let $x = a_1(2, 1) + a_2(1, -1)$

$$(2, 3) = (2a_1 + a_2, a_1 - a_2)$$

i.e.,
$$2a_1 + a_2 = 2$$
$$a_1 - a_2 = 3$$

Solving $a_1 = 5/3$ and $a_2 = -4/3$.

$$\therefore \quad [x]_S = \begin{bmatrix} 5/3 \\ -4/3 \end{bmatrix}$$

We have $(2, 3) = 2(1, 0) + 3(0, 1)$

$$\therefore \quad [x]_T = \begin{bmatrix} 2 \\ 3 \end{bmatrix}$$

$[x]_S$ and $[x]_T$ are different.

Example 31. *Consider the following two bases of R^3; S = {(1, 1, 1), (0, 2, 3), (0, 2, –1)} and T = {(1, 1, 0), (1, – 1, 0), (0, 0, 1)}. Find the co-ordinate vector of x = (3, 5, – 2) relative to S and T.*

Sol. Let $x = a_1(1, 1, 1) + a_2(0, 2, 3) + a_3(0, 2, -1)$

i.e., $a_1 = 3,\ a_1 + 2a_2 + 2a_3 = 5,\ a_1 + 3a_2 - a_3 = -2$

Solving, $2a_2 + 2a_3 = 2$ and $3a_2 - a_3 = -5$

$a_2 = -1$ and $a_3 = 2$

$$\therefore \quad [x]_S = \begin{bmatrix} 3 \\ -1 \\ 2 \end{bmatrix}$$

In a similar way,

$$[x]_T = \begin{bmatrix} 4 \\ -1 \\ -2 \end{bmatrix}.$$

Example 32. *Let V be the vector space of 2 × 2 symmetric matrices over R. Find the co-ordinate vector of the matrix (i) $x = \begin{pmatrix} 4 & -11 \\ -11 & -7 \end{pmatrix}$ relative to the basis*

$$T = \left\{\begin{pmatrix} 1 & -2 \\ -2 & 1 \end{pmatrix}, \begin{pmatrix} 2 & 1 \\ 1 & 3 \end{pmatrix}, \begin{pmatrix} 4 & -1 \\ -1 & -5 \end{pmatrix}\right\}$$

(*ii*) $x = \begin{pmatrix} 1 & -5 \\ -5 & 5 \end{pmatrix}$ *relative to the basis* $S = \left\{\begin{pmatrix} 1 & -1 \\ -1 & 2 \end{pmatrix}, \begin{pmatrix} 4 & 1 \\ 1 & 0 \end{pmatrix}, \begin{pmatrix} 3 & -2 \\ -2 & 1 \end{pmatrix}\right\}$

(*iii*) $x = \begin{pmatrix} 1 & 2 \\ 2 & 4 \end{pmatrix}$ *relative to S.*

Sol. (*i*) Let $\begin{pmatrix} 4 & -11 \\ -11 & -7 \end{pmatrix} = a_1\begin{pmatrix} 1 & -2 \\ -2 & 1 \end{pmatrix} + a_2\begin{pmatrix} 2 & 1 \\ 1 & 3 \end{pmatrix} + a_3\begin{pmatrix} 4 & -1 \\ -1 & -5 \end{pmatrix}$

$$= \begin{pmatrix} a_1 + 2a_2 + 4a_3 & -2a_1 + a_2 - a_3 \\ -2a_1 + a_2 - a_3 & a_1 + 3a_2 - 5a_3 \end{pmatrix}$$

i.e.,
$$a_1 + 2a_2 + 4a_3 = 4$$
$$-2a_1 + a_2 - a_3 = -11$$
$$-2a_1 + a_2 - a_3 = -11$$
$$a_1 + 3a_2 - 5a_3 = -7$$

Reducing the augmented matrix into echelon form,

$$\begin{bmatrix} 1 & 2 & 4 & 4 \\ -2 & 1 & -1 & -11 \\ -2 & 1 & -1 & -11 \\ 1 & 3 & -5 & -7 \end{bmatrix} \sim \begin{bmatrix} 1 & 2 & 4 & 4 \\ 0 & 5 & 7 & -3 \\ 0 & 0 & 0 & 0 \\ 0 & 0 & 52 & 52 \end{bmatrix} \sim \begin{bmatrix} 1 & 2 & 4 & 4 \\ 0 & 5 & 7 & -3 \\ 0 & 0 & 52 & 52 \\ 0 & 0 & 0 & 0 \end{bmatrix}$$

which is in echelon form.

Solving $a_1 = 4, a_2 = -2, a_3 = 1$

$$\therefore \qquad [x]_T = \begin{bmatrix} 4 \\ -2 \\ 1 \end{bmatrix}.$$

(*ii*) $[x]_S = \begin{bmatrix} 2 \\ -1 \\ 1 \end{bmatrix}$ (verify)

(*iii*) $[x]_S = \begin{bmatrix} 3 \\ 1 \\ -2 \end{bmatrix}$ (verify)

3.10. TRANSITION MATRIX

If $S = \{x_1, x_2, ..., x_n\}$ and $T = \{y_1, y_2, ..., y_n\}$ are two bases of an n-dimensional vector space V.

Since $\{x_i\}_1^n$ is a basis,

$$y_1 = a_{11}x_1 + a_{12}x_2 + ... + a_{1n}x_n$$
$$y_2 = a_{21}x_1 + a_{22}x_2 + ... + a_{2n}x_n$$
$$\vdots$$
$$y_n = a_{n1}x_1 + a_{n2}x_2 + ... + a_{nn}x_n$$

The transpose of the coefficient matrix is called the transition matrix from the basis S to the basis T and it is denoted by the matrix P.

i.e.,
$$P_{\text{from S to T}} = \begin{pmatrix} a_{11} & a_{21} & \cdots & a_{n1} \\ a_{12} & a_{22} & \cdots & a_{n2} \\ \vdots & \vdots & & \vdots \\ a_{1n} & a_{2n} & \cdots & a_{nn} \end{pmatrix} = P_{s \to T}$$

In a similar way we can find the transition matrix Q from the basis T to S. *i.e.,* $Q_{T \to S}$

Since $\{y_i\}_1^n$ is linearly independent P is invertible. $\therefore \quad PP^{-1} = I$.

Also P^{-1} is the transition matrix from the basis T to S *i.e.*, $P^{-1} = Q$.

Thus PQ = I.

Example 33. *Find the transition matrix P from S to T of R^2 for the following bases $S = \{(1, 0), (0, 1)\}$ and $T = \{(1, 1,), (-1, 0)\}$. Also find $Q_{T\to S}$.*

Sol. To find $P_{S\to T}$, express vectors in T as a linear combination of vectors in S.

We have $(1, 1) = 1(1, 0) + (0, 1)$ and

$$(-1, 0) = -1(1, 0) + 0(0, 1)$$

$$\therefore \quad P_{S\to T} = \begin{pmatrix} 1 & -1 \\ 1 & 0 \end{pmatrix}$$

To find $Q_{T\to S}$, express vectors in S as a linear combination of vectors in T.

Let $(1, 0) = a(1, 1) + b(-1, 0)$

Solving, $a = 0$ and $b = -1$

$$\therefore \quad (1, 0) = 0(1, 1) + (-1)(-1, 0)$$

$$(0, 1) = 1(1, 1) + 1(-1, 0)$$

$$\therefore \quad Q_{T\to S} = \begin{pmatrix} 0 & 1 \\ -1 & 1 \end{pmatrix}$$

Now $$PQ = \begin{pmatrix} 1 & -1 \\ 1 & 0 \end{pmatrix}\begin{pmatrix} 0 & 1 \\ -1 & 1 \end{pmatrix} = \begin{pmatrix} 1 & 0 \\ 0 & 1 \end{pmatrix} = I.$$

Example 34. *Consider the natural basis $S = \{(1, 0), (0, 1)\}$ and the basis $T = \{(1, 2), (2, 3)\}$ of R^2. Find $P_{S\to T}$, $Q_{T\to S}$, $[x]_S$ and $[x]_T$ for any x in R^2. Also prove PQ = I.*

Sol. Let $x = (x, y) \in R^2$ and $(x, y) = a(1, 0) + b(0, 1)$

$$\therefore \quad a = x \text{ and } b = y$$

$$[x]_S = \begin{pmatrix} x \\ y \end{pmatrix}$$

Now $(x, y) = a(1, 2) + b(2, 3)$

i.e., $x = a + 2b$ and $y = 2a + 3b$

Solving $b = 2x - y$ and $a = -3x + 2y$

$$\therefore \quad [x]_T = \begin{pmatrix} -3x + 2y \\ 2x - y \end{pmatrix}$$

To find $P_{S\to T}$

Express elements of T in terms of elements of S.

$$(1, 2) = 1(1, 0) + 2(0, 1)$$

$$(2, 3) = 2(1, 0) + 3(0, 1)$$

$$\therefore \quad P = \begin{pmatrix} 1 & 2 \\ 2 & 3 \end{pmatrix}$$

To find $Q_{T\to S}$

Express elements of S in terms of elements of T.

$$(1, 0) = -3(1, 2) + 2(2, 3)$$

$$(0, 1) = 2(1, 2) - 1(2, 3), \quad \text{since} \quad [x]_T = \begin{pmatrix} -3x + 2y \\ 2x - y \end{pmatrix}$$

$$\therefore \qquad Q_{T\to S} = \begin{pmatrix} -3 & 2 \\ 2 & -1 \end{pmatrix}$$

$$PQ = \begin{pmatrix} 1 & 2 \\ 2 & 3 \end{pmatrix}\begin{pmatrix} -3 & 2 \\ 2 & -1 \end{pmatrix} = \begin{pmatrix} 1 & 0 \\ 0 & 1 \end{pmatrix} = I.$$

Theorem. *If P is the transition matrix from the basis* $S = \{x_i\}_1^n$ *to a basis* $T = \{y_i\}_1^n$ *of a vector space V, then for any* $x \in V$, $P[x]_T = [x]_S$. *Hence* $[x]_T = P^{-1}[x]_S$.

Example 35. *Prove this result for the above example if* $x \in V$.

Sol. $$P[x]_T = \begin{pmatrix} 1 & 2 \\ 2 & 3 \end{pmatrix}\begin{pmatrix} -3x+2y \\ 2x-y \end{pmatrix} = \begin{pmatrix} x \\ y \end{pmatrix} = [x]_S$$

Also $$P^{-1}[x]_S = Q[x]_S$$

$$= \begin{pmatrix} -3 & 2 \\ 2 & -1 \end{pmatrix}\begin{pmatrix} x \\ y \end{pmatrix} = \begin{pmatrix} -3x+2y \\ 2x-y \end{pmatrix} = [x]_T$$

Hence the proof.

Example 36. *Consider the vector space* R^3. *The bases*

$S = \{(1, 0, 0), (0, 1, 0), (0, 0, 1)\}$ *and* $T = \{(1, 1, 1), (1, 1, 0), (1, 0, 0)\}$ *verify* $P[x]_T = [x]_S$ *and* $P^{-1}[x]_S = [x]_T$ *for any* $x \in R^3$.

Sol. Let $$x = (x, y, z) \in R^3$$

Then $$[x]_S = \begin{pmatrix} x \\ y \\ z \end{pmatrix} \text{ and } P_{S\to T} = \begin{pmatrix} 1 & 1 & 1 \\ 1 & 1 & 0 \\ 1 & 0 & 0 \end{pmatrix}$$

To find $[x]_T$

Let $$(x, y, z) = a(1, 1, 1) + b(1, 1, 0) + c(1, 0, 0)$$
$$= (a + b + c, a + b, a)$$

Solving $$a = z, b = y - z, c = x - y$$

$$\therefore \qquad [x]_T = \begin{pmatrix} z \\ y-z \\ x-y \end{pmatrix}$$

$$Q_{T\to S} = \begin{pmatrix} 0 & 0 & 1 \\ 0 & 1 & -1 \\ 1 & -1 & 0 \end{pmatrix}, \quad \begin{bmatrix} \text{Since } (1,0,0) = 0(1,1,1) + 0(1,1,0) + 1(1,0,0), \\ (0,1,0) = 0(1,1,1) + 1(1,1,0) - 1(1,0,0) \text{ and} \\ (0,0,1) = 1(1,1,1) - 1(1,1,0) + 0(1,0,0) \end{bmatrix}$$

$$P[x]_T = \begin{pmatrix} 1 & 1 & 1 \\ 1 & 1 & 0 \\ 1 & 0 & 0 \end{pmatrix}\begin{pmatrix} z \\ y-z \\ x-y \end{pmatrix} = \begin{pmatrix} x \\ y \\ z \end{pmatrix} = [x]_S$$

We have $PQ = I \quad \therefore \quad Q = P^{-1}$

$$\therefore \qquad P^{-1}[x]_S = Q[x]_S = \begin{pmatrix} 0 & 0 & 1 \\ 0 & 1 & -1 \\ 1 & -1 & 0 \end{pmatrix}\begin{pmatrix} x \\ y \\ z \end{pmatrix} = \begin{pmatrix} z \\ y-z \\ x-y \end{pmatrix} = [x]_S.$$

Example 37. *Let V be the vector space of all polynomials of degree ≤ 1. Two bases of V are S = {t, t – 3} and T = {t – 1, t + 1}. Find* $P_{S \to T}$ *and* $Q_{T \to S}$.

Sol. Express vectors of T in terms of vectors in S.

Let $$t - 1 = at + b(t - 3) = (a + b)t - 3b$$

∴ $$a + b = 1 \text{ and } 3b = 1$$

∴ $$a = 2/3 \text{ and } b = 1/3$$

∴ $$t - 1 = \frac{2}{3}(t) + \frac{1}{3}(t - 3)$$

Now, $$t + 1 = at + b(t - 3) = (a + b)t - 3b$$

Solving $$a = \frac{4}{3} \text{ and } b = -1/3$$

∴ $$t + 1 = \frac{4}{3}(t) - \frac{1}{3}(t - 3)$$

∴ $$P_{S \to T} = \begin{pmatrix} 2/3 & 4/3 \\ 1/3 & -1/3 \end{pmatrix}$$

To find $Q_{T \to S}$

Express vectors in S in terms of vectors in T.

Let $$t = a(t - 1) + b(t + 1)$$

∴ $$a + b = 1 \text{ and } -a + b = 0.$$

∴ $$a = b = 1/2 \quad i.e., \quad t = \frac{1}{2}(t - 1) + \frac{1}{2}(t + 1)$$

Also $$t - 3 = a(t - 1) + b(t + 1)$$

$$a + b = 1 \text{ and } -a + b = -3$$

∴ $$a = 2 \text{ and } b = -1, \quad \therefore \quad t - 3 = 2(t - 1) - (t + 1)$$

∴ $$Q_{T \to S} = \begin{pmatrix} \frac{1}{2} & 2 \\ \frac{1}{2} & -1 \end{pmatrix}.$$

Example 38. *If V = R^3 and the bases S = {(2, 0, 1), (1, 2, 0), (1, 1, 1)} and T {(6, 3, 3), (4, – 1, 3), (5, 5, 2)}. Compute* $P_{S \to T}$, $Q_{T \to S}$ *and verify* $P[x]_T = [x]_S$ *and* $Q[x]_S = [x]_T$ *for any* $x \in R^3$.

Sol. $$P = \begin{pmatrix} 2 & 2 & 1 \\ 1 & -1 & 2 \\ 1 & 1 & 1 \end{pmatrix},$$

$$Q = \begin{pmatrix} \frac{3}{2} & 1/2 & -5/2 \\ \frac{-1}{2} & -1/2 & 3/2 \\ -1 & 0 & 2 \end{pmatrix}$$

3.11. INNER PRODUCT SPACE

Let V be a finite dimensional real vector space. Let $x, y \in$ V. To each pair of vectors $x, y \in$ V, there assigned a scalar denoted by $<x, y>$ or (x, y) called inner product in V satisfying the following axioms.

(*i*) $<x, x> \geq 0$; $<x, x> = 0$ if and only if $x = 0$, the zero vector in V.

(*ii*) $<x, y> = \overline{<y, x>}$ for any $x, y \in$ V, where $\overline{<y, x>}$ is the complex conjugate of $<x, y>$.

(*iii*) $<ax + by, z> = a<x, z> + b<y, z>$; $a, b \in$ R

The vector space V with an inner product is called an inner product space.

A real inner product space is called Euclidean space.

- R^n is an inner product space with the inner product.

$$<x, y> = x_1y_1 + x_2y_2 + ... + x_ny_n \; ; \; x = (x_1, x_2, ..., x_n), y = (y_1, y_2, ..., y_n)$$

- The vector space of real continuous functions in $a \leq x \leq b$ with the inner product $<f, g> = \int_a^b f(x) g(x)\, dx$ is an inner product space.

3.12. PROPERTIES OF AN INNER PRODUCT

1. $<x, ay + bz> = \bar{a} <x, y> + \bar{b} <x, z>$.
2. For any x in an inner product space, $<0, x> = <x, 0> = 0$.
3. $\| kx \| \leq | k | \| x \|$.
4. $\| x + y \| \leq \| x \| + \| y \|$ (Triangle inequality).

For a real inner product space, $<x, y> = <y, x>$

and $<x, y><y, x> = |<x, y>|^2$, $[\because \; z\bar{z} = |z|^2$ for any complex number $z]$

3.13. CAUCHY-SCHWARZ INEQUALITY

For any two vectors x and y of a real inner product space, $|<x, y>| \leq \| x \| \| y \|$

Proof. If $y = 0$, then $<x, y> = 0$ and $<y, y> = 0$. Then the result is obviously true. Suppose that $y \neq 0$. Let a be any scalar.

$$\begin{aligned} \| x - ay \|^2 &= <x - ay, x - ay> \\ &= <x, x - ay> - a<y, x - ay> \\ &= <x, x> - \bar{a}<x, y> - a<y, x> + a\bar{a}<y, y> \\ &= \| x \|^2 - 2a<x, y> + a^2\| y \|^2, \quad [\text{Since } <x, y> = <y, x>] \end{aligned}$$

Now set $a = \dfrac{<x, y>}{\| y \|^2}$,

$$\begin{aligned} \| x - ay \|^2 &= \| x \|^2 - 2\frac{<x, y><x, y>}{\| y \|^2} + \frac{<x, y><x, y>}{\| y \|^2} \\ &= \| x \|^2 - \frac{|<x, y>|^2}{\| y \|^2} \end{aligned}$$

But $\| x - ay \|^2 \geq 0$.

$$\therefore \quad \| x \|^2 - \frac{|<x, y>|^2}{\| y \|^2} \geq 0$$

i.e., $\| x \|^2 \| y \|^2 \geq |<x, y>|^2$

i.e., $|<x, y>| \leq \| x \| \| y \|$.

3.14. ORTHOGONAL AND ORTHONORMAL VECTORS

Let V be an inner product space. Two vectors x and y in V are said to be **orthogonal** if their inner product is zero. *i.e.*, if $<x, y> = 0$.

Consider the inner product space R^n with usual inner product.

The distance between x and y, denoted by $d(x, y)$ is

$$\sqrt{(x_1 - y_1)^2 + (x_2 - y_2)^2 + \ldots + (x_n - y_n)^2}, \; x = (x_1, x_2, \ldots, x_n) \text{ and } y = (y_1, y_2, \ldots, y_n).$$

The norm of x or length of x is defined as the non-negative square root of $<x, x>$, denoted by $\| x \|$.

$$\therefore \qquad \| x \| = \sqrt{x_1^2 + x_2^2 + \ldots + x_n^2}$$

$$\text{Now} \qquad \| x - y \| = \sqrt{(x_1 - y_1)^2 + \ldots + (x_n - y_n)^2} = d(x, y)$$

$$\text{In } R^2, \qquad \| x \| = \sqrt{x_1^2 + x_2^2} \text{ and}$$

$$d(x, y) = \sqrt{(x_1 - y_1)^2 + (x_2 - y_2)^2}$$

$$\text{In R}, \qquad \| x \| = x \text{ and } d(x, y) = x - y$$

If the norm of a vector is 1, we call it as **unit vector.**

The norm in an inner product space has the following properties.

(*i*) $\| x \| \geq 0$ and $\| x \| = 0$ if and only if $x = 0$

(*ii*) $\| kx \| = \| k \| \, \| x \|$

(*iii*) $\| x + y \| \leq \| x \| + \| y \|$

For any non-zero vector $x \in R^n$, $\dfrac{x}{\| x \|}$ is a unit vector in the same direction as x

$$\left[\because \left\langle \frac{x}{\| x \|}, \frac{x}{\| x \|} \right\rangle = \frac{1}{\| x \| \| x \|} <x, x> = \frac{\| x \|^2}{\| x \|^2} = 1\right].$$

3.15. ORTHONORMAL SET

A set $\{n_1, n_2, \ldots, x_n\}$ of vectors in an inner product space is said to be orthonormal if

$$<x_i, x_j> = \begin{cases} 0 & \text{for } i \neq j \\ 1 & \text{for } i = j \end{cases}$$

i.e., the distinct elements are orthogonal and each x_i has unit length.

Theorem. *An orthogonal set $\{x_1, x_2, \ldots, x_n\}$ of non-zero vectors is linearly independent.*

Proof.

Let $a_1x_1 + a_2x_2 + \ldots + a_nx_n = 0$. To prove $a_1 = a_2 = \ldots = a_n = 0$.

We have
$$0 = <0, x_i> = <a_1x_1 + \ldots + a_ix_i + \ldots + a_nx_n, x_i>$$
$$= a_1<x_1, x_i> + a_2<x_2, x_i> + \ldots + a_i<x_i, x_i> + \ldots + a_n<x_n, x_i>$$
$$= a_i<x_i, x_i>, \qquad (\because \; <x_i, x_j> = 0, \text{ for } i \neq j)$$

But $<x_i, x_i> \neq 0$, as $x_i \neq 0$

$\therefore \qquad a_i = 0$, for all i

Thus $\qquad a_1 = a_2 = \ldots = a_n = 0$

Hence $\{x_1, x_2, \ldots, x_n\}$ is linearly independent.

3.16. ORTHONORMAL BASIS

A basis $\{x_i\}_1^n$ of an inner product space is called orthonormal basis if every vector is orthogonal to each other and each vector is of unit length.

Example 39. *Verify that the following is an inner product in* R^2. $<x, y> = x_1y_1 - x_1y_2 - x_2y_1 + 3x_2y_2$ *where* $x = (x_1, x_2)$ *and* $y = (y_1, y_2)$. *Find the norm of (5, 2) in* R^2. (C.U. Dec. 2006)

Sol. (*i*) $<x, x> = x_1^2 - x_1x_2 - x_2x_1 + 3x_2^2$

$= x_1^2 - 2x_1x_2 + 3x_2^2 = (x_1 - x_2)^2 + 2x_2^2 \geq 0$

Also $<x, x> = 0$ if and only if $(x_1 - x_2)^2 + 2x_2^2 = 0$

i.e., if and only if $x_1 = 0, x_2 = 0$

Thus $<x, x> = 0$ if and only if $x = 0$

(*ii*) $<y, x> = y_1x_1 - y_2x_1 - y_1x_2 + 3y_2x_2$

$= x_1y_1 - x_1y_2 - x_2y_1 + 3x_2y_2$ $[\because \ x, y \in R^2]$

$= <x, y>$

(*iii*) Let $a, b \in$ R and $z = (z_1, z_2) \in R^2$

$<ax + by, z> = <(ax_1 + by_1, ax_2 + by_2), (z_1, z_2)>$

$= (ax_1 + by_1)z_1 - (ax_1 + by_1)z_2 - (ax_2 + by_2)z_1 + 3(ax_2 + by_2)z_2$

$= a(x_1z_1 - x_1z_2 - x_2z_1 + 3x_2z_2) + b(y_1z_1 - y_1z_2 - y_2z_1 + 3y_2z_2)$

$= a(x, z) + b(y, z)$

Thus all the axioms are satisfied. Hence an inner product in R^2.

$\| (5, 2) \| = <(5, 2), (5, 2)>$

$= 5^2 - 2 \times 5 \times 2 + 3 \times 2^2 = 17.$

Example 40. *Show that (1, 1, 1), (1, 0, – 1), (1, – 2, 1) are mutually orthogonal. Also normalize the vectors.*

Sol. Let $x = (1, 1, 1), y = (1, 0, -1), z = (1, -2, 1)$

$<x, y> = <(1, 1, 1), (1, 0, -1)>$

$= 1 + 0 - 1 = 0$

$<x, z> = <(1, 1, 1), (1, -2, 1)>$

$= 1 - 2 + 1 = 0$

$<y, z> = <(1, 0, -1), (1, -2, 1)>$

$= 1 + 0 - 1 = 0$

Hence the vectors are mutually orthogonal.

The normalized vectros are $\dfrac{x}{\| x \|}, \dfrac{y}{\| y \|}$ and $\dfrac{z}{\| z \|}$.

$$\| x \| = \sqrt{<x, x>} = \sqrt{1^2 + 1^2 + 1^2} = \sqrt{3}$$

$$\| y \| = \sqrt{<y, y>} = \sqrt{1^2 + 0 + (-1)^2} = \sqrt{2}$$

$$\| z \| = \sqrt{<z, z>} = \sqrt{1^2 + 4 + 1^2} = \sqrt{6}$$

$\left(\dfrac{1}{\sqrt{3}}, \dfrac{1}{\sqrt{3}}, \dfrac{1}{\sqrt{3}}\right), \left(\dfrac{1}{\sqrt{2}}, 0, \dfrac{-1}{\sqrt{2}}\right), \left(\dfrac{1}{\sqrt{6}}, \dfrac{-2}{\sqrt{6}}, \dfrac{1}{\sqrt{6}}\right)$ are the normalized vectors.

Example 41. *Verify that the following is an inner product in* R^2.

$$<x, y> = x_1y_1 - 2x_1y_2 - 2x_2y_1 + 5x_2y_2 \text{ where } x = (x_1, x_2) \text{ and } y = (y_1, y_2)$$

Sol. (*i*) $<x, x> = x_1^2 - 4x_1x_2 + 5x_2^2 = (x_1 - 2x_2)^2 + x_2^2 \geq 0$

Also $<x, x> = 0$ if and only if $(x_1 - 2x_2)^2 + x_2^2 = 0$

i.e., if and only if $x_1 = 0$ and $x_2 = 0$

i.e., if and only if $x = 0$

(*ii*)
$$\begin{aligned} <y, x> &= y_1x_1 - 2y_2x_1 - 2y_1x_2 + 5y_2x_2 \\ &= x_1y_1 - 2x_1y_2 - 2x_2y_1 + 5x_2y_2, \quad \because \quad x_1, x_2, y_1, y_2 \in R \\ &= <x, y> \end{aligned}$$

(*iii*) Let $a,b \in$ R and $z = (z_1, z_2)$

$$\begin{aligned} (ax + by, z) &= <(ax_1 + by_1, ax_2 + by_2), (z_1, z_2)> \\ &= (ax_1 + by_1)z_1 - 2(ax_1 + by_1)z_2 - (ax_2 + by_2)z_1 + 5(ax_2 + by_2)z_2 \\ &= a(x_1z_1 - 2x_1z_2 - 2x_2z_1 + 5x_2z_2) + b(y_1z_1 - 2y_1z_2 - 2y_2z_1 + 5y_2z_2) \\ &= a(x, z) + b(y, z) \end{aligned}$$

Hence all the axioms of an inner product are satisfied.

Example 42. *For what values of k is the following an inner product in* R^2 ?

$$<x, y> = x_1y_1 - 3x_1y_2 - 3x_2y_1 + kx_2y_2 .$$

Sol. Consider the first axiom, $<x, x> \geq 0$

Here
$$\begin{aligned} <x, x> &= x_1^2 - 6x_1x_2 + kx_2^2 = (x_1 - 3x_2)^2 + kx_2^2 - 9x_2^2 \\ &= (x_1 - 3x_2)^2 + (k - 9)x_2^2. \end{aligned}$$

$$<x, x> \geq 0 \quad \Rightarrow \quad (x_1 - 3x_2)^2 + (k - 9)x_2^2 \geq 0$$

i.e., $(x_1 - 3x_2)^2 \geq (9 - k)x_2^2$

i.e., $0 \geq 9 - k$ *i.e.,* $\boldsymbol{k \geq 9}$.

3.17. GRAM-SCHMIDT ORTHOGONALIZATION PROCESS

A subspace V of R^n spanned by m (> 1) linearly independent vectors $x_1, x_2, ..., x_m$ has an orthogonal basis $\{y_1, y_2, ..., y_n\}$ where $y_1 = x_1$,

$$y_2 = x_2 - \frac{<x_2, y_1>}{<y_1, y_1>} y_1,$$

$$y_3 = x_3 - \frac{<x_3, y_1> y_1}{<y_1, y_1>} - \frac{<x_3, y_2> y_2}{<y_2, y_2>}, ...,$$

$$y_m = x_m - \frac{<x_m, y_1> y_1}{<y_1, y_1>} - \frac{<x_m, y_2> y_2}{<y_2, y_2>} - ... - \frac{<x_m, y_{m-1}> y_{m-1}}{<y_{m-1}, y_{m-1}>}.$$

Proof. Set $y_1 = x_1$

Since $x_1, x_2, ..., x_m$ are linearly independent, $x_i \neq 0$ for all i,

Hence $\| y_1 \| \neq 0$.

Define
$$y_2 = x_2 - \frac{<x_2, y_1>}{<y_1, y_1>} y_1.$$

Clearly y_1 and y_2 are linear combination of x_1 and x_2 and conversely.

Now
$$<y_2, y_1> = <x_2, y_1> - \frac{<x_2, y_1>}{<y_1, y_1>} <y_1, y_1> = <x_2, y_1> - <x_2, y_1> = 0.$$

$\therefore$ $\{y_1, y_2\}$ is an orthogonal basis of the linear space spanned by $\{x_1, x_2\}$.

Since $y_1 = x_1$ and x_2 is not a linear combination of x_1, $\| y_2 \| \neq 0$.

For $m > 2$, define $y_3 = x_3 - \frac{<x_3, y_1>}{<y_1, y_1>} y_1 - \frac{<x_3, y_2>}{<y_2, y_2>} y_2$

y_1, y_2, y_3 are linear combination of x_1, x_2, x_3 and vice versa.

$$<y_3, y_1> = <x_3, y_1> - \frac{<x_3, y_1>}{<y_1, y_1>} <y_1, y_1> - \frac{<x_3, y_2>}{<y_2, y_2>} <y_2, y_1>$$

$$= <x_3, y_1> - <x_3, y_1> - 0, \text{ since } <y_2, y_1> = 0$$

$$= 0.$$

$$<y_3, y_2> = <x_3, y_2> - \frac{<x_3, y_1>}{<y_1, y_1>} <y_1, y_2> - \frac{<x_3, y_2>}{<y_2, y_2>} <y_2, y_2>$$

$$= 0.$$

So $\{y_1, y_2, y_3\}$ is an orthogonal basis of linear space spanned by $\{x_1, x_2, x_3\}$.

Since x_3 is not a linear combination of x_1 and x_2, $\| y_3 \| \neq 0$.

If $m > 3$, by the same argument we can prove that $\{y_1, y_2, ..., y_m\}$ is an orthogonal basis of the subspace of R^n spanned by $\{x_1, x_2, ..., x_m\}$.

Remark 1. $\{y_1, y_2, ..., y_m\}$ is an orthogonal basis. Hence $\left\{\frac{y_1}{\|y_1\|}, \frac{y_2}{\|y_2\|}, \ldots \frac{y_m}{\|y_m\|}\right\}$ is an orthonormal basis of R^n.

Remark 2. If $<x, y> = 0$, then $<x, ky> = 0$ for any scalar k.

Example 43. *Using Gram-Schmidth orthogonalization process, obtain an orthonormal basis for R^2 from the basis $\{(1, 1, 1), (-1, 0, -1), (-1, 2, 3)\}$.*

Sol. Let $x_1 = (1, 1, 1), x_2 = (-1, 0, -1), x_3 = (-1, 2, 3)$

Set $y_1 = x_1 = (1, 1, 1)$

Using Gram-Schmidth Process,

$$y_2 = x_2 - \frac{<x_2, y_1>}{<y_1, y_1>} y_1, \; y_3 = x_3 - \frac{<x_3, y_1>}{<y_1, y_1>} y_1 - \frac{<x_3, y_2>}{<y_2, y_2>} y_2$$

$$y_2 = (-1, 0, -1) + \frac{2}{3}(1, 1, 1) = \left(\frac{-1}{3}, \frac{2}{3}, \frac{-1}{3}\right)$$

choose $y_2 = (-1, 2, -1)$, [Using remark (2)]

$$y_3 = (-1, 2, 3) - \frac{4}{3}(1, 1, 1) - \frac{2}{6}(-1, 2, -1) = (-2, 0, 2)$$

Now, $\| y_1 \| = \sqrt{<y_1, y_1>} = \sqrt{<(1, 1, 1), (1, 1, 1)>} = \sqrt{3}$

$$\| y_2 \| = \sqrt{<y_2, y_2>} = \sqrt{1 + 4 + 1} = \sqrt{6}$$

$$\| y_3 \| = \sqrt{<y_3, y_3>} = \sqrt{4 + 0 + 4} = \sqrt{8}$$

Thus $\left\{\frac{y_1}{\|y_1\|}, \frac{y_2}{\|y_2\|}, \frac{y_3}{\|y_3\|}\right\} = \left\{\left(\frac{1}{\sqrt{3}}, \frac{1}{\sqrt{3}}, \frac{1}{\sqrt{3}}\right), \left(\frac{-1}{\sqrt{6}}, \frac{2}{\sqrt{6}}, \frac{-1}{\sqrt{6}}\right), \left(\frac{-1}{\sqrt{2}}, 0, \frac{1}{\sqrt{2}}\right)\right\}$ is the required orthonormal basis.

Example 44. *Using Gram-Schmidth orthogonalization process, find an orthonormal basis for the subspace of R^4 spanned by (2, – 8, 2, 3), (9, – 12, 9, 10), (9, – 4, 5, 7).*

(C.U. June 2005)

Sol. Let $x_1 = (2, -8, 2, 3), x_2 = (9, -12, 9, 10), x_3 = (9, -4, 5, 7)$.

Given that $\{x_1, x_2, x_3\}$ generate the inner product space.

First we've to check whether these vectors are linearly independent or not.

Form the matrix A with these vectors as rows.

$$A = \begin{bmatrix} 2 & -8 & 2 & 3 \\ 9 & -12 & 9 & 10 \\ 9 & -4 & 5 & 7 \end{bmatrix} \sim \begin{bmatrix} 1 & -4 & 1 & 3/2 \\ 9 & -12 & 9 & 10 \\ 9 & -4 & 5 & 7 \end{bmatrix}$$

$$\sim \begin{bmatrix} 1 & -4 & 1 & 3/2 \\ 0 & 24 & 0 & -7/2 \\ 0 & 32 & -4 & -13/2 \end{bmatrix} \sim \begin{bmatrix} 1 & -4 & 1 & 3/2 \\ 0 & 1 & 0 & -7/48 \\ 0 & 0 & -4 & 211/2 \end{bmatrix}$$; which is in the echelon form.

Rank (A) = 3. Hence the given vectors are independent and form a basis.

By Gram-Schmidth process, $y_1 = x_1, y_2 = x_2 - \frac{<x_2, y_1>}{<y_1, y_1>} y_1 - \frac{<x_2, y_2>}{<y_2, y_2>} y_2$

$y_3 = x_3 - \frac{<x_3, y_1>}{<y_1, y_1>} y_1 - \frac{<x_3, y_2>}{<y_2, y_2>} y_2$ are the orthogonal vectors.

$$y_1 = x_1 = (2, -8, 2, 3)$$

$$y_2 = (9, -12, 9, 10) - \frac{18 + 96 + 18 + 30}{4 + 64 + 4 + 9}(2, -8, 2, 3)$$

$$= (9, -12, 9, 10) - \frac{162}{81}(2, -8, 2, 3)$$

$$= (5, 4, 5, 4)$$

$$y_3 = (9, -4, 5, 7) - \left(\frac{18 + 32 + 10 + 21}{81}\right) y_1 - \frac{45 - 16 + 25 + 28}{25 + 16 + 25 + 16} y_2$$

$$= (9, -4, 5, 7) - \frac{81}{81}(2, -8, 2, 3) - \frac{82}{82}(5, 4, 5, 4)$$

$$= (2, 0, -2, 0)$$

Now $\| y_1 \| = \sqrt{<y_1, y_1>} = \sqrt{81} = 9$

$\| y_2 \| = \sqrt{<y_2, y_2>} = \sqrt{82}$

$\| y_3 \| = \sqrt{<y_3, y_3>} = \sqrt{8}$

The normalized basis is $\left\{\left(\frac{2}{9}, \frac{-8}{9}, \frac{2}{9}, \frac{1}{3}\right), \left(\frac{5}{\sqrt{82}}, \frac{4}{\sqrt{82}}, \frac{5}{\sqrt{82}}, \frac{4}{\sqrt{82}}\right), \left(\frac{1}{\sqrt{2}}, 0, \frac{-1}{\sqrt{2}}, 0\right)\right\}$.

UNIVERSITY QUESTIONS WITH SOLUTION

Q. 1. *Determine whether the following vectors are linearly dependent.*

(i) $U = (3, 4), V = (1, -3)$ *(ii)* $U = (2, -3), V = (6, -9)$ (C.U. June 2009, Dec. 2006)

(iii) $U = (1, -2, 1), V = (2, 1, -7), W = (7, -4, 11)$ (C.U. June 2009, 2006, Dec. 2007)

(iv) $(2, -3, 7), (0, 0, 0), (3, -1, -4)$ (C.U. June 2006)

(v) $(1, 2, 3), (3, 2, 1), (5, 5, 5)$ (C.U. June 2008)

Sol. (*i*) Let $au + bv = 0$. If a or $b \neq 0$, the given vectors are linearly dependent.

i.e., $$a(3, 4) + b(1, -3) = (0, 0)$$

i.e., $$3a + b = 0 \text{ and } 4a - 3b = 0$$

Solving, $a = 0$ and $b = 0$, *i.e.*, $au + bv = 0$ with $a = b = 0$.

Hence u and v are not dependent.

(*ii*) Clearly v is a multiple of u. $v = 3u$

We have the result, two non-zero vectors are dependent if and only if one of them is a multiple of the other.

Hence the given vectors are dependent.

(*iii*) Let $$au + bv + cw = 0.$$

i.e., $$a(1, -2, 1) + b(2, 1, -7) + c(7, -4, 1) = (0, 0, 0)$$

Comparing, $$a + 2b + 7c = 0$$
$$-2a + b - 4c = 0 \quad \textit{i.e.}, \text{AX} = 0, \text{A is the coefficient matrix.}$$
$$a - 7b + c = 0.$$

If this homogeneous system have a non-trivial solution, the given vectors are dependent. The system AX = 0 has non-trivial solution if $|A| = 0$.

Now, $|A| = \begin{vmatrix} 1 & 2 & 7 \\ -2 & 1 & -4 \\ 1 & -7 & 1 \end{vmatrix} \neq 0$. Hence the vectors are independent.

Alternate Method

Form the matrix with the given **vectors as rows.** If its determinant is zero, the vectors are dependent. Otherwise independent.

(*iv*) Form the matrix A with these vectors as rows.

Now $$|A| = \begin{vmatrix} 2 & -3 & 7 \\ 0 & 0 & 0 \\ 3 & -1 & -4 \end{vmatrix} = 0.$$

Hence dependent.

OR, since one of the vectors is zero, the given vectors are dependent.

(*v*) Let A be the matrix with these vectors as rows.

$$|A| = \begin{vmatrix} 1 & 2 & 3 \\ 3 & 2 & 1 \\ 5 & 5 & 5 \end{vmatrix} = 0.$$

Hence dependent.

Q. 2. *Show that if two of the vectors $x_1, x_2, ..., x_m$ are equal, say $x_1 = x_2$, then the vectors are dependent.* (C.U. Dec. 2009)

Sol. Given $x_1 = x_2$

So $$1.x_1 - 1.x_2 + 0.x_3 + ... + 0x_m = 0 \text{ with } a_1 = 1 \text{ and } a_2 = -1$$

i.e., $$a_1x_1 + a_2x_2 + ... + a_mx_m = 0 \text{ with } (a_1 \neq 0 \text{ and } a_2 \neq 0) \text{ some } a_i \neq 0.$$

$\therefore$ The given vectors are linearly dependent.

Q. 3. *Represent $x = (3, 9, -4, -2)$ in R^4 in terms of $(1, -2, 0, 3)$, $(2, 3, 0, -1)$ and $(2, -1, 2, 1)$.* (C.U. June 2007)

Sol. Let x be a linear combination of the given vectors.

Choose scalars a, b, c such that,

$$x = a(1, -2, 0, 3) + b(2, 3, 0, -1) + c(2, -1, 2, 1)$$

i.e.,
$$a + 2b + 2c = 3,$$
$$-2a + 3b - c = 9,$$
$$2c = -4,$$
$$3a - b + c = -2$$

i.e., $c = -2, b = 3$ and $a = 1$

Thus $\mathbf{x = (1, -2, 0, 3) + 3(2, 3, 0, -1) - 2(2, -1, 2, 1).}$

Q. 4. *Show that the vectors $x_1 = (1, 2, 3)$, $x_2 = (0, 1, 2)$ and $x_3 = (0, 0, 1)$ generate R^3.* (Dec. 2009)

Sol. If any vector (x, y, z) in R^3 can be represented as a linear combination of x_1, x_2 and x_3, then $\{x_1, x_2, x_3\}$ generates R^3.

Let
$$(x, y, z) = ax_1 + bx_2 + cx_3$$
$$= a(1, 2, 3) + b(0, 1, 2) + c(0, 0, 1)$$
$$= (a, 2a + b, 3a + 2b + c)$$

Comparing, $x = a, y = 2a + b, z = 3a + 2b + \mathbf{c}$

$\therefore$ $a = x, b = y - 2a = y - 2x$ and $c = z - 3a - 2b$

i.e., $c = z - 3x - 2(y - 2x) = z + x - 2y$

Thus the given vectors generate R^3.

Q. 5. *Let V be the vector space of functions from R into R. Show that f, g, h $\in$ V are linearly independent where $f(t) = e^{2t}$, $g(t) = t^2$, $h(t) = t$.* (June 2009)

Sol. Let $af(t) + bg(t) + ch(t) = 0$. To prove $a = b = c = 0$, for all values of t.

$$ae^{2t} + bt^2 + ct = 0.$$

For $t = 0$, $ae^0 + 0b + 0c = 0$ *i.e.,* $a = 0$.

For $t = 1$, $ae^2 + b1 + c1 = 0$.

For $t = 2$, $ae^4 + 4b + 2c = 0$. Solving these $a = 0, b = 0, c = 0$.

$\therefore$ f, g and h are linearly independent.

Q. 6. *Determine the subspace spanned by $H = \{(1, -2, 3), (3, 0, 1)\}$ in R^3.* (Dec. 2010)

Sol. The required subspace is the set of vectors (x, y, z) which are linear combination of the given vectors $(1, -2, 3), (3, 0, 1)$.

Let (x, y, z) be an arbitrary element in R^3.

Let $(x, y, z) = a(1, -2, 3) + b(3, 0, 1)$, a and b are unknowns.

i.e., $(x, y, z) = (a + 3b, -2a, 3a + b)$

Equating,
$$x = a + 3b$$
$$y = -2a + 0b$$
$$z = 3a + b \Rightarrow AX = B, \text{(say)}$$

$$\begin{bmatrix} 1 & 3 \\ -2 & 0 \\ 3 & 1 \end{bmatrix} \begin{bmatrix} a \\ b \end{bmatrix} = \begin{bmatrix} x \\ y \\ z \end{bmatrix}.$$ Solving for a and b.

Augmented matrix,

$$(A : B) = \begin{bmatrix} 1 & 3 & x \\ -2 & 0 & y \\ 3 & 1 & z \end{bmatrix} \sim \begin{bmatrix} 1 & 3 & x \\ 0 & 6 & y+2x \\ 0 & -8 & z-3x \end{bmatrix} \sim \begin{bmatrix} 1 & 3 & x \\ 0 & 1 & \dfrac{y+2x}{6} \\ 0 & 0 & \dfrac{3x-2}{8} - \dfrac{y+2x}{6} \end{bmatrix}$$

(x, y, z) belongs to the space generated by the given vectors if and only if this system is consistent.

i.e., only if $\text{rank}(A : B) = \text{rank}(A)$

i.e., only if $r(A : B) = r(A) = 2$

i.e., only if $\dfrac{3x-z}{8} - \dfrac{y+2x}{6} = 0$

i.e., only if $x - 4y - 3z = 0$

$\therefore$ The required subspace is $\{(x, y, z) ; x - 4y - 3z = 0\}$.

Q. 7. *Show that the set* $\{(x, y, z) \in R^3 ; 2x + 5y - 7z = 0\}$ *is a subspace of* R^3.

(C.U. Dec. 2010)

Sol. Let $U = \{(x, y, z) ; 2x + 5y - 7z = 0\}$

To prove U is a subspace of R^3, it is enough to prove $au + bv \in U$ if $u, v \in U$ and $a, b \in R$. Clearly U is a subset of R^3.

Let $u = (x_1, y_1, z_1)$ and $v = (x_2, y_2, z_2)$ belong to U and $a, b \in R$.

Now

$$\begin{aligned} au + bv &= a(x_1, y_1, z_1) + b(x_2, y_2, z_2) \\ &= (ax_1 + bx_2, ay_1 + by_2, az_1 + bz_2) \end{aligned}$$

$$\begin{aligned} 2(ax_1 + bx_2) + 5(ay_1 + by_2) - 7(az_1 + bz_2) &= a(2x_1 + 5y_1 - 7z_1) + b(2x_2 + 5y_2 - 7z_2) \\ &= a \times 0 + b \times 0 \\ &= 0 \end{aligned}$$

i.e., $(ax_1 + bx_2, ay_1 + by_2, az_1 + bz_2) \in U$

i.e., $au + bv \in U$

Hence U is a subspace of R^3.

Q. 8. *Show that in* R^3, $U = \{(x, y, 0) \in R^3\}$ *is a subspace.* (C.U. June 2006, Dec. 2007)

Sol. $U \subset R^3$. As in the above problem, it is enough to prove $au + bv \in v$, for $u. v \in v$ and $a, b \in R$.

Let $u = (x_1, y_1, 0)$ and $v = (x_2, y_2, 0)$ be two elements in U and let $a, b \in R$.

Now

$$\begin{aligned} au + bv &= a(x_1, y_1, 0) + b(x_2, y_2, 0) \\ &= (ax_1 + bx_2, ay_1 + by_2, 0) \in U \end{aligned}$$

$\therefore$ U is a subspace of R^3.

Q. 9. *Prove that the vectors (1, 1, 0, 0), (0, 1, 0, 1), (0, 1, 1, 1) and (1, 1, 1, 1) form a basis of the vector space* R^4. *Express (2, 1, 1, 2) as a linear combination of these vectors.*

(C.U. June 2008)

Sol. The given vectors form a basis of R^4 if they generate R^4 and are linearly independent. Let (x, y, z, t) be any element in R^4 and let it be a linear combination of the given vectors.

Let $(x, y, z, t) = a(1, 1, 0, 0) + b(0, 1, 0, 1) + c(0, 1, 1, 1) + d(1, 1, 1, 1)$ ...(1)

i.e.,
$$a + d = x$$
$$a + b + c + d = y$$
$$c + d = z$$
$$b + c + d = t.$$

Solving $a = y - t$, $b = t - z$, $c = z - t + y - x$ and $d = t - y + x$.

i.e., we can find unknowns a, b, c, d such that (1) is satisfied. *i.e.,* given vectors generate R^4.

Now to prove the vectors are independent.

Let $a(1, 1, 0, 0) + b(0, 1, 0, 1) + c(0, 1, 1, 1) + d(1, 1, 1, 1) = (0, 0, 0, 0)$.

If $a = b = c = d = 0$, the vectors are independent

Now, $a = y - t = 0,$
$b = t - z = 0,$
$c = 0$ and $d = 0$

Thus the given vectors form a basis of R^4.

Let $(2, 1, 1, 2) = a(1, 1, 0, 0) + b(0, 1, 0, 1) + c(0, 1, 1, 1) + d(1, 1, 1, 1)$

As above, $a = y - t = -1, b = 1, c = -2$ and $d = 3$.

So $(2, 1, 1, 2) = (-1)(1, 1, 0, 0) + 1(0, 1, 0, 1) - 2(0, 1, 1, 1) + 3(1, 1, 1, 1)$.

Q. 10. *Let $u_1 = (1, 0, 0)$, $u_2 = (-3, 4, 0)$ and $u_3 = (3, -6, 3)$. Show that (i) $B = \{u_1, u_2, u_3\}$ is a basis of R^3 (ii) Find the co-ordinate vector for $u = (-8, 2, 3)$.*

(C.U. Dec. 2010)

Sol. (*i*) To prove B is linearly independent and spans R^3. Since dim $(R^3) = 3$, any basis of R^3 has 3 linearly independent vectors. Form the matrix A with u_1, u_2 and u_3 as rows.

$$|A| = \begin{vmatrix} 1 & 0 & 0 \\ -3 & 4 & 0 \\ 3 & 6 & 3 \end{vmatrix} \neq 0. \text{ i.e., These vectors are linearly independent.}$$

$\because$ dim$(R^3) = 3$. These 3 linearly independent vectors form a basis.

(*ii*) To find the co-ordinate vector for $u = (-8, 2, 3)$.

Let $U = au_1 + bu_2 + cu_3$.

i.e.,
$$(-8, 2, 3) = a(1, 0, 0) + b(-3, 4, 0) + c(3, -6, 3)$$
$$= (a - 3b + 3c, 4b - 6c, 3c)$$

Equating, $3c = 3 \Rightarrow c = 1$
$$4b - 6c = 2 \Rightarrow 4b = 2 + 6c = 8$$
$\Rightarrow$ $b = 2$
$$a - 3b + 3c = -8, a = -8 + 3b - 3c = -5$$

Thus $U = -5u_1 + 2u_2 + u_3$

Q. 11. *Let $V = R^4$ and U be a subspace spanned by $(1, -2, 5, -3)$, $(2, 3, 1, -4)$ and $(3, 8, -3, -5)$. Find a basis and dim U. Extend the basis of U to a basis of R^4.* (C.U. Dec. 2010)

Sol. Form the matrix 'A' with these vectors as rows and change it into row reduced echelon form. The number of non-zero rows of a matrix in the echelon form are linearly independent.

$$A = \begin{bmatrix} 1 & -2 & 5 & -3 \\ 2 & 3 & 1 & -4 \\ 3 & 8 & -3 & -5 \end{bmatrix} \sim \begin{bmatrix} 1 & -2 & 5 & -3 \\ 0 & 7 & -9 & 2 \\ 0 & 14 & -18 & 4 \end{bmatrix}$$

$$\sim \begin{bmatrix} 1 & -2 & 5 & -3 \\ 0 & 7 & -9 & 2 \\ 0 & 0 & 0 & 0 \end{bmatrix} \text{ which is in the echelon form.}$$

The non-zero rows (1, – 2, 5, – 3) and (0, 7, – 9, 2) are independent and form a basis of the row space, U. $\therefore$ dim $U = 2$.

To extend this basis of a basis of R^4.

The vectors (1, – 2, 5, – 3), (0, 7, – 9, 1), (0, 0, 1, 0) and (0, 0, 0, 1) are independent, ($\because$ they form a matrix in echelon form) and hence form a basis of R^4.

Q. 12. *Does the set of vectors (i) (1, 1, 1) and (1, – 1, 5), (ii) (1, 2, 3), (1, 0, – 1), (3, – 1, 0) and (2, 1, – 2) form a basis of R^3?*

Sol. No, the basis of R_3 contains exactly three vectors.

Q. 13. *Find the basis and dimension of the subspace generated by (2, 3, – 1, 2), (– 1, 4, 3, 0) and (7, – 6, – 11, 4) in R^4.* (C.U. June 2008)

Sol. Let U be the subspace generated by the given vectors. Reduce the matrix formed with these vectors as rows into echelon form,

$$A = \begin{bmatrix} 2 & 3 & -1 & 2 \\ -1 & 4 & 3 & 0 \\ 7 & -6 & -11 & 4 \end{bmatrix} \sim \begin{bmatrix} 1 & -4 & -3 & 0 \\ 2 & 3 & -1 & 2 \\ 7 & -6 & -11 & 4 \end{bmatrix} \sim \begin{bmatrix} 1 & -4 & -3 & 0 \\ 0 & 11 & 5 & 2 \\ 0 & 22 & 10 & 4 \end{bmatrix}$$

$$\sim \begin{bmatrix} 1 & -4 & -3 & 0 \\ 0 & 11 & 5 & 2 \\ 0 & 0 & 0 & 0 \end{bmatrix}$$

The non-zero rows (1, – 4, – 3, 0) and (0, 11, 5, 2) are linearly independent and form a basis of U.

dim U = 2.

Q. 14. *Find the orthonormal basis for the subspace spanned by the vectors (1, 2, 1), (1, 0, 1), (3, 1, 0) of R^3.* (C.U. Dec. 2010)

Sol. Let A be the matrix with these vectors as rows.

$$|A| = \begin{vmatrix} 1 & 2 & 1 \\ 1 & 0 & 1 \\ 3 & 1 & 0 \end{vmatrix} \neq 0 \quad \therefore \quad \text{These vectors are linearly independent and hence a basis of } R^3.$$

Now to find an orthonormal basis. Let $x_1 = (1, 2, 1)$, $x_2 = (1, 0, 1)$ and $x_3 = (3, 1, 0)$. Using Gram-Schmidth orthogonalization process we've, $y_1 = x_1 = (1, 2, 1)$.

$$y_2 = x_2 - \frac{<x_2, y_1>}{<y_1, y_1>} y_1 = (1, 0, 1) - \frac{1+0+1}{1+4+1}(1, 2, 1)$$

$$= (1, 0, 1) - \left(\frac{1}{3}, \frac{2}{3}, \frac{1}{3}\right) = \left(\frac{2}{3}, \frac{-2}{3}, \frac{2}{3}\right).$$

$$y_3 = x_3 - \frac{<x_3, y_1>}{<y_1, y_1>} y_1 - \frac{<x_2, y_2>}{<y_2, y_2>} y_2$$

$$= (3, 1, 0) - \frac{3+2+0}{6}(1, 2, 1) - \frac{\left(2 - \frac{2}{3} + 0\right)}{4/3}\left(\frac{2}{3}, \frac{-2}{3}, \frac{2}{3}\right)$$

$$= (3, 1, 0) - \left(\frac{5}{6}, \frac{10}{6}, \frac{1}{6}\right) - \left(\frac{2}{3}, \frac{-2}{3}, \frac{2}{3}\right)$$

$$= \left(\frac{3}{2}, 0, \frac{-3}{2}\right), \qquad \left[\because \ <y_2, y_2> = \frac{4}{9} + \frac{4}{9} + \frac{4}{9} = \frac{12}{9} = \frac{4}{3}\right]$$

The orthonormal vectors are $\frac{y_1}{\| y_1 \|}, \frac{y_2}{\| y_2 \|}, \frac{y_3}{\| y_3 \|}$

$$\| y_1 \| = \sqrt{<y_1, y_1>} = \sqrt{6}$$

$$\| y_2 \| = \sqrt{<y_2, y_2>} = \sqrt{4/3}$$

$$\| y_3 \| = \sqrt{<y_3, y_3>} = \sqrt{18/4}$$

Thus $\left\{\left(\frac{1}{\sqrt{6}}, \frac{2}{\sqrt{6}}, \frac{1}{\sqrt{6}}\right), \left(\frac{1}{\sqrt{3}}, \frac{-1}{\sqrt{3}}, \frac{1}{\sqrt{3}}\right), \left(\frac{1}{\sqrt{2}}, 0, \frac{-1}{\sqrt{2}}\right)\right\}$ is the orthonormal basis of R^3.

Q. 15. *Let V be the vector space of polynomials $f(t)$ with the inner product $<f, g> = \int_{-1}^{1} f(t)\, g(t)\, dt$. Apply Gram-Schmidth algorithm to the set $\{1, t, t^2, t^3\}$ to obtain an orthonormal set $\{f_0, f_1, f_2, f_3\}$.* (C.U. June 2009)

Sol. Let $x_1 = 1, x_2 = t, x_3 = t^2, x_4 = t^3$

We have $\{1, t, t^2, t^3)$ is the natural basis.

Hence linearly independent.

Using Gram-Schmidth orthogonalization process.

$$y_1 = x_1 = 1,$$

$$y_2 = x_2 - \frac{<x_2, y_1>}{<y_1, y_1>} y_1 = t - 0 = t.$$

Since $\quad <x_2, y_1> = \int_{-1}^{1} t.1\, dt = 0.$

$$y_3 = x_3 - \frac{<x_3, y_1> y_1}{<y_1, y_1>} - \frac{<x_3, y_2> y_2}{<y_2, y_2>} = t^2 - \frac{2/3}{2} \times 1 - 0 = t^2 - \frac{1}{3}.$$

Since $\quad <x_3, y_1> = \int_{-1}^{1} t^2\, dt = 2/3$

$$<x_3, y_2> = \int_{-1}^{1} t^2 . t\, dt = 0$$

$$<y_1, y_1> = \int_{-1}^{1} 1\, dt = 2$$

Also $\quad <x_4, y_1> = \int_{-1}^{1} t^3\, dt = 0, \qquad <x_4, y_3> = \int_{-1}^{1} t^3 \left(t^2 - \frac{1}{3}\right) dt = 0$

$$<x_4, y_2> = \int_{-1}^{1} t^3 . t\, dt = 2/5, \quad <y_2, y_2> = \int_{-1}^{1} t^2\, dt = 2/3$$

$$<y_3, y_3> = \int_{-1}^{1}\left(t^4 - \frac{2}{3}t^2 + \frac{1}{9}\right)dt = \frac{28}{45}$$

$$\therefore \quad y_4 = x_4 - \frac{<x_4, y_1>y_1}{<y_1, y_1>} - \frac{<x_4, y_2>y_2}{<y_2, y_2>} - \frac{<x_4, y_3>y_3}{<y_3, y_3>}$$

$$= t^3 - 0 - \frac{2}{5}\times\frac{3}{2}t - 0 = t^3 - \frac{3}{5}t$$

The orthonormal basis, $f_0 = \frac{y_1}{\| y_1 \|}, f_1 = \frac{y_2}{\| y_2 \|}, f_2 = \frac{y_3}{\| y_3 \|}, f_3 = \frac{y_4}{\| y_4 \|}$.

where $\| y_1 \| = \sqrt{<y_1, y_1>} = \sqrt{2}$, $\| y_2 \| = \sqrt{2/3}$, $\| y_3 \| = \sqrt{\frac{28}{45}}$

$$<y_4, y_4> = \int_{-1}^{1}\left(t^6 - \frac{6}{5}t^4 + \frac{9}{25}t^2\right)dt = \frac{8}{175}$$

$$\therefore \quad \| y_4 \| = \sqrt{8/175}$$

Thus $\left\{1, \frac{\sqrt{3}}{2}t, \frac{\sqrt{45}}{\sqrt{28}}t^2, \frac{\sqrt{175}}{\sqrt{8}}\left(t^3 - \frac{3}{5}t\right)\right\}$ is an orthonormal basis.

Q. 16. *If $\{x_i\}_1^n$ is a basis of a vector space, then $\{cx_i\}_1^n$, $c \neq 0$ is also a basis. i.e., the basis of a non-zero vector space is not unique.*

Sol. Since $\{x_i\}_1^n$ is a basis, it is linearly independent. $\therefore$ $a_1x_1 + ... + a_nx_n = 0$ implies $a_1 = a_2 = ... = a_n = 0$.

Now let $a_1 cx_1 + a_2 cx_2 + ... + a_n cx_n = 0$ *i.e.*, $c(a_1x_1 + ... + a_nx_n) = 0$. But $a_1 = a_2 = ... = a_n = 0$.

$\therefore$ $\{cx_1, cx_2, ..., cx_n\}$ is independent and hence a basis.

Q. 17. *Show that $v_1 = (1, 1, 1)$, $v_2 = (0, 1, 1)$, $v_3 = (0, 0, 1)$ form a basis of R^3. Apply Gram-Schmidth orthogonalization process to find an orthonormal basis using the above vectors.*

(C.U. June 2006, Dec. 2007, 2009)

Sol. Let A be the matrix formed with v_1, v_2, v_3 as rows.

$$|A| = \begin{vmatrix} 1 & 1 & 1 \\ 0 & 1 & 1 \\ 0 & 0 & 1 \end{vmatrix} \neq 0.$$ Hence v_1, v_2 and v_3 are 3 independent vectors and form a basis of R^3,

$\because$ dim $(R^3) = 3$.

$$y_1 = (1, 1, 1), y_2 = \left(\frac{-2}{3}, \frac{1}{3}, \frac{1}{3}\right) \text{ and } y_3 = \left(0, \frac{-1}{2}, \frac{+1}{2}\right) \qquad \text{[verify]}$$

So $\left\{\frac{y_1}{\| y_1 \|}, \frac{y_2}{\| y_2 \|}, \frac{y_3}{\| y_3 \|}\right\}$ form an orthonormal basis.

i.e., $\left\{\left(\frac{1}{\sqrt{3}}, \frac{1}{\sqrt{3}}, \frac{1}{\sqrt{3}}\right), \left(\frac{-\sqrt{2}}{\sqrt{3}}, \frac{1}{\sqrt{6}}, \frac{1}{\sqrt{6}}\right), \left(0, \frac{-1}{\sqrt{2}}, \frac{+1}{\sqrt{2}}\right)\right\}$ is the required basis.

Q. 18. *Verify whether the following represents an inner product in* R^2. $<u, v> = 2x_1y_1 + x_2y_1 + x_1y_2$ *where* $u = (x_1, x_2)$ *and* $v = (y_1, y_2)$. (C.U. June 2008)

Sol. Write the definition of an inner product.

Now, $<u, u> = 2x_1x_1 + x_2x_1 + x_1x_2 = 2x_1^2 + 2x_1x_2$ which is not ≥ 0 always.

also
$$<u, u> = 0 \iff 2x_1^2 + 2x_1x_2 = 0$$
$$\iff x_1^2 + x_1x_2 = 0$$
$$\iff x_1(x_1 + x_2) = 0$$
$$\iff x_1 = 0 \quad \text{or} \quad x_1 + x_2 = 0.$$

$\therefore$ $<u, u> = 0$ iff $u = 0$ is not satisfied. Hence not an inner product in R^2.

MORE UNIVERSITY QUESTIONS

1. Find the dimension of the vector space spanned by (1, – 2, 3, – 1) and (1, 1, – 2, 3). *(C.U. June 2006)*
2. Define a vector space and give an example. *(C.U. June 2007, 2005)*
3. Explain Gram-Schmidth orthogonalization process. *(C.U. June 2007, July 2002, Dec. 2005)*
4. Find a basis and dimension of the subspace generated by the vectors (2, 1, 1, – 1), (0, 1, 2, 2), (1, – 1, 1, 0) and (1, 4, 4, 3) in R^4. *(C.U. June 2008)*
5. Find an orthonormal basis for the set of basis {(1, 1, 1), (1, – 1, 0), (0, 1, – 1)} in R^3. *(C.U. June 2008)*
6. Find an orthonormal basis of the subspace of R^5 spanned by $x_1 = (1, 1, 1, 0, 1)$, $x_2 = (1, 0, 0, -1, 1)$, $x_3 = (3, 1, 1, -2, 3)$ and $x_4 = (0, 2, 1, 1, -1)$. *(C.U. June, 2009)*
7. Define basis and dimension of a vector space. Also define subspace. *(C.U. Dec. 2006, 2009, 2005, 2007)*
8. For what value of k, will the vectors $x = (1, -2, k) \in R^3$ is a linear combination of the vectors $x_1 = (3, 0, -2)$, $x_2 = (2, -1, -5)$. *(C.U. Dec. 2009)*
9. Prove that the vectors (1, 2, 3), (2, 3, – 1), (1, – 1, 1) are independent in R^3. *(C.U. Dec. 2007)*
10. Find the subspace S in R^3 spanned by the vectors (1, – 2, 1), (– 2, 0, 3), (3, – 2, – 2). *(C.U. Dec. 2007)*
11. Find the basis and dimension of the vector space spanned by the vectors (3, 9, 3, 5), (4, 12, 4, 5), (2, 6, 1, 0), (5, 15, 3, 2). *(C.U. Dec. 2007)*
12. Verify all the axioms of the vector space on the set $V = \{(x, y) \in R^2 ; x + 2y = 10\}$. *(C.U. Dec. 2007)*
13. Define linear dependence, independence, subspace and inner product space. *(C.U. 2005, 2006)*
14. Show that if, x and y are linearly independent vectors of V and $U = ax + by$ and $V = cx + dy$, then U and V are independent if and only if $ad - bc \neq 0$.
15. Show that the space U generated by the vectors $u_1 = (1, 2, -1, 3)$, $u_2 = (2, 4, 1, -2)$ and $u_3 = (3, 6, 3, -7)$ and the space V generated by the vectors $v_1 = (1, 2, -4, 11)$ and $v_2 = (2, 4, -5, 14)$ are equal. *(C.U. June 2007)*
16. Find the basis and dimension of the subspace $\{(a, b, c, d) : b + c + d = 0\}$ of R^4.
17. Find the dimension of the vector space spanned by 1 and – 1.
18. Show that if $\{x_1, x_2, x_3\}$ is a basis of a vector space V, then $\{x_1 + x_2 + x_3, x_2 + x_3, x_3\}$ is also a basis of V.

19. Find an orthonormal basis of R^4 using Gram-Schmidth process from the following basis {(1, – 2, 0, 1), (– 1, 0, 0, – 1), (1, 1, 0, 0)}.

20. Apply Gram-Schmidth orthogonalization process to the basis $\{1, t, t^2\}$ to obtain an orthonormal basis $\{u_1(t), u_2(t), u_3(t)\}$ of the vector space of polynomials of degree ≤ 2, given

$$\langle f, g\rangle = \int_0^1 f(t)\, g(t)\; dt.$$ *(Dec. 2006)*

21. Show that the vectors $u = (1, 2, -1)$, $v = (2, 1, -2)$, and $w = (1, 4, 3)$ generate R^3. *(C.U. Oct. 2011)*

22. Apply the Gram-Schmidth orthogonalization process to obtain an orthonormal basis for R^3 from the basis given by $v_1 = (3, 0, 4)$, $v_2 = (-1, 0, 7)$, $v_3 = (2, 9, 11)$. *(C.U. Oct. 2011)*

23. Verify triangle inequality for the vectors (0, 1, 1) and (1, 1, 0) in R^3. *(C.U. Oct. 2011)*

Answers

1. 2

4. {(1, – 1, 1, 0), (0, 1, 2, 2), (0, 0, 1, 1)}, 3

5. $$\left\{\left(\frac{1}{\sqrt{3}}, \frac{1}{\sqrt{3}}, \frac{1}{\sqrt{3}}\right), \left(\frac{1}{\sqrt{2}}, \frac{-1}{\sqrt{2}}, 0\right), \left(\frac{1}{\sqrt{6}}, \frac{1}{\sqrt{6}}, \frac{-\sqrt{2}}{\sqrt{3}}\right)\right\}$$

6. **Hint:** First find the basis of the subspace spanned by the given vectors.
{(1, 1, 1, 0, 1), (0, 1, 1, 1, 0), (0, 0, 0, 0, – 1)} is a basis of the subspace.

Orthonormal basis is $\left\{\frac{1}{2}(1,1,1,0,1), \frac{1}{\sqrt{3}}\left(\frac{-1}{2}, \frac{1}{2}, \frac{1}{2}, 1, \frac{-1}{2}\right), \frac{1}{\sqrt{10}}\left(\frac{3}{2}, \frac{1}{2}, \frac{1}{2}, -1, \frac{-5}{2}\right)\right\}$

8. $k = -8$

10. $S = \{(x, y, z) \,;\, 14x - 4z = 25\}$

11. {(1, 3, 1, 5/3), (0, 0, 2, 19/3), (0, 0, 0, 1)} ; dim = 3.

16. dimension = 3; basis = {(1, 0, 0, 0), (0, – 1, 1, 0), (0, – 1, 0, 1)}

17. 1

19. $$\left\{\left(\frac{1}{\sqrt{6}}, \frac{-2}{\sqrt{6}}, 0, \frac{1}{\sqrt{6}}\right), \left(\frac{-1}{\sqrt{3}}, \frac{-1}{\sqrt{3}}, 0, \frac{-1}{\sqrt{3}}\right), \left(\frac{1}{\sqrt{2}}, 0, 0, \frac{-1}{\sqrt{2}}\right)\right\}$$

20. $$u_1(t) = 1, u_2(t) = \sqrt{2}\left[t - \frac{1}{2}\right], u_3(t) = \sqrt{180}\left(t^2 - t + \frac{1}{6}\right)$$

22. $$\left(\frac{3}{5}, 0, \frac{4}{5}\right), \left(\frac{-4}{5}, 0, \frac{3}{5}\right), (0, 1, 0)$$

EXAMINATION PAPERS

THIRD SEMESTER B. TECH. (ENGINEERING) DEGREE EXAMINATION, OCTOBER 2011 **D20603**

EN 09 301–ENGINEERING MATHEMATICS—III

(2009 Admissions)

[Common to All Branches]

Time: Three Hours *Maximum: 70 Marks*

PART–A

Answer **all** *questions.* **(5 × 2 = 10 marks)**

1. Determine where the Cauchy-Riemann conditions are satisfied for the function $w = xy^2 + iyx^2$.
2. Define isogonal mapping.
3. Express the residue of a function of an isolated singularity as a contour integral.
4. How do you define the linear span of a set of vectors in a vector space.
5. Write down the complex Fourier transform pair.

PART–B

Answer any **four** *questions.* **(4 × 5 = 20 marks)**

6. Find a function w such that $w + u + iv$ is analytic, given that $v = 3x^2y - y^3$.
7. Find the image of the semi-infinite strip $x > 0$, $0 < y < 2$ under the transformation $w = iz + 1$. Show the regions graphically.
8. Evaluate $\int \frac{\sin \pi z^2 + \cos \pi z^2}{(z-1)(z-2)} dz$, around $|z| = 3$.
9. Show that the vecotrs $u = (1, 2, -1)$, $v = (2, 1, -2)$, and $w = (1, 4, 3)$ generate R^3.
10. Verify that the triangle inequality is satisfied by the vectors (0, 1, 1) and (1, 1, 0) in R^3.
11. Show that $f(x) = e^{-x^2/2}$ is self reciprocal under Fourier transform.

PART–C

Answer **all** *questions as per choice given.* **(4 × 10 = 40 marks)**

12. (*a*) Determine the analytic function $f(z) = u + iv$ if $u - v = \frac{\cos x + \sin x - e^{-y}}{2(\cos x - \cosh y)}$ given that $f\left(\frac{\pi}{2}\right) = 0$.

Or

(*b*) Find the invariant points of the transformation $w = -\dfrac{2z + 4i}{iz + 1}$, and prove that these two points together with any point z and its image w, form a set of four points having a constant cross ratio. What is this cross ratio?

13. (*a*) Find the Laurent series expansion of the function $f(z) = \dfrac{z^2 - 6z - 1}{(z - 1)(z - 3)(z + 2)}$ valid in the region $3 < | z + 2 | < 5$.

Or

(*b*) Find the value of the integral $\displaystyle\int_C \frac{dz}{z^2(z + 4)}$ taken counter clockwise around the circle

(*i*) $| z | = 2$ (*ii*) $| z + 2 | = 3$.

14. (*a*) Find the co-ordinates of the vector (2, 1, – 6) of V_3 (R) relative to the basis $F_1 = (1, 1, 2)$, $F_2 = (3, -1, 0)$ and $F_3 = (2, 0, -1)$.

Or

(*b*) Apply the Gram-Schmidt orthogonalisation process to obtain an orthonormal basis for R^3 from the basis given by $v_1 = (3, 0, 4)$, $v_2 = (-1, 0, 7)$, $v_3 = (2, 9, 11)$.

15. (*a*) Find the Fourier sine and cosine transforms of $f(x) = 2e^{-5x} + 5e^{-2x}$.

Or

(*b*) Find the Fourier transform of

$$f(x) = \begin{cases} 2 - |x|, & \text{in } |x| \le 2 \\ 0, & \text{in } |x| \ge 2 \end{cases}.$$

Hence find the value of $\displaystyle\int_0^\infty \left(\frac{\sin t}{t}\right)^4 dt$.

THIRD SEMESTER B. TECH. (ENGINEERING) DEGREE EXAMINATION, NOVEMBER 2010 **D10025**

EN 09 301–ENGINEERING MATHEMATICS—III

Time: Three Hours *Maximum: 70 Marks*

PART–A

Answer **all** *questions.* **(5 × 2 = 10 marks)**

1. Prove that $f(z) = z\,J_{mz}$ is differentiable only at $z = 0$.
2. Obtain the expansion of $\dfrac{z-1}{z^2}$ in a Taylor series in powers of $(z - 1)$.
3. Find the invariant points of the transformation $w = \dfrac{3z - 5i}{iz - 1}$.
4. Determine the subspace spanned by $H = \{(1, -2, 3), (3, 0, 1)\}$ in $\mathbf{R}^3$.
5. Find the Fourier sine transform of

$$f(x) = \begin{cases} 1, & 0 \le x < a \\ 0, & x \ge a \end{cases}.$$

PART–B

Answer any **four** *questions.* **(4 × 5 = 20 marks)**

6. Find the image of the line $y - x + 1 = 0$ under the transformation $w = 1/z$.
7. Evaluate $\int_C \dfrac{3z^2 + 7z + 1}{3+1}\,dz$ where C is the circle $|z + i| = 1$.
8. Let $V = \mathbf{R}^4$ and W be a subspace generated by $(1, -2, 5, -3)$, $(2, 3, 1, -4)$ and $(3, 8, -3, -5)$. Find a basis and dim (W).
9. Show that the set $\{(x, y, z) \in \mathbf{R}^3 : 2x + 5y - 7z = 0\}$ is a vector subspace of $\mathbf{R}^3$.
10. Find the Fourier transform of the function $f(t) = e^{-a|t|}, -\infty < t < \infty, a > 0$.
11. Find the Fourier cosine transform of $f(x) = \dfrac{e^{-ax}}{x}$.

PART–C

Answer **all** *questions as per choice given.* **(4 × 10 = 40 marks)**

12. (*a*) Find the bilinear transformation which maps the points $z = 1, i, -1$ on to the points $w = i, 0, -i$. Hence find the image of $|z| < 1$.

Or

(*b*) Determine the analytic function whose real part is $\dfrac{\sin 2x}{\cosh 2y - \cos 2x}$.

13. (*a*) Evaluate $\oint_C \frac{e^z \, dz}{\cos \pi z}$ where C is the unit circle $|z| = 1$.

Or

(*b*) Evaluate $\int_0^{2\pi} \frac{d\theta}{5 - 3\cos\theta}$.

14. (*a*) Let $u_1 = (1, 0, 0)$, $u_2 = (-3, 4, 0)$ and $u_3 = (3, -6, 3)$.

(*i*) Show that $B = \{u_1, u_2, u_3\}$ is a basis of $\mathbf{R}^3$.

(*ii*) Find the co-ordinate vector for $v = (-8, 2, 3)$.

Or

(*b*) Find an orthonormal basis for the subspace spanned by (1, 2, 1), (1, 0, 1), (3, 1, 0) of $\mathbf{R}^3$.

15. (*a*) Using the Fourier Integral representation, show that $\int_0^{\infty} \frac{w \sin xw}{1 + w^2} \, dw = \frac{\pi}{2} e^{-x}, (x > 0)$.

Or

(*b*) Show that the Fourier transform of $e^{-x^2/2}$ is self reciprocal.

APPENDIX—I

Table 1 : NORMAL TABLE
AREAS UNDER THE STANDARD NORMAL

$$\text{CURVE} = \frac{1}{\sqrt{2\pi}} \int_0^z e^{-\frac{z^2}{2}} dz$$

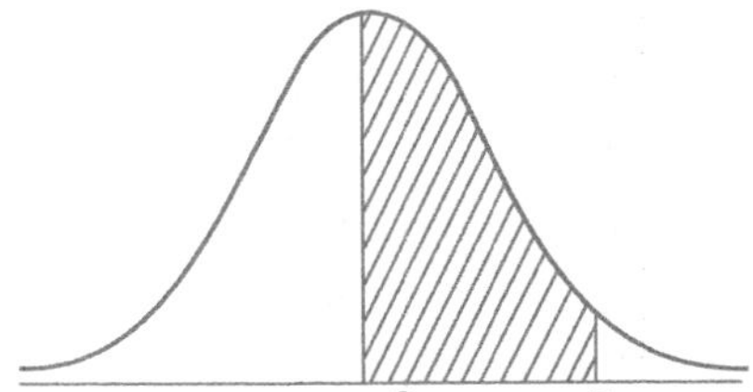

z	.00	.01	.02	.03	.04	.05	.06	.07	.08	.09
0.0	.0000	.0040	.0080	.0120	.0160	.0199	.0239	.0279	.0319	.0359
0.1	.0398	.0438	.0478	.0517	.0557	.0596	.0636	.0675	.0714	.0754
0.2	.0793	.0832	.0871	.0910	.0948	.0987	.1026	.1064	.1103	.1141
0.3	.1179	.1217	.1255	.1293	.1331	.1368	.1406	.1443	.1480	.1517
0.4	.1554	.1591	.1628	.1664	.1700	.1736	.1772	.1808	.1844	.1879
0.5	.1915	.1950	.1985	.2019	.2054	.2088	.2123	.2157	.2190	.2224
0.6	.2257	.2291	.2324	.2357	.2389	.2422	.2454	.2485	.2517	.2549
0.7	.2580	.2611	.2642	.2673	.2704	.2734	.2764	.2794	.2823	.2852
0.8	.2881	.2910	.2939	.2967	.2995	.3023	.3051	.3078	.3106	.3133
0.9	.3159	.3186	.3212	.3238	.3264	.3289	.3315	.3340	.3365	.3389
1.0	.3413	.3438	.3461	.3485	.3508	.3531	.3554	.3577	.3599	.3621
1.1	.3643	.3665	.3686	.3708	.8729	.3749	.3770	.3790	.3810	.3830
1.2	.3849	.3869	.3888	.3907	.3925	.3944	.3962	.3980	.3997	.4015
1.3	.4032	.4049	.4066	.4082	.4099	.4115	.4131	.4147	.4162	.4177
1.4	.4192	.4207	.4222	.4236	.4251	.4255	.4279	.4292	.4306	.4319
1.5	.4332	.4345	.4357	.4370	.4382	.4394	.4406	.4418	.4429	.4441
1.6	.4452	.4463	.4474	.4484	.4495	.4505	.4515	.4525	.4535	.4545
1.7	.4554	.4564	.4573	.4582	.4591	.4599	.4608	.4616	.4625	.4633
1.8	.4641	.4649	.4656	.4664	.4671	.4678	.4686	.4693	.4699	.4706
1.9	.4713	.4719	.4726	.4732	.4738	.4744	.4750	.4756	.4761	.4767
2.0	.4772	.4778	.4783	.4788	.4793	.4798	.4803	.4808	.4812	.4817
2.1	.4821	.4826	.4830	.4834	.4838	.4842	.4846	.4850	.4854	.4857
2.2	.4861	.4864	.4868	.4871	.4875	.4878	.4881	.4884	.4887	.4890
2.3	.4893	.4896	.4898	.4901	.4904	.4906	.4909	.4911	.4913	.4916
2.4	.4918	.4920	.4922	.4925	.4927	.4929	.4931	.4932	.4934	.4936
2.5	.4938	.4940	.4941	.4943	.4945	.4946	.4948	.4949	.4951	.4952
2.6	.4953	.4955	.4956	.4957	.4959	.4930	.4961	.4962	.4963	.4964
2.7	.4965	.4966	.4967	.4968	.4969	.4970	.4971	.4972	.4973	.4974
2.8	.4974	.4975	.4976	.4977	.4977	.4978	.4979	.4979	.4980	.4981
2.9	.4981	.4982	.4982	.4983	.4984	.4984	.4985	.4985	.4986	.4986
3.0	.4987	.4987	.4987	.4988	.4988	.4989	.4999	.4989	.4990	.4990
3.1	.4990	.4991	.4991	.4991	.4992	.4992	.4992	.4992	.4993	.4993

Table 2 : SIGNIFICANT VALUES t_v (α) OF t-DISTRIBUTION (TWO TAIL AREAS) [| t | > $t_v(\alpha)$] = α

d.f.	*Probability (Level of Significance)*					
(ν)	*0.50*	*0.10*	*0.05*	*0.02*	*0.01*	*0.001*
1	1.00	6.31	12.71	31.82	63.66	636.62
2	0.82	0.92	4.30	6.97	6.93	31.60
3	0.77	2.32	3.18	4.54	5.84	12.94
4	0.74	2.13	2.78	3.75	4.60	8.61
5	0.73	2.02	2.57	3.37	4.03	6.86
6	0.72	1.94	2.45	3.14	3.71	5.96
7	0.71	1.90	2.37	3.00	3.50	5.41
8	0.71	1.80	2.31	2.90	3.36	5.04
9	0.70	1.83	2.26	2.82	3.25	4.78
10	0.70	1.81	2.23	2.76	3.17	4.59
11	0.70	1.80	2.20	2.72	3.11	4.44
12	0.70	1.78	2.18	2.68	3.06	4.32
13	0.69	1.77	2.16	2.05	3.01	4.22
14	0.69	1.76	2.15	2.62	2.98	4.14
15	0.69	1.75	2.13	2.60	2.95	4.07
16	0.69	1.75	2.12	2.58	2.92	4.02
17	0.69	1.74	2.11	2.57	2.90	3.97
18	0.69	1.73	2.10	2.55	2.88	3.92
19	0.69	1.73	2.09	2.54	2.86	3.88
20	0.69	1.73	2.09	2.53	2.85	3.85
21	0.69	1.72	2.08	2.52	2.83	3.83
22	0.69	1.72	2.07	2.51	2.42	3.79
23	0.69	1.71	2.07	2.50	2.81	3.77
24	0.69	1.71	2.06	2.49	2.80	3.75
25	0.68	1.71	2.06	2.49	2.79	3.73
26	0.68	1.71	2.06	2.48	2.78	3.71
27	0.68	1.70	2.05	2.47	2.77	3.69
28	0.68	1.70	2.05	2.47	2.76	3.67
29	0.68	1.70	2.05	2.46	2.76	3.66
30	0.68	1.70	2.04	2.46	2.75	3.65
∞	0.67	1.65	1.96	2.33	2.58	3.29

Table 3 : F-Distribution

Values of F for F-Distributions with 0.05 of the Area in the Right Tail

	Degrees of freedom for numerator																		
	1	*2*	*3*	*4*	*5*	*6*	*7*	*8*	*9*	*10*	*12*	*15*	*20*	*24*	*30*	*40*	*60*	*120*	∞
1	161	200	216	225	230	234	237	239	241	242	244	246	248	249	250	251	252	253	254
2	18.5	19.0	19.2	19.2	19.3	19.3	19.4	19.4	19.4	19.4	19.4	19.4	19.4	19.5	19.5	19.5	19.5	19.5	19.5
3	10.1	9.55	9.28	9.12	9.01	9.94	8.89	8.85	8.81	8.79	8.74	8.70	8.66	8.64	8.62	8.59	8.57	8.55	8.53
4	7.71	6.94	6.59	6.39	6.26	6.16	6.09	6.04	6.00	5.96	5.91	5.86	5.80	5.77	5.75	5.72	5.69	5.66	5.63
5	6.61	5.79	5.41	5.19	5.05	4.95	4.88	4.82	4.77	4.74	4.68	4.62	4.56	4.53	4.50	4.46	4.43	4.40	4.37
6	5.99	5.14	4.76	4.53	4.39	4.28	4.21	4.15	4.10	4.06	4.00	3.94	3.87	3.84	3.81	3.77	3.74	3.70	3.67
7	5.59	4.74	4.35	4.12	3.97	3.87	3.79	3.73	3.68	3.64	3.57	3.51	3.44	3.41	3.38	3.34	3.30	3.27	3.23
8	5.32	4.46	4.07	3.84	3.69	3.58	3.50	3.44	3.39	3.35	3.28	3.22	3.15	3.12	3.08	3.04	3.01	2.97	2.93
9	5.12	4.26	3.86	3.63	3.48	3.37	3.29	3.23	3.18	3.14	3.07	3.01	2.94	2.90	2.86	2.83	2.79	2.75	2.71
10	4.96	4.10	3.71	3.48	3.33	3.22	3.14	3.07	3.02	2.98	2.91	2.85	2.77	2.74	2.70	2.66	2.62	2.58	2.54
11	4.84	3.98	3.59	3.36	3.20	3.09	3.01	2.95	2.90	2.85	2.79	2.72	2.65	2.61	2.57	2.53	2.49	2.45	2.40
12	4.75	3.89	3.49	3.26	3.11	3.00	2.91	2.85	2.80	2.75	2.69	2.62	2.54	2.51	2.47	2.43	2.38	2.34	2.30
13	4.67	3.81	3.41	3.18	3.03	2.92	2.83	2.77	2.71	2.67	2.60	2.53	2.46	2.42	2.38	2.34	2.30	2.25	2.21
14	4.60	3.74	3.34	3.11	3.96	2.85	2.76	2.70	2.65	2.60	2.53	2.46	2.39	2.35	2.31	2.27	2.22	2.18	2.13
15	4.54	3.68	3.29	3.06	3.90	2.79	2.71	2.64	2.59	2.54	2.48	2.40	2.33	2.29	2.25	2.20	2.16	2.11	2.07
16	4.49	3.63	3.24	3.01	2.85	2.74	2.66	2.59	2.54	2.49	2.42	2.35	2.28	2.24	2.19	2.15	2.11	2.06	2.01
17	4.45	3.59	3.20	2.96	2.81	2.70	2.61	2.55	2.49	2.45	2.38	2.31	2.23	2.19	2.15	2.10	2.06	2.01	1.96
18	4.41	3.55	3.16	2.93	2.77	2.66	2.58	2.51	2.46	2.41	2.34	2.27	2.19	2.15	2.11	2.06	2.02	1.97	1.92
19	4.38	3.52	3.13	2.90	2.74	2.63	2.54	2.48	2.42	2.38	2.31	2.23	2.16	2.11	2.07	2.03	1.98	1.93	1.88
20	4.35	3.49	3.10	2.87	2.17	2.60	2.51	2.45	2.39	2.35	2.28	2.20	2.12	2.08	2.04	1.99	1.95	1.90	1.84
21	4.32	3.47	3.07	2.84	2.68	2.57	2.49	2.42	2.37	2.32	2.25	2.18	2.10	2.05	2.01	1.96	1.92	1.87	1.81
22	4.30	3.44	3.05	2.82	2.66	2.55	2.46	2.40	2.34	2.30	2.23	2.15	2.07	2.03	1.98	1.94	1.89	1.84	1.78
23	4.28	3.42	3.03	2.80	2.64	2.53	2.44	2.37	2.32	2.27	2.20	2.13	2.05	2.01	1.96	1.91	1.86	1.81	1.76
24	4.26	3.40	3.01	2.78	2.62	2.51	2.42	2.36	2.30	2.25	2.18	2.11	2.03	1.98	1.94	1.98	1.84	1.79	1.73
25	4.24	3.39	2.99	2.76	2.60	2.94	2.40	2.34	2.28	2.24	2.16	2.29	2.01	1.96	1.92	1.87	1.82	1.77	1.71
30	4.17	3.32	2.92	2.69	2.53	2.42	2.33	2.27	2.21	2.16	2.09	2.01	1.93	1.89	1.84	1.79	1.74	1.64	1.62
40	4.08	3.23	2.84	2.61	2.45	2.34	2.25	2.18	2.12	2.08	2.00	1.92	1.84	1.79	1.74	1.69	1.64	1.58	1.51
60	4.00	3.15	2.76	2.53	2.37	2.25	2.17	2.10	2.04	1.99	1.92	1.84	1.75	1.70	1.65	1.59	1.53	1.47	1.39
120	3.92	3.07	2.68	2.45	2.29	2.18	2.09	2.02	1.96	1.91	1.83	1.75	1.66	1.61	1.55	1.50	1.43	1.35	1.25
∞	3.84	3.00	2.60	2.37	2.21	2.10	2.01	1.94	1.88	1.83	1.75	1.67	1.57	1.52	1.46	1.39	1.32	1.22	1.00

Table 4 : CHI-SQUARE

Significant Values χ^2 (α) of Chi-Square Distribution Right Tail Areas for Given Probability α,

$P = P_r (\chi^2 > \chi^2 (\alpha)) = \alpha$

And is Degrees of Freedom (d.f.)

Degree of freedom (v)	*Probability (Level of Significance)*						
	0 = .99	*0.95*	*0.50*	*0.10*	*0.05*	*0.02*	*0.01*
1	.000157	.00393	.455	2.706	3.841	5.214	6.635
2	.0201	.103	1.386	4.605	5.991	7.824	9.210
3	.115	.352	2.366	6.251	7.815	9.837	11.341
4	.297	.711	3.357	7.779	9.488	11.668	13.277
5	.554	1.145	4.351	9.236	11.070	13.388	15.086
6	.872	2.635	5.348	10.645	12.592	15.033	16.812
7	1.239	2.167	6.346	12.017	14.067	16.622	18.475
8	1.646	2.733	7.344	13.362	15.507	18.168	20.090
9	2.088	3.325	8.343	14.684	16.919	19.679	21.669
10	2.558	3.940	9.340	15.987	18.307	21.161	23.209
11	3.053	4.575	10.341	17.275	19.675	22.618	24.725
12	3.571	5.226	11.340	18.549	21.026	24.054	26.217
13	4.107	5.892	12.340	19.812	22.362	25.472	27.688
14	4.660	6.571	13.339	21.064	23.685	26.873	29.141
15	4.229	7.261	14.339	22.307	24.996	28.259	30.578
16	5.812	7.962	15.338	23.542	26.296	29.633	32.000
17	6.408	8.672	15.338	24.769	27.587	30.995	33.409
18	7.015	9.390	17.338	25.989	28.869	32.346	34.805
19	7.633	10.117	18.338	27.204	30.144	33.687	36.191
20	8.260	10.851	19.337	28.412	31.410	35.020	37.566
21	8.897	11.591	20.337	29.615	32.671	36.343	38.932
22	9.542	12.338	21.337	30.813	33.924	37.659	40.289
23	10.196	13.091	22.337	32.007	35.172	38.968	41.638
24	10.856	13.848	23.337	32.196	36.415	40.270	42.980
25	11.524	14.611	24.337	34.382	37.65	41.566	44.314
26	12.198	15.379	25.336	35.363	38.885	41.856	45.642
27	12.879	16.151	26.336	36.741	40.113	41.140	46.963
28	13.565	16.928	27.336	37.916	41.337	45.419	48.278
29	14.256	17.708	28.336	39.087	42.557	46.693	49.588
30	14.933	18.493	29.336	40.256	43.773	47.962	50.892

Note. For degrees of freedom (v) greater than 30, the quantity $\sqrt{2\chi^2} - \sqrt{2v-1}$ may be used as a normal variate with unit variance.

APPENDIX—II

SOME IMPORTANT CURVES

Cissoid (Imp.)

$y^2(2a - x) = x^3$

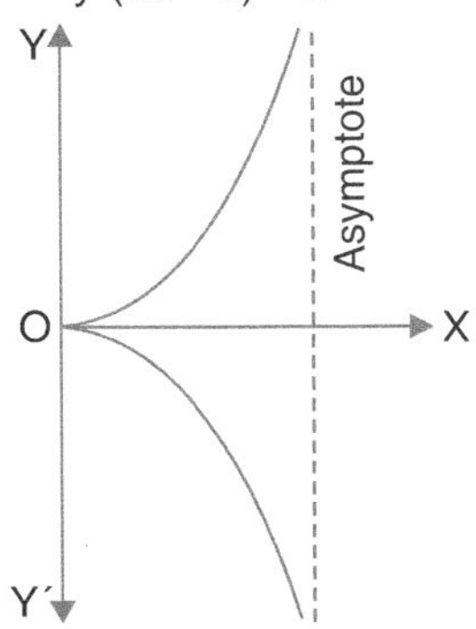

Catenary

$y = a \cosh \frac{x}{a}$

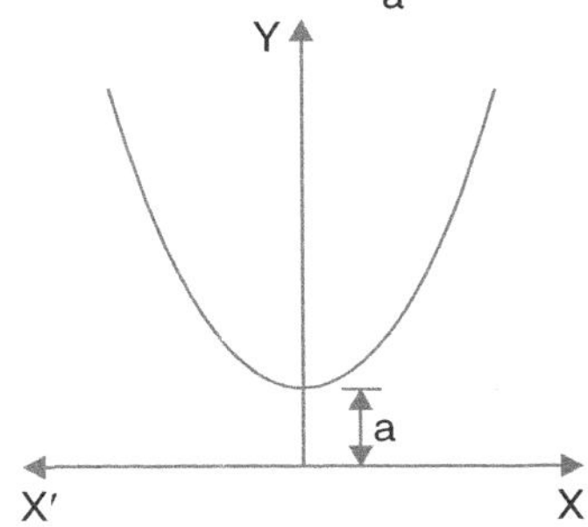

Cubical Parabola

$a^2y = x^3$

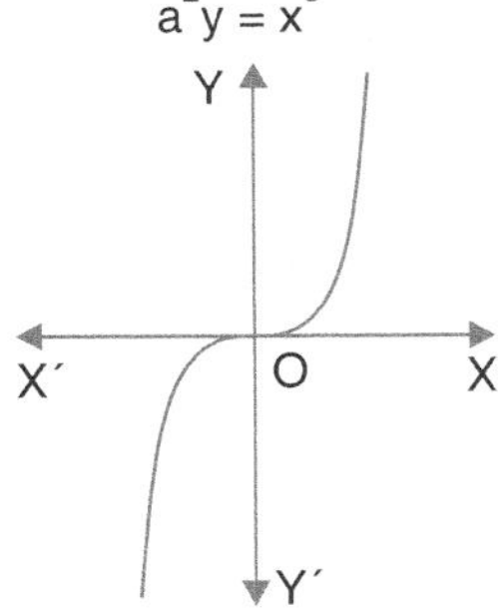

Semicubical Parabola

$ay^2 = x^3$

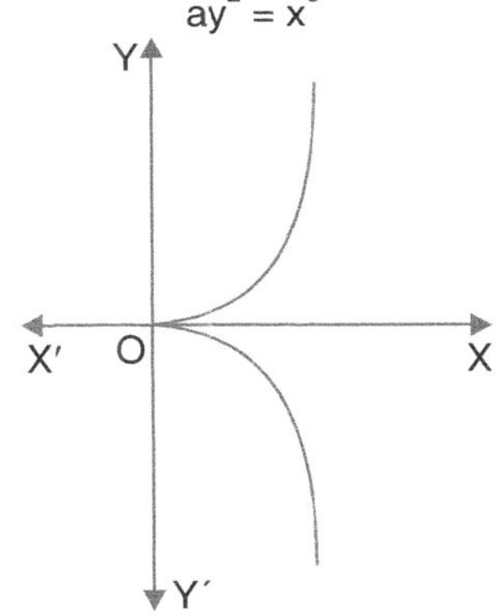

Strophoid

$y^2(a - x) = x^2(a + x)$

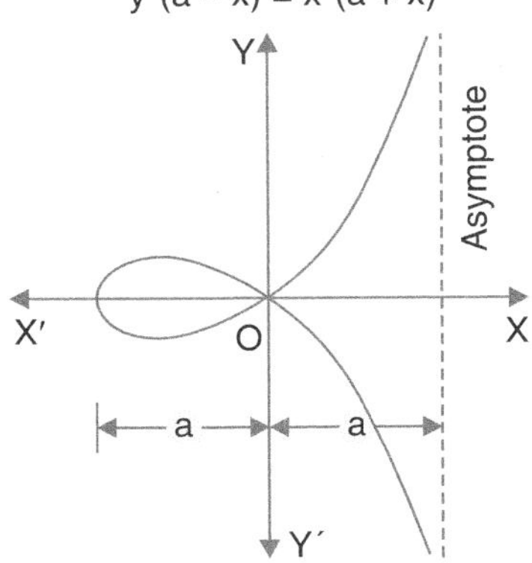

Folium of Descartes

$x^3 + y^3 = 3axy$

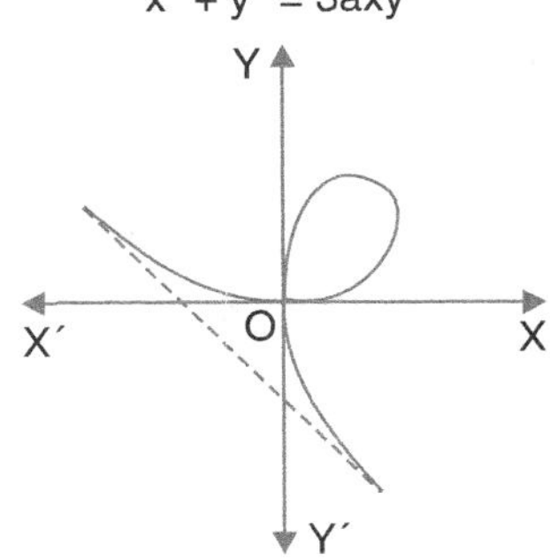

Hypocycloid (Imp.)

$x^{2/3} + y^{2/3} = a^{2/3}$

$x = a\cos^3\theta \quad y = a\sin^3\theta$

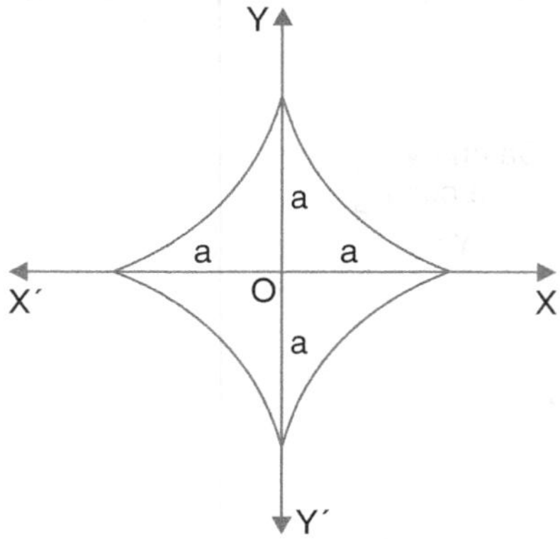

Witon of Agnesi

$xy^2 = 4a^2(2a - x)$

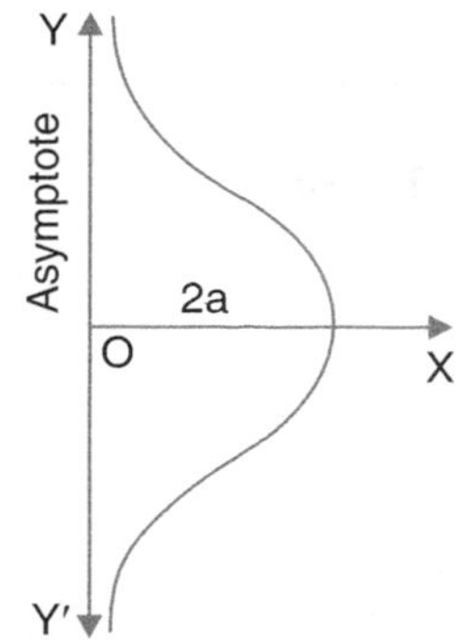

Cardioid (Imp.)

$r = a(1 + \cos\theta)$

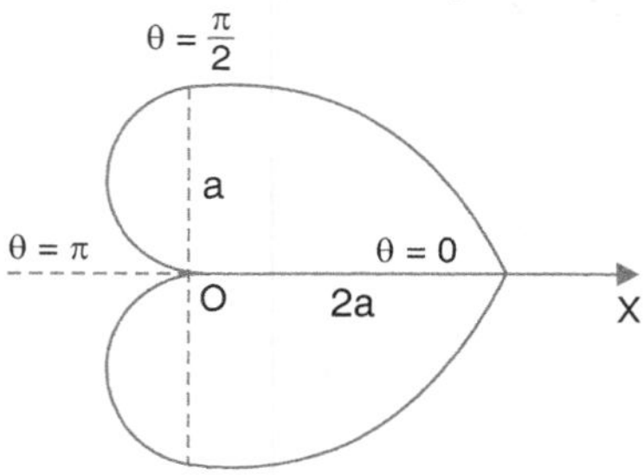

Cardioid (Imp.)

$r = a(1 - \cos\theta)$

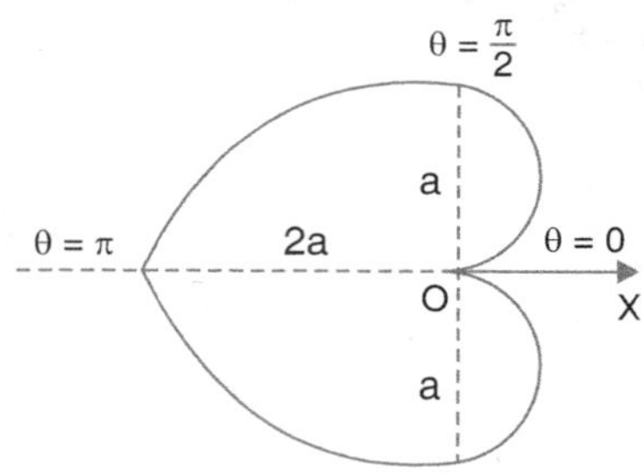

Cycloid (Most Imp.)

$x = a(\theta + \sin\theta)$

$y = a(1 - \cos\theta)$

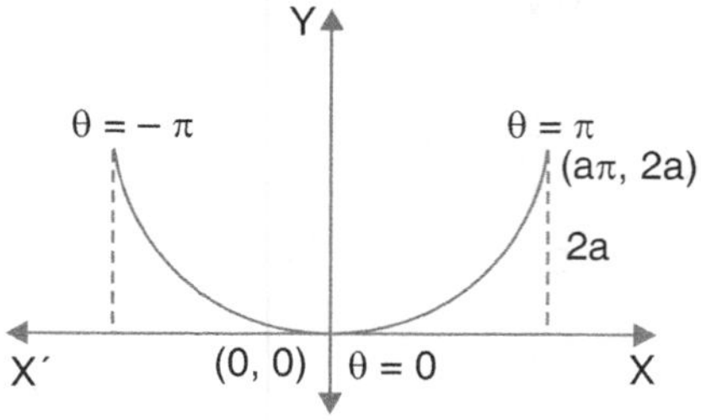

Cycloid

$x = a(\theta - \sin\theta)$

$y = a(1 + \cos\theta)$

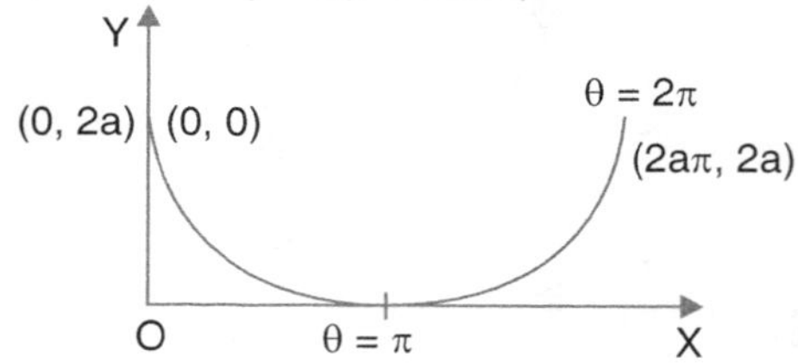

Cycloid (Imp.)

$x = a(\theta - \sin\theta)$

$y = a(1 - \cos\theta)$

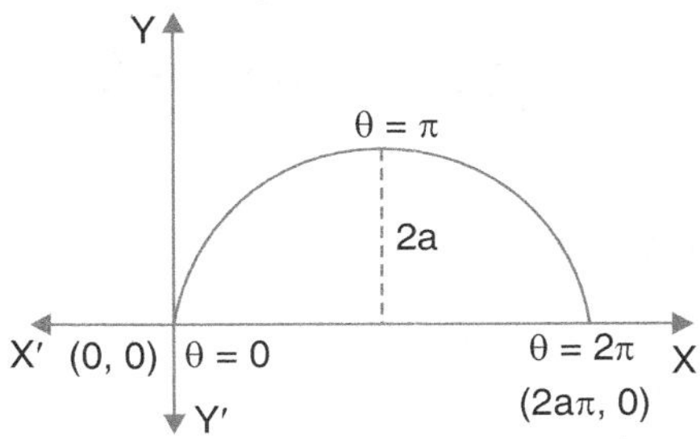

Cycloid

$x = a(\theta + \sin\theta)$

$y = a(1 + \cos\theta)$

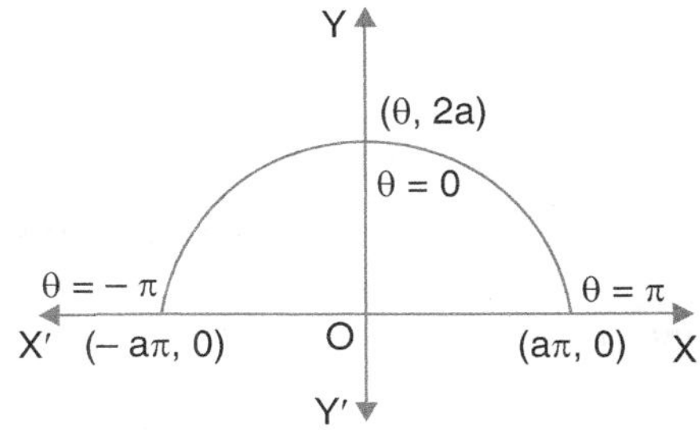

Lemniscate

$r^2 = a^2 \cos 2\theta$

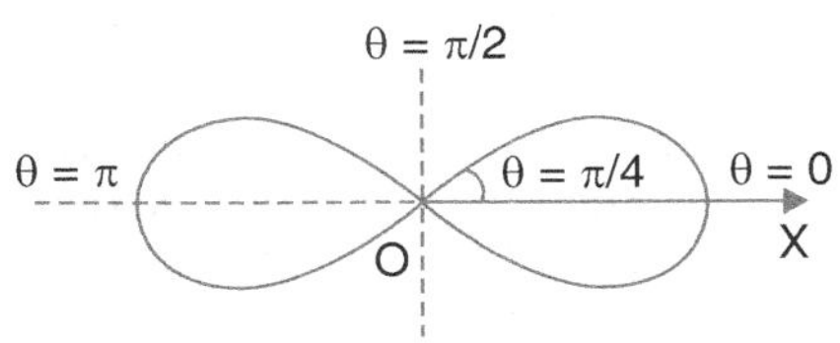

The three leaved rose

$r = a \sin 3\theta$

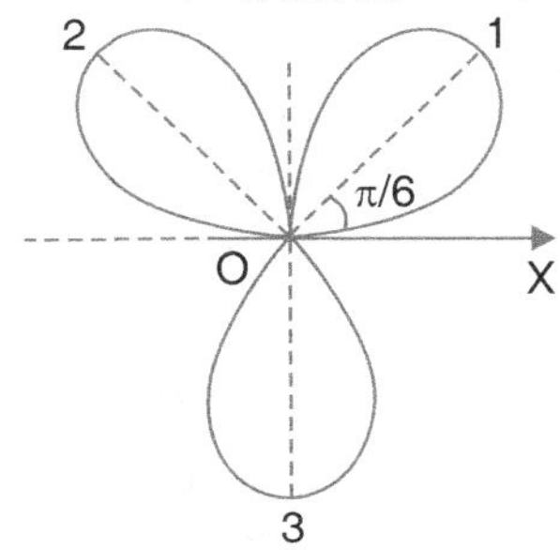

APPENDIX—III

CONVERSION FACTORS

To convert	*into*	*Multiple by*	
LINEAR MEASURE			
Inch	Millimetre	25.40	0.03937
Inch	Centimetre	2.54	0.3937
Inch	Metre	0.0254	39.37
Feet	Metre	0.3048	3.281
Yard	Metre	0.9144	1.0936
Mile	Kilometre	1.6093	0.62137
Furlong	Metre	201.1678	0.004971
Miles	Nautical miles (int.)	0.858975	1.15078
WEIGHT MEASURE			
Ounces	Grammes	28.3495	0.035274
Pounds	Kilogrammes	0.4536	2.20462
Cwt.	Quintal (100 kg.)	0.50802	1.9684
Ton	Kilogrammes	1016.05	0.0009842
U.S. Ton	Kilogrammes	907.18	0.0011
Ton (2240 lb)	Metric ton (Tonne)	1.01605	0.9842
Maunds	Ton	0.036735	27.2222
Tola	Ounce	0.411429	2.43056
Tola	Gramme	11.6628	0.087535
SQUARE MEASURE			
Square inches	Square millimetres	645.16	0.00155
Square inches	Square centimetres	6.4516	0.155
Square feet	Square metre	0.0929	10.764
Square Yard	Square metre	0.836	1.196
Acre	Square metre	4046.9	0.00025
Square mile	Square kilometre	2.59	0.3861
Acre (4840 sq.yd.)	Hectare (10,000 sq. m)	0.40468	2.4711
CUBIC MEASURE			
Cubic inch	Cubic centimetre	16.387	0.061
Cubic feet	Cubic metre	0.02832	35.315
Cubic Yard	Cubic metre	0.76455	1.308
Cubic foot	Gallon (Imp.)	6.2288	0.16054

Cubic foot	Litres (1000 cc)	28.3161	0.0353156
Gollon (Imp.)	Litres	4.54596	0.219976
Pint (0.124 Imp. Gln)	Litres	0.568	1.76
U.S. Gallon	Litres	3.78533	0.264178
	PRESSURES AND DENSITIES		
Pounds per sq in.	Kg. per sq. cm.	0.070307	14.2233
Pounds per sq. ft.	Kg. per sq. metre	4.88243	0.204816
Tonnes per sq. ft.	Tonnes per sq. metre	10.937	0.091436
Atmospheres	Pounds per sq. in.	14.6959	0.06804
Inch of Hg	Pounds per sq. in.	0.491154	2.036
Inch of Hg	Pounds per sq. in.	0.0345316	28.959
Pounds per sq. ft.	mm. of Hg.	0.035913	2.78450
Pounds per sq. in.	Feet of water	2.30672	0.433516
Feet of water	Kg. per sq. cm	0.0304792	32.81
Pounds per cu. m.	Grammes per cc	27.6799	0.0361273
Pounds per cft.	Kg. per cu. m.	16.02	0.052422
	MISCELLANEOUS		
Pounds per foot	Kg. per metre	1.48816	0.67197
Miles per hour	Feet per metre	1.46667	0.68182
Feet per Second	Km per hour	1.09728	0.91134
H.P. (550 ft. lb/sec.)	Metric H.P.	1.01387	0.98632
To obtain	From		Multiple by